25—

W9-CND-449

WITH
WILLIAM
BURROUGHS

Also by Victor Bockris

FIGHTER, POET, PROPHET: THE POETRY OF MUHAMMAD ALI

NOTHING HAPPENS: PHOTOGRAPHS OF MUHAMMAD ALI
AND ANDY WARHOL

Photo by Robert Mapplethorpe

WITH
WILLIAM
BURROUGHS
A REPORT FROM THE BUNKER

BY VICTOR BOCKRIS

SEAVER BOOKS   NEW YORK

Copyright © 1981 by Victor Bockris and William Burroughs
All Rights Reserved
No part of this book may be reproduced, for any reason,
by any means, including any method of photographic
reproduction, without the permission of the publisher.
First Edition 1981
First Printing 1981
ISBN: 0-394-51809-8 (hardbound)
0-394-17828-9 (paperbound)
Seaver Books ISBN: 0-86579-006-X
Library of Congress Catalog Card Number: 80-24905

LIBRARY OF CONGRESS CATALOGING IN PUBLICATION DATA
Burroughs, William S. 1914-
With William Burroughs.
Includes index.
1. Burroughs, William S., 1914-   —Biography—Sources.
2. Novelists, American—20th century—Biography.
I. Bockris, Victor, 1949-   II. Title.
PS3552.U75Z478   813'.54 B   80-24905
ISBN 0-86579-006-X
ISBN 0-394-51809-8
ISBN 0-394-17828-9 (pbk.)

Manufactured in the United States of America
Distributed by Grove Press, Inc., New York
SEAVER BOOKS, 333 Central Park West, New York, N.Y. 10025

DESIGNED BY BETH TONDREAU

for Muhammad Ali, Andy Warhol, Allen Ginsberg
and all the Grey Gentlemen out there and in here

"As I write this I have barricaded myself in the ward room against the 2nd Lieutenant who claims he is 'God's little hang boy sent special to me' that fucking shave tail I can hear him out there whimpering and slobbering and the Colonel is jacking off in front of the window pointing to a Gemini Sex Skin. The Captain's corpse hangs naked at the flagpole. I am the only sane man left on the post. I know now when it is too late what we are up against."

    —*The Ticket That Exploded,* William S. Burroughs, 1967

"We must hold the Bunker at all costs."

    —William Burroughs in conversation, New York, 1977

"I am a man of the world. Going to and fro and walking up and down in it."

    —*Cities of the Red Night,* William S. Burroughs, 1981

CONTENTS

A PASSPORT FOR WILLIAM BURROUGHS INTRODUCTION

"As a child I wanted to be a writer because writers were rich and famous," Burroughs begins. "They lounged around Singapore and Rangoon smoking opium in yellow pongee silk suits. They sniffed cocaine in Mayfair and they penetrated forbidden swamps with a faithful native boy and lived in the native quarter of Tangier smoking hashish and languidly caressing a pet gazelle.

"My first literary essay was called *The Autobiography of a Wolf*. People laughed and said: 'You mean the *biography* of a wolf.' No, I mean the *autobiography* of a wolf and still do. I was quite sure I wanted to be a writer when I was eight. There was something called *Carl Cranbury in Egypt* that never got off the ground. . . . Carl Cranbury frozen back there on yellow lined paper, his hand an inch from his blue steel automatic. In this set I also wrote westerns, gangster stories, and haunted houses. I was quite sure that I wanted to be a writer."

Burroughs was born February 5, 1914. He spent his childhood in a solid, three-story brick house in St. Louis in what he later described as "a malignant matriarchal society." He was the grandson of the inventor of the adding machine, and his parents, Mr. and Mrs. Mortimer Burroughs, were comfortable. "My father owned and ran a glass business." He has one brother, Mortimer Burroughs, Jr. The family of four lived with their English governess, whose name was Mary Evans (she left quite suddenly for England when Bill was five) at 4664 Pershing Avenue until William was twelve. As a child his hair was blond.

"My mother's character was enigmatic and complex. Sometimes old and knowing, mostly with a tremulous look of doom and sadness, she suffered from head and back aches, was extremely psychic, and was interested in magic. She had a dream one night that my brother Mort came to the door, his face covered with blood, and said, 'Mother, we've had an accident.' And at that very moment, Mort was in a car accident and suffered a few minor cuts. She had a very definite intuition about people—'like an animal,' she described it. And she would make flat judgments, warning my father of a business contact: 'I think he's crooked all over.' She was not a lady of reserve and nineteenth-century refinements; she was clearly crippled by her Bible Belt upbringing, which had imposed an abhorrence of bodily functions. She was indeed a lady of great poise and charm, and ran a gift and art shop for many years and wrote a book on flower arranging for the Coca-Cola Company. She was a complete alien to the icy, remote strata of the serene, rich matrons she saw every day in the shop. . . . 'We must get together,' they would say, but they rarely did. She didn't belong in the 'in' group. Neither did my father, who certainly had nothing to recommend him in the way of lineage. Son of an originally penniless bank clerk from Massachusetts—nobody knew where he came from or who he was.

"So the family was never *in*. This feeling I experienced from early childhood, of living in a world where I was not accepted, caused me to develop a number of displeasing characteristics. I was shy and awkward, and at the same time furtive and purposeful. An old St. Louis aristocrat with cold blue eyes chews his pipe . . . 'I don't want that boy in the house again. He looks like a sheep-killing dog.' And a St. Louis matron said: 'He is a walking corpse.' No, I was not escaping my elitist upbringing through crime: I was not searching for an identity denied me by the Wasp elite, who have frequently let me know just where I stand.

"My earliest memories were colored by a nightmare fear. I was afraid to be alone, and afraid of the dark, and afraid to go to sleep because of dreams where a supernatural horror seemed always on the point of taking shape. I was afraid someday the dream would still be there when I woke up. I recall hearing a maid talk about opium and

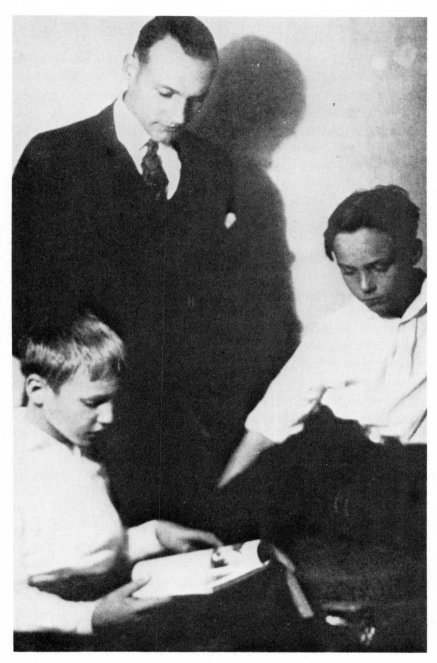

William Burroughs (left) with his father, Mortimer Burroughs, and brother Mortimer Burroughs, Jr. Photographer unknown

how smoking opium brings sweet dreams, and I said, 'I will smoke opium when I grow up.'

"I was subject to hallucinations as a child. Once I woke up in the early-morning light and saw little men playing in a blockhouse I had made. I felt no fear, only a feeling of stillness and wonder. Another recurrent hallucination or nightmare concerned 'animals in the wall,' and started with the delirium of a strange undiagnosed fever that I had at the age of four or five.

"I was timid with other children and afraid of physical violence. One aggressive little lesbian would pull my hair whenever she saw me. I would like to shove her face in right now, but she fell off a horse and broke her neck years ago."

When William was twelve, his parents decided to move to a house in the suburbs with five acres of ground on Price Road. "My parents decided to 'get away from people.' They bought a large house with grounds and woods and a fish pond where there were squirrels instead of rats. They lived there in a comfortable capsule, with a beautiful garden and cut off from contact with the life of the city." He attended the John Burroughs (no relation) private high school. "I was not particularly good or bad at sports. I had a definite blind spot for anything mechanical. I never liked competitive games and avoided these whenever possible. I became, in fact, a chronic malingerer. I did like fishing, hunting, and hiking." He also read Wilde, Anatole France, Baudelaire, and Gide.

At fifteen Bill was sent to Los Alamos Ranch School in New Mexico for his health. He had a bad sinus condition. "I formed a romantic attachment for one of the boys at Los Alamos and we spent time together bicycling, fishing, and exploring old quarries. I kept a diary about 'our relationship.' I was sixteen and I'd just read *Dorian Gray* . . . you can imagine. Even now I blush to remember the contents of that *grimoire*. It put me off writing for many years. During the Easter vacation of my second year I persuaded my family to let me stay in St. Louis, so my things were packed and sent to me from school and I used to turn cold thinking that maybe the boys were reading my diary out loud to each other. When the box finally arrived I pried it open and threw away everything until I found the diary and destroyed it forthwith, without even a glance at the appalling pages."

At that time, Burroughs read the autobiography of a burglar, called

You Can't Win by Jack Black. "It sounded good to me compared with the dullness of a Midwest suburb where all contact with life was shut out." He and his friend found an abandoned factory, broke all the windows, and stole one chisel. They were caught, and their fathers had to pay for the damages. "After that my friend packed me in because our relationship was endangering his standing with the group. I saw there was no compromise with the group, the others, and I found myself a good deal alone. I drifted into solo adventure. My criminal acts were gestures, unprofitable and for the most part unpunished. I would break into houses and walk around without taking anything. . . . Sometimes I would drive around in the country with a .22 rifle, shooting chickens. I made the roads unsafe with reckless driving until an accident, from which I emerged miraculously and portentously unscratched, scared me into normal caution."

Burroughs went on to Harvard, living first at Adams House and then Claverly Hall. "I majored in English literature for lack of interest in any other subject. I hated the university and I hated the town it was in. Everything about the place was dead. The university was a fake English setup taken over by the graduates of fake English public schools. I was lonely. I knew no one and strangers were regarded with distaste by the closed corporation of the desirables. Nobody asked me to join a club at Harvard. They didn't like the looks of me. And when I tried to join the OSS under Bill Donovan with a letter from my uncle, I encountered, as the deciding factor, a professor who was head of the house I was living in at Harvard, who particularly didn't like the looks of me. And later when I tried to join the American Field Service, this snotty young English school tie says, 'Oh, uh, by the way, Burroughs, what were your clubs at Harvard? No clubs?' He goes all dim and gray like the room was full of fog. 'And what was your house?' I named an unfashionable house. 'We'll consider your application. . . .'

"And the physical exam when I applied for a Naval commission. . . . The doctor said flatly, 'His feet are flat, his eyesight bad, and put down that he is a very poor physical specimen.' He gave me a tough aside: 'You may get your commission, if you can throw some weight around.' Needless to say, I had no weight to throw around anywhere. I wanted some. And that is what brought me to dabble in crime."

"The only possible thing to do is what one wants to do," Burroughs wrote years later in a letter to Jack Kerouac, who planned to write a book called *Secret Mullings About Bill*. *With William Burroughs* could just as well have been called *Secret Mullings About Bill Updated*, if the title hadn't been too Kerouackian to steal, because as I got to know him I found myself increasingly mulling over Bill's thoughts and actions. At sixty-seven he has become the wise old wolf who escapes from a forest fire at the end of his first literary essay: *The Autobiography of a Wolf*. In the words of one of his young friends, Stewart Meyer, "I saw that William not only holds water, but when he doesn't he changes. This guy is everything he pretends to be. In fact, he's not pretending. Isn't that rare among famous people?" In this sense Burroughs is revealingly similar to Muhammad Ali and Andy Warhol, two

Burroughs and Mailer at dinner for Allen Ginsberg's Gold Medal Award presentation at The Gramercy Arts Club. Note photo of Burroughs by Peter Hujar above Mailer's head. Photo by Marcia Resnick

other stars I've written portraits of. All three are exactly what they appear to be. They are, as Burroughs says of Genet, "right there." And they are willing to let others benefit from their experiences.

William Burroughs is, as Patti Smith has often pointed out, "the father of heavy metal," who helped make the present possible by writing maps of territory that had previously been considered out of bounds. "It only takes one man to reject all this crap," he states flatly, "and it can disappear for everybody."

"Burroughs is a real man," I heard Norman Mailer tell writer Legs McNeil.

"But . . . but," Legs, an avid exponent of heterosexuality, spluttered.

"Oh no, that's bullshit," Norman insisted. "That is a man. I remember when we read the first sections of *Naked Lunch* we felt so relieved. We knew a great man had spoken."

"Any writer who does not consider writing his only salvation, I—'I trust him little in the commerce of the soul,' " says Burroughs.

The most difficult thing in a writer's career is to keep on writing. The odds are very much against a writer's being able to write to his satisfaction throughout his life. He has to keep traveling intuitively. He has to get off boats and planes to keep looking for new scenes he will need to write twenty years later. He may have to involve himself in other people's dreams. He may have to spend weeks in bed with the covers pulled up over his head. Only by continual courage can this writer renew his essential writer's passport. For, as Burroughs constantly reminds his students, "a writer must write." Where Kerouac, who did not change, died at the hands of the writer in him, Burroughs found salvation in the vehicles writing gave him to continue traveling to Venus and other locations in.

The period *With William Burroughs* focuses on (1974-1980) has been extremely active, exciting and productive for Burroughs and constitutes a watermark in his career. He began the eighties by completing *Cities of the Red Night,* the novel that had occupied him since his return from London in '74; beginning *The Place of Dead Roads,* his long awaited western; and looking for a piece of property on which, as he approaches his seventies, he plans to purchase or build a country house, where he will be able to chop wood, take walks, practice shooting his guns in between writing, and become a country gentleman.

Being a writer becomes largely a matter of character. It is the writer's personality and attitudes that allow him to find a new way to go on, or stop him dead in his tracks. In *With William Burroughs,* I provide an introduction to the character of Burroughs through the mirror of these conversations with the characters who wander in and out of our pages. It is a portrait-in-the-round of a man whose writings and opinions have had great effect throughout the world of letters for the last twenty years, and whose work continues to be important to all those concerned with language and the question of survival. As he continues to travel it becomes evident that his writer's passport will never be revoked. I hope this book may also stand as a celebration of William Burroughs.

WITH
WILLIAM
BURROUGHS

ON WRITING

DINNER WITH SUSAN SONTAG, STEWART MEYER, AND GERARD MALANGA: NEW YORK 1980

BOCKRIS: What is writing?

BURROUGHS: I don't think there is any definition. *Mektoub: It is written.* Someone asked Jean Genet when he started to write, and he answered, "At birth." A writer writes about his whole experience, which starts at birth. The process begins long before the writer puts pencil or typewriter to paper.

SUSAN SONTAG: Do you write every day?

BURROUGHS: I feel terrible if I don't; it's a real agony. I'm addicted to writing. Do you?

SONTAG: Yes. I feel restless if I don't write.

BURROUGHS: The more you write the better you feel, I find.

SONTAG: I've trained myself to be able to produce some writing that I tell myself quite sincerely is never going to be published. Sometimes something comes out of those things.

BURROUGHS: People will get ahold of them unless you destroy them. Papa Hemingway got caught short with a whole trunkload of stuff!

SONTAG: Do you write on the typewriter?

BURROUGHS: Entirely. I can hardly do it with the old hand. I remember that Sinclair Lewis was asked what to do about becoming a writer and he always said, "Learn to type."

STEWART MEYER: I remember waking up at the Bunker and hearing the

1

typewriter going like thunder. James Grauerholz told me every morning Bill just gets up, has coffee and cake, and hits the typewriter . . .

BURROUGHS: The world is not my home, you understand. I am primarily concerned with the question of survival—with Nova conspiracies, Nova criminals, and Nova police. A new mythology is possible in the Space Age, where we will again have heroes and villains, as regards intentions towards this planet. I feel that the future of writing is in space, not time—

SONTAG: This book [*Cities of the Red Night*], which is 720 pages long, did you just write it out? I'm not asking if you revise. Is your method to write it out and then you have a version to revise, or do you write it in pieces?

BURROUGHS: I used a number of methods, and some of them have been disastrously wrong. In this book I tended to go ahead and write a hundred pages of first draft and then I'd get bogged down in revisions. What I do personally is make ten-page hops. I do a version of a chapter, go over it a couple of times, get it approximately the way I want it, and then go on from there, because I find that if I let it pile up I suddenly get a sickening feeling of overwrite. The whole matter of writer's block often comes from overwrite. You see, they've overwritten themselves, whereas they should have stopped, gone back and corrected. No writer who's worth his salt has not experienced the full weight of writer's block.

BOCKRIS: How long did it take you to write your book about cancer?

SONTAG: That was easy and fast. Everything is hard for me, but it was easy. I was inspired. When you're really full of a subject and you're thinking about it all the time, that's when the writing comes, also when you're angry. The best emotions to write out of are anger and fear or dread. If you have emotions like that you just sail.

GERARD MALANGA: I used to think it was love until love took a third place.

SONTAG: Love is the third. The least energizing emotion to write out of is admiration. It is very difficult to write out of because the basic feeling that goes with admiration is a passive contemplative mood. It's a very big emotion, but it doesn't give you much energy. It makes you passive. If you use it for something you want to write, some strange languor creeps over you, which militates against the aggressive energy

2

that you need to write, whereas if you write out of anger, rage, or dread, it goes faster.

BOCKRIS: William, have you ever written anything out of admiration?

BURROUGHS: I don't know what this term means. It does seem to me an anemic emotion.

SONTAG: Bill, suppose you agreed, which maybe you couldn't even conceive of doing, to write about Beckett. Somebody offered you a situation at which you said, yes, I'd like to say what I want to say about Beckett, and my feeling about Beckett is mainly positive. I think that's harder to get down in a way that's satisfactory than when you're attacking something.

BURROUGHS: I don't see what's being said here at all.

SONTAG: Victor asked me how long it took to write the little book about illness. I wrote it in two weeks because I was so angry I was writing out of rage at the incompetence of doctors and the ignorance and mystifications and stupidities that caused people's deaths, and that just pulled me along. Whereas I just finished writing an essay on something I really adore, Syberberg's seven-hour movie about Hitler, and it took months to write.

BURROUGHS: I see what you mean, but it doesn't correspond to my experience.

SONTAG: I think you write more exclusively out of some kind of objection or admonitory impulse.

BURROUGHS: A great deal of my writing which I most identify with is not written out of any sort of objection at all, it's more poetic messages, the still sad music of humanity, my dear, simply poetic statements. If I make a little bit of fun of control with Dr. Schaeffer, the Lobotomy Kid, they say, "This dark pacifist who's paranoid, who's motivated completely by rejection of technology." This is a bunch of crap. I just make a little skit that's all. I am so sick of having this heavy thing laid on me where I just make a little slapstick and someone comes upon me with this "Oh, God, he's rejecting everything!" shit. I always get this negative image from critics, but the essays in *Light Reading for Light Years* will make me sound like some sort of great nineteenth-century crank who thought that brown sugar was the answer to everything and was practicing something he called brain breathing. You know, he believed in Reich's orgone box. I think the real end of any

William and Susan after dinner at my apartment. Photo by Gerard Malanga

civilization is when the last eccentric dies. The English eccentric was one of the great fecund figures. They're the lazy men. One man just took to his bed and died from sheer inertia, another would just walk around his estate and he was so lazy that he would have to eat the fruit without plucking it, see, which caused a lot more trouble than if he had actually plucked it. Yes, the English eccentrics were a great breed.

SONTAG: There are southern eccentrics.

BURROUGHS: Oh, by heavens yes, living on their crumbling estates controlled by their slaves . . .

DINNER AT BURROUGHS' APARTMENT: BOULDER 1977

BOCKRIS: Why do you feel that writing is still behind painting?

BURROUGHS: There is no invention that has forced writers to move, corresponding to photography, which forced painters to move. A hundred years ago they were painting cows in the grass—representational painting—and it looks just like cows in the grass. Well, a photograph

4

could do it better. Now one invention that would certainly rule out one kind of writing would be a tape recorder that could record subvocal speech, the so-called stream of consciousness. In writing we are always interpreting what people are thinking. It's just a guess on my part, an approximation. Suppose I have a machine whereby I could actually record subvocal speech. If I could record what someone thought, there'd be no necessity for me to interpret.

BOCKRIS: How would this machine work?

BURROUGHS: We know that subvocal speech involves actual movement of the vocal cords, so it's simply a matter of sensitivity. There is a noise connected with subvocal speech, but we can't pick it up. They probably could do it within the range of modern technology, but it hasn't been done yet.

BOCKRIS: People absorb and repeat the words of rock songs, which make them very effective. Do you think the printed word can become a more effective tool for communication than it is? People do not go around reciting passages of books in their heads.

BURROUGHS: Yes, they do.

BOCKRIS: Not a lot of people.

BURROUGHS: A lot of them don't know where what's in their heads came from. A lot of it came from books.

BOCKRIS: However, words accompanied by music tend to have a bigger effect.

BURROUGHS: This fits right into the bicameral brain theory. If you can get right to the nondominant side of the brain, you've got it made. That's where the songs come from that sing themselves in your head, the right side of the brain. Curiously enough, the most interesting thing about Julian Jaynes' book *The Origins of Consciousness in the Breakdown of the Bicameral Mind* is all Jaynes' clinical evidence on people who've had various areas destroyed. The nondominant side of the brain can sing, but it can't talk. You can say to it: "Okay, if you can't say it, sing it."

BOCKRIS: When did you first meet Brion Gysin?

BURROUGHS: He'd just come back from the Sahara and I went to see an exhibit of his paintings. I met him then. He was a tremendously powerful personality and I was very much impressed with the paintings. I didn't really get to know him until he came to Paris in 1958.

Then I saw his paintings and he was the one who taught me everything I know about painting. He said, "Writing is fifty years behind painting," and started the cut-up method, which is simply applying the montage method of writing which had been used in painting for fifty years. As you see, painters are now getting off the canvas with all these happenings. I suppose that writing will eventually get off the page following painting. What exactly will happen then I don't know. They may start writing things in real life. A crime writer will actually go out and shoot people. There's been a lot of talk about crimes incited by writing, but actually very few authenticated cases of anyone who has committed a crime as a result of reading a work of fiction. Any number of crimes have been committed by people who've read about it in the newspapers. Like the man who killed eight nurses in Chicago and then some kid in Arizona got the idea that this might be a good thing to do and killed five women. So all the censorship arguments should be applied first to the daily press because they're the ones that actually cause people to commit crimes. This man who shot Deutsches [a Communist student leader] in Berlin said he'd gotten the idea from the assassination of King, so the daily press, as far as causing crimes goes, is the real offender, and not the works of fiction. People read a work of fiction and they know it's a work of fiction. They don't necessarily rush out and do these things.

BOCKRIS: What is Gysin's interest in writing?

BURROUGHS: He said, "Well, here's a simple little thing—the cut-ups—painters have been doing it for fifty years, why don't you writers try it?" He wants to bring writing up to where painting is. The montage method is much closer to the facts of actual human perception than representational writing, which corresponds to cows-in-the-grass painting.

BOCKRIS: How do you feel about using the tape recorder at the moment?

BURROUGHS: I did some experiments with tape recorders, but using a tape recorder for composition has never worked for me. In the first place, talking and writing are quite different. So far as writing goes I do need a typewriter. I have to write it down and see it rather than talk it. I know that some writers get their notes together for a chapter, then get it into a tape recorder. They got a secretary who brings that back to them and then they make some corrections.

Burroughs in Towers Open Fire, *a film he made with Anthony Balch in London in the early sixties. Film still by Anthony Balch*

BOCKRIS: Have you ever taped television?

BURROUGHS: Lots of times. I had tapes of television shows, then I did all these experiments of putting the soundtrack of one television show onto another similar one and people would come in and it would take ten minutes before anyone realized there was anything wrong if the programs were at all similar. Say the soundtrack of one western on another, they work uncannily well. There's a shot just where it should be and so on. Then there'll be a moment and people will say wait a minute there's something wrong there. But it has taken fifteen or twenty minutes before someone has realized this is not the soundtrack that went with that particular program. It's very amusing.

———

7

A LETTER FROM CARL WEISSNER:
MANNHEIM, WEST GERMANY 1974

In 1966 I was living at 1-3a Mühltalstrasse, Heidelberg, West Germany, in a room about the size of a 3rd-class passenger berth of an Estonian saltpeter freighter on the Riga-Valparaiso run. On June 6, at precisely 8.20 P.M., there was a knock on the door. I opened the door and for a fraction of a second before the hall light went out I caught a glimpse of a tall thin man, about 52 years of age, black suit black tie white shirt w/ black needle stripes black phosphorescent eyes black hat. He looked like Opium Jones.

"Hello," he said in a voice hard and black as smoked metal.

"Hello, Mr. Burroughs," I said. "Come in."

He had come from Paris where he had worked on the soundtrack of *Chappaqua,* with Conrad Rooks. He took three or four steps and stood by the narrow table in front of the window. He put his hands into his pockets and in one smooth movement brought out two reels of mylar tape and put them on the table.

"Got your tape recorder?" he asked.

"Yes."

"Let's compare tapes."

We played his tapes, then some of mine. Nothing was said. Except at one point he stopped his tape, wound it back for a second or two, and played it again. "You hear that?" he asked. ". . . 'wiring wiring'. . . It's the voice of a friend of mine from the south. Haven't seen him in twenty years. Don't know how his voice got on there."

Then we put a microphone on the table and took turns talking to the tape recorder switching back and forth between tracks at random intervals. We played it all back and sat there listening to our conversation:

"The other veins crawl through mine," he said. Adjusting his throat microphone. Breathing heavily in the warm anaesthetic mist that filled the old Studio.

"Mind you take film. I want to see that. Grammars of distant differential tissue.

"Agony to breathe here.

"Muy alone in such tense and awful silence and por eso have I survived.

"Echoes of sticky basements. From Lyon to Marseilles. Fossil flesh stormed the exits.

"Carl made words in the air without a throat without a tongue. Vestigial penis figures to the sky now isn't that cute?

"Yes that's what makes a real 23 as the focus snaps like this & you are actually *there*.

"Junkie there at the corner flicking empty condoms H caps KY tubes?

"Now what I was telling you about the Police Parallele. The Manipulator takes pictures for 24 hours. His eyes unbluffed unreadable.

"His face melted under the flickering arc lights. Most distasteful thing I ever stand still for."

At approximately 1.30 A.M. Mr. Burroughs took a cab to the Hotel Kaiserhof. At approximately 1.36 the receptionist handed him the key to his room. It was the key to room 23.

DINNER AT BURROUGHS' APARTMENT: BOULDER 1977

BOCKRIS: When you were writing *Naked Lunch* you told Jack Kerouac that you were apparently an agent from some other planet who hadn't gotten his messages clearly decoded yet. Has all your work been sent from other places and your job been to decode it?

BURROUGHS: I think this is true with any writer. The best seems to come from somewhere . . . perhaps from the nondominant side of the brain. There's a very interesting book I mentioned earlier called *The Origins of Consciousness in the Breakdown of the Bicameral Mind* by Julian Jaynes. His theory is that the first voices were hallucinated voices, that everyone was schizophrenic up till about 800 B.C. The voice of God came from the nondominant side of the brain, and the man who was obeying these voices, to put it in Freudian terms, would have a superego and an id but no ego at all. Therefore no responsibility.

This broke down in a time of great chaos, and then you got the concepts of morality, responsibility, law, and also divination. If you really know what to do, you don't have to ask. Jaynes' idea was that early men knew what to do at all times; they were told, and this was coming from outside, as far as they were concerned. This was not fancy, because they were actually seeing and hearing these gods. So they didn't have anything that we call "I." Your "I" is a completely illusory concept. It has a space in which it exists. They didn't have that space, there wasn't any "I" or anything corresponding to it.

BOCKRIS: Is human nature to blame for . . .

BURROUGHS: Human nature is another figment of the imagination.

BOCKRIS: What do I mean when I say human nature?

BURROUGHS: You mean there is some implicit way that people are. I don't think this is true at all. The tremendous range in which people can be conditioned would call in question any such concept.

BOCKRIS: There seems to be an alarmingly large number of meaningless words polluting our language.

BURROUGHS: The captain says, "The ship is sinking." People say he's a pessimist. He says, "The ship will float indefinitely." He's an optimist. But this has actually nothing to do with whatever is happening with the leak and the condition of the ship. Both pessimist and optimist are meaningless words. All abstract words are meaningless. They will lump such disparate political phenomena as Nazi Germany, an expansionist militaristic movement in a highly industrialized country, together with South Africa and call them both fascism. South Africa is just a white minority trying to hang on to what they got. It's not expansionist. They're not the same phenomena at all. To call both fascist is like saying there's no difference between a wristwatch and a grandfather clock.

BOCKRIS: Do you think what appears in newspapers, on television, and in daily intercourse is quite meaningless?

BURROUGHS: Absolutely, because they're always using such generalities. There is no such entity as Americans, there's no such entity as "most people." These are generalities. All generalities are meaningless. You've got to pin it down to a specific person doing a specific thing at a specific time and space. "People say . . ." "People believe . . ." "In the consensus of informed medical opinion . . ." Well, the minute you hear this, you know if the man can't pin down who he's talking about, where and when, you know you're listening to meaningless statements.

The consensus of medical opinion was that marijuana drove people insane. Well, we pinned Anslinger down on this. All he could come up with was one Indian doctor who stated that he considered the use of marijuana grounds for incarceration in a mental institution. Therefore it was proven that marijuana drove people insane. One should always challenge a generality. Police Chief Davis of Los Angeles wrote a column on pornography. He says, "Studies have shown that pornography leads to economic disaster." *What* studies? *Where* are these wondrous studies?

BOCKRIS: In your new novel, *Cities of the Red Night,* you write about body transference.

BURROUGHS: I'm convinced the whole cloning book was a fraud, but it's within the range of possibilities: and there's no doubt that what you call your "I" has a definite location within the brain, and if they can transplant it, they can transplant *it.* In fact, what these transplant doctors are working up to is brain transplants.

BOCKRIS: Have you had any out-of-the-body experiences?

BURROUGHS: Who hasn't?

BOCKRIS: I'm not quite sure what they are.

BURROUGHS: I'll give you one right now. You're staying where?

BOCKRIS: The Lazy L Motel.

BURROUGHS: What does your room look like?

BOCKRIS: Standard motel, double bed, rust-colored rug and . . .

BURROUGHS: You're having an out-of-the-body experience. Right now you're there.

BOCKRIS: I was standing in the middle of the room looking around it.

BURROUGHS: That's good, isn't it? But dreams are also, of course . . .

BOCKRIS: Have you ever dreamed that you were someone else?

BURROUGHS: Frequently. I looked in a mirror and found that I was black. Looked down at my hands and they were still white. This is quite common. It's usually someone I don't know. I look at my face and it's quite different, and not only my face but my thoughts. I've come in in the middle of someone else's identity and feel usually quite comfortable with the person I've become.

BOCKRIS: Often I find when I tell a lie it becomes true. I say to someone, "Well, no, I'm awfully sorry I can't come over tonight because I'm going to see so and so," and I actually end up going to see so and so, but it wasn't true at all when I said it.

BURROUGHS: I've had that happen lots of times.

BOCKRIS: I've become more careful what lies I tell.

BURROUGHS: Talking about writers who write things that actually happen, take Graham Greene. I went to Algiers during the Algerian war in 1956. All the planes were jammed with people trying to leave and I couldn't get out. I was staying in this dumpy hotel, and I used to eat every day in this Milk Bar which had big jars of passion fruit, various banana splits, all kinds of juices and little sandwiches; there were pillars made of mirror all around. About a week after I left, a bomb exploded in that Milk Bar and there was this terrible mess. Brion [Gysin] was there very shortly after the bomb exploded and he later described the scene. People were lying around with their legs cut off, spattered with maraschino cherries, passion fruit, ice cream, brains, pieces of mirror and blood. Now, at approximately the same time this happened, Graham Greene was writing *The Quiet American* in Saigon, and he described an explosion in a Milk Bar in almost exactly the same details. So, years later when I was reading the book and came to the Milk Bar explosion scene, I said, "Uh oh, time to duck," because I knew exactly what was going to happen.

DINNER WITH NICOLAS ROEG, LOU REED, BOCKRIS-WYLIE AND GERARD MALANGA: NEW YORK 1978

BURROUGHS [*talking about Graham Greene's* Brighton Rock]: It's a good book. It's got a strange shape. He's suddenly saying you're a bad Catholic. That's a very good book.

NICOLAS ROEG: I'm interested by your liking *Brighton Rock*. It is an overlooked book in literature. Hands up those who read *Brighton Rock*? Excellent! Go to the top of the form. And *stay* there till I come for you.

BOCKRIS: What's that one about?

BURROUGHS: It's about boys—seventeen-year-old boooooooiiiiiyyyysss. With razor blades strapped on their fingertips or something. I never got into that razor blade thing exactly . . . Do you know a writer named Denton Welch?

ROEG: Who was that?

BURROUGHS: He was sort of the original punk, and his father called him Punky. He was riding on a bicycle when he was twenty, and some complete cunt hit him and crippled him for the rest of his life. He died in 1948 at the age of thirty-three after writing four excellent books. He was a very great writer, very precious.

ROEG: Punk is a very good word. It's an old English word. Shakespeare used it and it originally meant prostitute. In fact, it used to appear in the forties in the movies. I guess it must have different connotations in America. I love the subtle differences in the language. Americans are able to cut it down and make it much slicker. Where we say lift you say elevator. Where you say automobile we say car.

Lou Reed came in with his Chinese girlfriend and some guitarists, sat down and immediately launched into a playful attack. He told Burroughs that he'd read his great essay called *Kerouac* in *High Times* and asked why he didn't write more stuff like that.

BURROUGHS: I write quite a lot.

Reed wondered whether Bill had written any more books with a straight narrative since *Junky*.

BURROUGHS: Certainly. Certainly. *The Last Words of Dutch Schultz,* for

Peter Beard, Nicolas Roeg, and William Burroughs at my apartment after their conversations. Photo by Bobby Grossman

example. And my new novel, *Cities of the Red Night,* has a fairly straight narrative line.

I got up, went across the room and returned with a copy of *The Last Words of Dutch Schultz.* Reed asked if it was an opera.

BURROUGHS: No man, no. You don't know about the last words of Dutch Schultz? You obviously don't know. They had a stenographer at his bedside in the hospital taking down everything he said. These cops are sitting around asking him questions, sending out for sandwiches, it went on for 24 hours. He's saying things like, "A boy has never wept nor dashed a thousand kim," and the cops are saying, "C'mon, don't give us that. Who shot ya?" It's incredible. Gertrude Stein said that he outdid her. Gertrude really liked Dutch Schultz.

BOCKRIS-WYLIE: Do you know where Genet is now?

BURROUGHS: Nobody knows. The people who know him just don't seem to know where he is. Brion knows him very well. I thought he was one of the most charming people I ever met. Most perceptive and extremely intelligent. While his English is nonexistent and my French very bad, we never had the slightest difficulty in communicating. That can be disastrous. You get a real intellectual French type like Sartre, the fact that I didn't speak French would just end the discussion right there.

BOCKRIS-WYLIE: Where'd you meet Genet?

BURROUGHS: I met him in Chicago at the convention.

BOCKRIS-WYLIE: What was he like? What was he wearing?

BURROUGHS: He was wearing corduroy trousers and some old beat up jacket, and no tie. For one thing he's just completely there, sincere and straight-forward. *Right there* is Genet. When people were chased out of Lincoln Park, there was a cop right behind Genet with a nightstick and Genet turned around and did like this, "I'm an old man." And the guy veered away, didn't hit him. There were more coming up, so he went into an apartment at random, knocked at a door, and someone said, "Who's there?" He said, "MONSIEUR GENET!" The guy opened the door and it turned out he was writing his thesis on Genet.

BOCKRIS-WYLIE: How do you feel about Cocteau? Proust?

BURROUGHS: I think Proust is a very great writer. Much greater writer than Cocteau or Gide. I was in the army hospital in the process of getting discharged. And because of the bureaucracy it took four months for this to come through, so I had the time to read *Re-*

14

membrance of Things Past from start to finish. It is a terrifically great work. Cocteau appears as a minor poseur next to this tremendous work of fiction. And Gide appears as a prissy old queen.

BOCKRIS: I understand you met Céline shortly before he died?

BURROUGHS: This expedition to see Céline was organized in 1958 by Allen Ginsberg who had got his address from someone. It is in Meudon, across the river from Paris proper. We finally found a bus that let us off in a shower of French transit directions: *"Tout droit, Messieurs . . ."* Walked for half a mile in this rundown suburban neighborhood, shabby villas with flaking stucco—it looked sort of like the outskirts of Los Angeles—and suddenly there's this great cacophony of barking dogs. Big dogs, you could tell by the bark. "This must be it," Allen said. Here's Céline shouting at the dogs, and then he stepped into the driveway and motioned to us to come in. He seemed glad to see us and clearly we were expected. We sat down at a table in a paved courtyard behind a two-story building and his wife, who taught dancing—she had a dancing studio—brought coffee.

Céline looked exactly as you would expect him to look. He had on a dark suit, scarves and shawls wrapped around him, and the dogs, confined in a fenced-in area behind the villa, could be heard from time to time barking and howling. Allen asked if they ever killed anyone and Céline said, "Nooo. I just keep them for the *noise.*" Allen gave him some books, *Howl* and some poems by Gregory Corso and my book *Junky.* Céline glanced at the books without interest and laid them sort of definitively aside. Clearly he had no intention of wasting his time. He was sitting out there in Meudon. Céline thinks of himself as the greatest French writer, and no one's paying any attention to him. So, you know, there's somebody who wanted to come and see him. He had no conception of who we were.

Allen asked him what he thought of Beckett, Genet, Sartre, Simone de Beauvoir, Henri Michaux, just everybody he could think of. He waved this thin, blue-veined hand in dismissal: "Every year there is a new fish in the literary pond.

"It is nothing. It is nothing. It is nothing," he said about all of them.

"Are you a good doctor?" Allen asked.

And he said: "Well . . . I am reasonable."

Was he on good terms with the neighbors? Of course not.

"I take my dogs to the village because of the *Jeeews.* The postmaster

destroys my letters. The druggist won't fill my prescriptions. . . ."
The barking dogs punctuated his words.

We walked right into a Céline novel. And he's telling us what shits the Danes were. Then a story about being shipped out during the war: the ship was torpedoed and the passengers are hysterical so Céline lines them all up and gives each of them a big shot of morphine, and they all got sick and vomited all over the boat.

He waved goodbye from the driveway and the dogs were raging and jumping against the fence.

BOCKRIS: Who else do you read?

BURROUGHS: A writer who I read and reread constantly is Conrad. I've read practically all of him. He has somewhat the same gift of transmutation that Genet does. Genet is talking about people who are very commonplace and dull. The same with Conrad. He's not dealing with unusual people at all, but it's his vision of them that transmutes them. His novels are very carefully written.

BOCKRIS: Is there anyone in particular who influenced your work?

BURROUGHS: I'd say Rimbaud is one of my influences, even though I'm a novelist rather than a poet. I have also been very much influenced by Baudelaire, and St.-John Perse, who in his turn was very much influenced by Rimbaud. I've actually cut out pages of Rimbaud and used some of that in my work. Any of the poetic or image sections of my work would show his influence.

MALANGA: Are you very self-critical or critical of others?

BURROUGHS: I'm certainly very self-critical. I'm critical of my work. And I do a great deal of editing. Sinclair Lewis said if you have just written something you think is absolutely great and you can't wait to publish it or show it to someone, throw it away. And I've found that to be very accurate. Tear it into small pieces and *throw* it into someone else's garbage can. It's terrible!

MALANGA: Do you have a lot of secrets?

BURROUGHS: I would say that I have no secrets. In the film *The Seventh Seal* the man asked Death, "What are your secrets?" Death replied, "I have no secrets." No writer has any secrets. It's all in his work.

MALANGA: In an article by your son that appeared in *Esquire* you were quoted as saying, "All past is fiction." Maybe you could explain this further.

BURROUGHS: Sure. We think of the past as being something that has

Burroughs being photographed by Warhol for a portrait at The Factory while a Wharholed Franz Kafka looks on discerningly. Photo by Bobby Grossman

just happened, right? Therefore, it is fact; but nothing could be further from the truth. This conversation is being recorded. Now suppose ten years from now you tamper with the recordings and change them around, after I was dead. Who could say that wasn't the actual recording? The past is something that can be changed, altered at your discretion. [*Burroughs points to the two Sonycorders facing each other that are taping this dinner.*] The only evidence that this conversation ever took place here is the recording, and if those recordings were altered, then that would be the only record. The past only exists in some record of it, right? There are no facts. We don't know how much of history is completely fiction. There was a young man named Peter Webber. He died in Paris, I believe, in 1956. His papers fell into my hands, quite by chance. I attempted to reconstruct the circumstances of his death. I talked to his girlfriend. I talked to all sorts of people. Everywhere I got a different story. He had died in this hotel. He had died in that hotel. He had died of an OD of heroin. He had died of withdrawal from heroin. He had died of a brain tumor. Everybody was either lying or covering up something; it was a regular *Rashomon* [reference is to the

Japanese film in which everybody gives a different account of the story; even the dead man who they bring back with a medium tells a completely different story] or they were simply confused. This investigation was undertaken two years after his death. Now imagine the inaccuracy of something that was one hundred years ago! The past is largely a fabrication by the living. And history is simply a bundle of fabrication. You see, there's no record this conversation ever took place or what was said, except what is on these machines. If the recordings were lost, or they got near a magnet and were wiped out, there would be no recordings whatever. So what were the actual facts? What was actually said here? There are no actual facts.

MALANGA: Is ESP something that has helped you in your writing?

BURROUGHS: Yes, I think all writers are actually dealing in this area. If you're not to some extent telepathic, then you can't be a writer, at least not a novelist where you have to be able to get into someone else's mind and *see* experience and what that person feels. I think that telepathy, far from being a special ability confined to a few psychics is quite widespread and used every day in all walks of life. Watch two horse traders. You can see the figures taking shape . . . "Won't go above . . . won't go below." Card players pride themselves on the ability to block telepathy, the "poker face." Anybody who is good at anything uses ESP.

Interrupting Bill again, Lou asked him which one of his books was his favorite.

BURROUGHS: Authors are notoriously bad judges of their own work. I don't really know . . .

Reed claimed that he had gone out and bought *Naked Lunch* as soon as it was published. He then asked what Burroughs thought of *City of Night* by John Rechy and *Last Exit to Brooklyn* by Hubert Selby, adding that these two books couldn't have been written without what Burroughs had done.

BURROUGHS: I admire *Last Exit to Brooklyn* very much. You can see the amount of time that went into the making of that book. It took seven years to write. And I like Rechy's work very much too. We met him out in L.A. Very pleasant man, I thought; we only saw him for about half an hour.

Reed asked whether Rechy had read Burroughs.

BURROUGHS: I didn't ask him, no.

18

Changing his tack radically, Lou said he'd heard that Burroughs had cut his toe off to avoid the draft.

BURROUGHS [*chuckling*]: I would prefer to neither confirm nor deny any of these statements.

Lou then wanted to know why Bill had used the name William Lee on *Junky*.

BURROUGHS: Because my parents were still alive and I didn't want them to be embarrassed.

Reed asked whether Burroughs' parents read.

BURROUGHS: They might have.

Reed told Bill that he felt *Junky* was his most important book because of the way it says something that hadn't been said before so straightforwardly. Reed then asked Bill if he was boring him.

BURROUGHS [*staring blankly at the table*]: Wha . . . ?

THREE SPEECHES

ALLEN GINSBERG: I nominated William Burroughs for membership in the *American Institute of Arts and Letters,* of which I'm a member, but I don't think he was accepted. So apparently the establishment still hasn't fully accepted him, although he is Supreme Establishment himself as far as literature: I think he's one of the immortals; he's had an enormous effect on succeeding generations of writers directly, and indirectly through my work and Kerouac's work in terms of his ideas, his ideologies, his Yankee pragmatic spiritual investigations. But directly—more importantly—through his own spectral prose. I think Burroughs should get the Nobel Prize. Genet never got it. Obviously Genet deserves it. Just Burroughs and Genet themselves are really two contenders for world honors.

MILES: William is a writer who has gone through a long period of addiction and survived. He spent twelve years as a drug addict and is one of the few people who have ever been able to really transform it into something solid, and use it. It really enabled him to understand a control system, and when he applied his understandings of the control systems to literature, which is essentially what he did, and what Brion helped him to do by introducing him to the cut-up technique, for instance, he automatically entered into a public field of information,

Driss ben Hamed Charhadi, author of A Life Full of Holes, *translated by Paul Bowles. Photo by Burroughs, taken in Madeira as they were both leaving Tangier*

Burroughs with books of ancient language. Note Brion Gysin drawings on wall behind him. Film still from Towers Open Fire *by Anthony Balch*

exposing control systems, which is what politics has been all about, the CIA, and word addiction and everything else Bill talks about, so his actual art and his literature have been about subjects which transcend literature and move out into everyday political experience as experienced by our generation, but not by his generation, oddly enough, which is why he's so important to the underground press and people like that. He is still probably the most relevant writer alive. He has that extraordinary combination of elements in his background which makes him that. He's able to transform things, and that's why people respond to him. He also has that cynical funny angle like Céline that appeals to a certain type of person who has taken a lot of drugs maybe. He's actually a humorist to a lot of people who transcend the superficial level of a lot of present-day humor that we get fed on. William is probably the funniest person you can come upon. As a writer, I think he's in a very crucial phase right now. He's obviously always going to be important, but he hasn't achieved the kind of success that he deserves. His career parallels Kerouac's in this respect. His early books are really significant but no one realized that until about six years later. Then he got really famous and kept on writing. But Kerouac's later books weren't as good. I think Bill's capable of better than that. He could grow to produce something that is better than *Naked Lunch.* I don't think William ever needs to justify himself as a writer. He's written a lot. He hasn't just written *Ulysses* and *Finnegans Wake.* William's had an absolute rebirth since he came back to the States. He's a very different person now, much more confident in his position as some kind of literary celebrity and I think it was moving back to New York that enabled him to do that. Shortly after he went back he told me, "It's really good, but one standing ovation is enough."

Certainly of the Beat Generation, Bill was the one that no one was ever able to put tabs on, because his approach was always so very different. For a start, Burroughs was in a funny kind of way openly gay. Even Allen's gayness was different. His was a kind of proselytizing, campaigning gayness, whereas Bill's was very different. Bill was always the absolute antithesis of what the society was doing, which is why he stayed out of America. He couldn't have made it here. Allen could make it. William went through a lot of very heavy times. Don't forget most people thought he was dead when he arrived back in the States. They thought he and Kerouac had just snuffed.

BURROUGHS: To my way of thinking the function of the poet is to make us aware of what we know and don't know we know. Allen Ginsberg's opinions, his writings, his works, and his outspoken attitudes towards sex and drugs, were once fully disreputable and unacceptable and now have become acceptable and in fact respectable. And this occasion is an indication of this shift in opinion. You remember it was extremely unacceptable once to say that the earth was round, and I think that this shift whereby original thinkers are accepted is very beneficial both to those who are accepting them and to the thinkers themselves. Somerset Maugham said that the greatest asset that any writer can have is longevity, and I think that in another ten or fifteen or twenty years, Allen may be a very deserving recipient of the Nobel Prize.

DINNER WITH LOU REED: NEW YORK 1979

BOCKRIS: Was Kerouac the writer you felt closest to in your generation?

BURROUGHS: He encouraged me to write when I was not really interested in it. There's that. But stylistically, or so far as influence goes, I don't feel close to him at all. If I should mention the two writers who had the most direct effect on my writing, they would be Joseph Conrad and Denton Welch, not Kerouac. In the 1940s, it was Kerouac who kept telling me I should write and call the book I would write *Naked Lunch*. I had never written anything after high school and did not think of myself as a writer and I told him so. I had tried a few times, a page maybe. Reading it over always gave me a feeling of fatigue and disgust and aversion toward this form of activity, such as a laboratory rat must experience when he chooses the wrong path and gets a sharp reprimand from a needle in his displeasure centers. Jack insisted quietly that I did have talent for writing and that I would write a book called *Naked Lunch*. To which I replied, "I don't want to hear anything literary." During all the years I knew Kerouac I can't remember ever seeing him really angry or hostile. It was the sort of smile he gave in reply to my demurs, in a way you get from a priest who knows you will come to Jesus sooner or later—you can't walk out on the Shakespeare Squad, Bill.

BOCKRIS: When did you write *Naked Lunch*?

BURROUGHS: In the summer of 1956 I went to Venice and made a few notes there, and then I had this trip to Libya. I went to the American Embassy there and said, "Well, how can I get out of here? All the planes are full, can I just get on a train?"

22

Burroughs in the garden of the Villa Muneiria, Tangier, in 1957, when he was in the middle of writing Naked Lunch. *Photo by Allen Ginsberg*

"Oh no," they said, "you have to have an exit permit." And so I went around. I remember going to this courtyard with porticos around and looking for some official who was supposed to do this and he wasn't ever there. In fact, he did not exist, as I came to suspect. So finally somebody told me, "Listen, just get on a train and leave." That's what I did, and when I got to the Moroccan border the French guard sort of looked at my papers, but I was leaving, see, and he didn't want to make a fuss so he just stamped it and said, "Go ahead," and I was back in Morocco. I could have been sitting around for months waiting for an exit visa according to the American Embassy: "Oh, you have to have this. It would be very inadvisable to leave without it. We couldn't help you . . ." So it was just at this time that I sat down and I had lots of notes that I'd made in Scandinavia, Venice, and Tangier previously, and started writing, and I wrote and I wrote and I wrote. I'd usually take majoun every other day and on the off days I would just have a bunch of big joints lined up on my desk and smoke them as I typed. I was getting up pretty early; I'd work most of the day, sometimes into the early evening. I used to go out and row in the bay every day for exercise. I had this room for which I was paying, God, $15 a month for a nice room on the garden of the Hotel Muneria there with a big comfortable bed and a dresser and a washstand and everything, with a toilet just around the corner. When Jack came to Tangier in 1957 I had decided to take his title and much of the book was already written.

BOCKRIS: When you were writing then, did you have any intimation of the effect it might have?

BURROUGHS: None whatever. I doubted that it would ever be published. I had no idea that the manuscript had any value. I was terrifically turned on by what I was writing.

BOCKRIS: Did Kerouac have all his experiences so he could write about them?

BURROUGHS: I'd say that he was there as a writer, and not as a brakeman or whatever he was supposed to be. He said, "I am a spy in somebody else's body. I am not here as what I am supposed to be."

BOCKRIS: Is that what ultimately made him unhappy?

BURROUGHS: Not at all. It's true of all artists. You're not there as a newspaper reporter, a doctor or a policeman, you're there as a writer.

BOCKRIS: He seemed to lose contact with people, so that he ended up . . .

BURROUGHS: All writers lose contact. I wouldn't say that he was particularly miserable. He had an alcohol problem. It killed him.

BOCKRIS: When was the last time you saw him?

BURROUGHS: 1968. I had been at the Democratic Convention in Chicago, and *Esquire* had placed at my disposal a room in the Delmonico Hotel to write the story. Kerouac came to see me, and he was living at that time in Lowell. He had these big brothers-in-law, one of whom ran a liquor store, and they were shepherding him around. He was really hittin' it heavy, because he got another room in the hotel and stayed overnight, and he was ordering up bottles of whiskey and drinking in the morning, which is a practice I regard with horror. So I talked to the Greek brothers . . . you know . . . "Terrible he's hittin' it like this and not doing any work . . ." That was the last time.

BOCKRIS: Did you have much conversation?

BURROUGHS: Well, he's hittin' it heavy. That was when he went on the Buckley show, and I told him, "No, Jack, don't go, you're not in any condition to go." But he did go that same night. I said, "I'm not even going to go along." Allen Ginsberg went. It was, of course, a disaster. Jack and his in-law brothers left the next day. That was the last time I ever saw him. He was dead a year later. Cirrhosis, massive hemorrhage.

Lou Reed seemed extremely interested in Kerouac and wanted to know why he had ended up in such bad shape, sitting in front of a television set in a tee shirt drinking beer with his mother. What had happened to make Kerouac change?

BURROUGHS: He didn't change that much, Lou. He was always like that. First there was a young guy sitting in front of television in a tee shirt drinking beer with his mother, then there was an older fatter person sitting in front of television in a tee shirt drinking beer with his mother.

Addressing Bill as Mr. Burroughs, Lou asked if Kerouac's books were published because he had slept with his publisher. He wondered if that happened a lot in the literary world.

BURROUGHS: Not nearly as much as in painting. No, thank God, it is not very often that a writer will have to actually make it with his publisher in order to get published, but there are a lot of cases of young artists who will have to sleep with an older woman gallery owner or something to get their first show, or get a grant. I can definitely assure you that *I* have never had sex with any of my publishers. Thank God, it has not been necessary.

DINNER WITH MAURICE GIRODIAS, GERARD MALANGA, AND GLENN O'BRIEN: BOSTON 1978

MAURICE GIRODIAS: I like Bill Burroughs very much. He is about the nicest person I have ever met in this literary game. He is a very naive man. There is something naive about him that explains a lot of the mythological strangeness that is attached to his image and reputation.

BOCKRIS: What were the circumstances of your publishing *Naked Lunch?*

GIRODIAS: Allen Ginsberg brought me the first manuscript of *Naked Lunch* in 1957. He was acting as Burroughs' friendly agent. It was such a mess, that manuscript! You couldn't physically read the stuff, but whatever caught the eye was extraordinary and dazzling. So I returned it to Allen saying, "Listen, the whole thing has to be re-shaped." The ends of the pages were all eaten away, by the rats or something. . . . The prose was transformed into verse, edited by the rats of the Paris sewers. Allen was very angry at me, but he went back to Bill, who was leading a very secret life in Paris, a gray phantom of a man in his phantom gabardine and ancient discolored phantom hat, all looking like his moldy manuscript. Six months or so later he came back with a completely reorganized, readable manuscript, and I published it in 1959. Burroughs was very hard to talk to because he didn't say anything. He had these incredibly masklike, ageless features—completely cold-looking. At this time ne was living with Brion Gysin and Gysin would do all the talking. I'd go down to Gysin's room and he would talk and show me his paintings and explain things. Then we'd go back to Burroughs' room and all three of us would sit on the bed—because there were no chairs—and try to make conversation. It was really funny. The man just didn't say anything. I had my Brazilian nightclub and the first time Burroughs came there—it was soon after I met him—I was in the cellar giving an impromptu lesson in the tango to one of John Calder's assistants who came over every summer for these tango lessons. I'm down there with her alone when Burroughs suddenly comes down the stairs and he says: "Girodias . . . I don't want to disturb anything at all that's going on down here, but . . ." It turned out the Beat Hotel had been raided and he'd been busted for possession of some hash or something and he wanted my help. He kept saying: "These French cops . . ." After I published *Naked Lunch,* I published a book of his every six months. *The Soft Machine, The Ticket That Exploded.* I never had much editorial conversation with him, actually none. He'd just bring in the manuscript and I'd knock it out. I think he was doing it to pay the rent. He really needed the money.

BURROUGHS: I would like to lay to rest for all time the myth of the Burroughs millions which has plagued me for many years. One reviewer has even gone as far as to describe me as "the world's richest ex-junkie" at a time when I had less than $1,000 in the bank. My grandfather, who invented the hydraulic device on which the adding machine is based, like many inventors received a very small share of the company stock; my father sold the few shares in his possession in the 1920s. My last bequest from the Burroughs estate on the death of my mother in 1970 was the sum of $10,000.

BOCKRIS: Do you ever get worried that being a writer provides a pretty thin income?

BURROUGHS: It's gotten very thin. I've sat down many times and tried to write a bestseller but something always goes wrong. It isn't that I can't bring myself to do it or that I feel I'm commercializing myself or anything like that, but it just doesn't work. If your purpose is to make a lot of money on a book or film, there are certain rules to observe. You're aiming for the general public, and there are all sorts of things the general public doesn't want to see or hear. A good rule is never ask the general public to experience anything they cannot easily experience. You don't want to scare them to death, knock them out of their seats, and above all, you don't want to puzzle them.

GLENN O'BRIEN: Maybe we have to go into show business.

BURROUGHS: We already have, for Godsakes, with all these readings. That's the way I make a living, man!

O'BRIEN: We'll probably wind up as stand-up comedians or something.

BURROUGHS: My God! I already have been described as a stand-up comedian.

MALANGA: Would you ever like to apply your knowledge of telepathy in areas other than writing? Let's say, the stock market?

BURROUGHS: A deep misuse of these powers is always going to fuck you up. I used to do some gambling. Horseraces. I've had dreams and intuitions, and something always went wrong. That is, I had a number but I didn't have the horse, or I had the horse and I didn't have the number. I think this is a misuse of telepathy. If you're trying to take something from this level and bring it down to this level, you're going to get fucked every time. The classical story about that was *The Queen of Spades*—a Russian story about someone who was getting telepathic tips on gambling and, of course, finally got fucked.

MALANGA: So you think using telepathy for gambling purposes is a disrespect of one's powers?

BURROUGHS: All gamblers use telepathy for gambling purposes; all gambling works on telepathy. But it's a tricky area. And gambling is something I absolutely don't want to know about anymore, or let's say the use of telepathic powers or extrasensory perception in those areas, because I know sooner or later you're going to get the shaft and you'll well deserve it.

BOCKRIS: How do they absorb used-up money?

BURROUGHS: They burn it. Ted Joans had an uncle who worked in the combustion department and he figured out some way to get this stuff out under his coat and he had a big stack of it under his porch. His wife saw somebody going by in an old beat-up car and she said, "It'd be nice to get one," and he said, "Well, pretty soon we will," and he told her. Next thing he knew they were knocking on his door. Telephone. Telegraph. Television. Tell a woman. He got twenty years.

DINNER WITH TENNESSEE WILLIAMS:
NEW YORK 1977

BURROUGHS: When someone asks me to what extent my work is auto-biographical, I say, "Every word is autobiographical, and every word is fiction." Now what would your answer be on that question?

TENNESSEE WILLIAMS: My answer is that every word is autobiographical and no word is autobiographical. You can't do creative work and adhere to facts. For instance, in my new play there is a boy who is living in a house that I lived in, and undergoing some of the experiences that I underwent as a young writer. But his personality is totally different from mine. He talks quite differently from the way that I talk, so I say the play is not autobiographical. And yet the events in the house did actually take place. I avoid talking about writing. Don't you, Bill?

BURROUGHS: Yes, to some extent. But I don't go as far as the English do. You know this English bit of never talking about anything that means anything to anybody . . . I remember Graham Greene saying, "Of course, Evelyn Waugh was a very good friend of mine, but we never talked about writing!"

———

WILLIAMS: There's something very private about writing, don't you think? Somehow it's better, talking about one's most intimate sexual practices—you know—than talking about writing. And yet it's what I think we writers live for: writing. It's what we live for, and yet we can't discuss it with any freedom. It's very sad . . . Anyway, I'm leaving America, more or less for good. Going to England first.

BURROUGHS: For good or for bad . . .

WILLIAMS: Well, when I get to Bangkok it may be for bad, I don't know [*laughter*]. And after I get through with this play in London, I should go to Vienna. I love Vienna. You remember the twenties?

BURROUGHS: Oh heavens, yes.

WILLIAMS: I only ask because there are few people living who do . . . That's the sad thing about growing old, isn't it—you learn you are confronted with loneliness. . . .

BURROUGHS: One of the many.

WILLIAMS: Yes, one of the many—that's the worst, yes.

Burroughs and Williams in the drawing room of the latter's suite at the Elysee Hotel. Photo by Michael McKenzie.

BURROUGHS: After all, if there wasn't age, there wouldn't be any youth, remember.

WILLIAMS: I'm never satisfied to look back on youth, though . . . not that I ever had much youth.

BURROUGHS: Writers don't, as a rule.

WILLIAMS: I was in Vienna in 1936. Remember the Römanische Baden?

BURROUGHS: The Roman Baths. I went to them . . . they're lovely, too.

WILLIAMS: Right near where the Prater used to be.

BURROUGHS: I've ridden on that ferris wheel in the park.

WILLIAMS: Me, too.

ON DREAMS

BURROUGHS: There couldn't be a society of people who didn't dream. They'd be dead in two weeks.

MALANGA: Do you have a certain technique for notating dreams?

BURROUGHS: If you don't write them down right away, in many cases you'll forget them. I keep a pencil and paper by my bed. I've had dreams where I've continued episodes—"to be continued"—and if they're goodies you want to get back there as quick as possible, but I always make a point, even though I want to get back there, of making just a few notes, otherwise the next day you'll lose the whole thing. If I just make two words here, that'll get me back there. There's some basic difference between memory traces of a dream and the actual event. Now I've had this happen: I'd wake up and I'm too lazy to get up and I'll go over it ten times in my mind and say, "Well, sure I'll certainly remember that." Gone. So memory traces are lighter for dreams than they are for so-called events. I keep a regular dream diary. Then, if they're particularly interesting or important I'll expand them into dream-scenes that might be usable in a fictional context by making a longer typewritten account. Sometimes I get long sequential narrative dreams just like a movie, and some of these have gone almost verbatim into my work. In some ways the most fruitful dreams have been when I find a book or magazine with a story in it I can read. It

William and James with first proof copies of Cities of the Red Night, *which Grauerholz worked on closely with Burroughs. Note the subtitle,* A Boy's Book, *which was later removed from the jacket and title page. Photo by Victor Bockris*

can be hard to remember, but sometimes I get a whole chapter that way and the next day I just sit down and write it out. The opening chapter of *Cities of the Red Night*—The Health Officer—was such a chapter, a dream that I had about a cholera epidemic in Southwest Africa, and I just sat down and wrote it out. I was reading rather than writing. And then the story *They Do Not Always Remember,* which appeared in *Exterminator,* was also a dream. I don't know if other writers have them, but it's certainly a writer's dream.

MALANGA: Learning to get hold of this material is a technical matter, so I presume it's something you get better at.

BURROUGHS: You can get feedback: I've had a dream and I write something about it; then, as a result of writing something, I have a further dream along the same lines. I'm getting feedback between what I write and what I'm dreaming about.

BOCKRIS: Have you always had this habit of waking up a lot during the night?

BURROUGHS: I've always been a very light sleeper. The slightest thing wakes me up. I wake up five or six times in the course of an average night. I get up and maybe have some milk or a glass of water, or write down some dreams, if I have any. I was once in a room with another person who set the mattress on fire. *His* mattress, but I was the one that woke up. Oooooh, smoke! Wide awake. I've always defied anyone to get in the room with me without waking me up. Just the presence of another person is enough. Sometimes if I can't go back to sleep I'll read for a while. I have about six books by my bed that I'm reading. And it's the only thing to do if you have a real nightmare. Get up and fix yourself a cup of coffee or tea and stay up for ten minutes to reorient yourself, because if you go right back to sleep you're going right back into it. Sometimes I'll have three real nightmares in a row, so I say now it's time to stop, break the chain. I will get up, maybe have some tea, smoke a joint, anything to break it up. The best thing to do is get up and have something to drink.

BOCKRIS: I've had nightmares in which it seems that somebody or something has gotten into the apartment.

BURROUGHS: I had this experience with James. When I first came back to New York we were sleeping in a loft over on Broadway and I had this dream: There was a knock at the back door, I went to the back door and there was this person known as Marty. I've got a little chapter in *Cities* about this, and he was there with a chauffeur, a bearded man, who was so drunk he could hardly stand up. It was all sort of 1890s, see. "Come along to the Metropole and have some bubbly," as he put it, some champagne. The Metropole was the old hangout in the 1890s. It was around Times Square. And I said, "Oh Marty, no." I said, "You know . . ."

He said, "What's the matter, your old pals aren't good enough for you anymore?"

"I don't remember that we were exactly *pals,* Marty!" I replied. This is someone I'd known, sort of *real bad news.* Then he said, "Let me in, I've come a long way," and he shoved his way into the apartment. Then I had pictures of James covered with a white foam and I was trying to wake up, saying, "James! James!" When I did finally wake up he was out of bed and he had picked up a pipe threader that was there and I said, "What's the matter?" He answered, "I just felt that there was someone in the apartment."

"Well," I said, "someone indeed was in the apartment. That was Marty." So I used Marty as a character in *Cities*. Marty Blum.

* * *

In 1977, Bob Dylan invited Burroughs to join the Rolling Thunder tour to participate in some way in the movie *Renaldo and Clara*. Burroughs declined on the grounds that the offer was too ill-defined to be worth his while. During this period he had two dreams about Dylan.

In the first dream he had the idea that he should suggest a benefit concert for junkies. After seeing Dylan's Madison Square Garden benefit performance for Rubin Hurricane Carter, Burroughs had a second dream that told him to forget the idea on the grounds that he would not be able to hold the attention of the vast audience that Dylan commands.

BOCKRIS: When did you first meet Bob Dylan?
BURROUGHS: In a small café in the Village, around 1965. A place where they only served wine and beer. Allen had brought me there. I had no idea who Dylan was, I knew he was a young singer just getting started. He was with his manager, Albert Grossman, who looked like a typical manager, heavy kind of man with a beard, and John Hammond, Jr., was there. We talked about music. I didn't know a lot about music—a lot less than I know now, which is still very little—but he struck me as someone who was obviously competent in his subject. If his subject had been something that I knew absolutely nothing about, such as mathematics, I would have still received the same impression of competence. Dylan said he had a knack for writing lyrics and expected to make a lot of money. He had a likable direct approach in conversation, at the same time cool, reserved. He was very young, quite handsome in a sharp-featured way. He had on a black turtleneck sweater.

DINNER WITH STEWART MEYER: NEW YORK 1979

MEYER: Bill, when I make something up out of the clear blue sky where is it coming from?
BURROUGHS: Man, nothing comes out of the clear blue sky. You've got your memory track . . . everything you've ever seen or heard is walk-

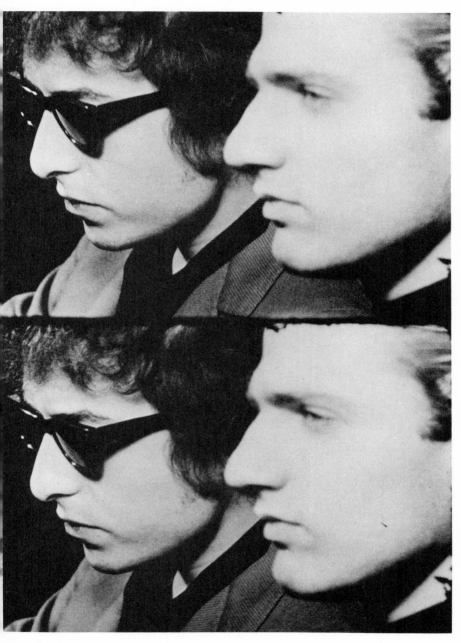

Bob Dylan and Gerard Malanga in a scene from Film Notebooks *(circa 1965, The Warhol Factory), a film by Gerard Malanga. Photo by Gerard Malanga*

Stewart Meyer and Burroughs after dinner at the Bunker. Note Burroughs' NO METRIC T-*shirt. Photo by Victor Bockris*

ing around with you. Remember the line "All a Jew wants to do is doodle a Christian girl, you know that yourself," from *Naked Lunch*? I heard that line verbatim. I thought to myself, "Goooooood Lord, now I've heard it all." But the line came in handy.

MEYER: Right away?

BURROUGHS: Give or take thirty years.

MEYER: What stops the flow for me is, I'm sitting there writing and dreaming freely, then I start to watch myself.

BURROUGHS: Who's watching you when you're watching yourself?

MEYER: Is a tightrope walker a tightrope walker all the time?

BURROUGHS: Well, yes. I'll just cower in the Bunker and leave that stuff to the professionals.

MEYER: Too bad the subconscious mind can't be triggered like the conscious.

BURROUGHS: It can.

MEYER: What? How?

BURROUGHS: Do nothing. Only secret to tapping the subconscious mind is do nothing. This corresponds to the Buddhist thing.

MEYER: But it isn't a direct trigger.

BURROUGHS: The conscious and subconscious work completely differently.

MEYER: How necessary do you think the conscious mind is?

BURROUGHS: I think the conscious mind will eventually be phased out as a failed experiment. Think of it: no conscious egos. All that negativity done away with.

BOCKRIS: What do you believe in?

BURROUGHS: Belief is a meaningless word. What does it mean? I believe something. Okay, now you have someone who is hearing voices and believes in these voices. It doesn't mean they have any necessary reality. Your whole concept of your "I" is an illusion. You have to give something called an "I" before you speak of what the "I" believes.

BOCKRIS: What's your greatest strength and weakness?

BURROUGHS: My greatest strength is to have a great capacity to confront myself no matter how unpleasant. My greatest weakness is that I don't. I know that's enigmatic, but that's sort of a general formula for anyone, actually.

DINNER WITH ALLEN GINSBERG: NEW YORK 1980

BOCKRIS: What frightens you most?

BURROUGHS: Possession. It seems to me this is the basic fear. There is nothing one fears more or is more ashamed of than not being oneself. Yet few people realize even an approximation of their true potential. Most people must live with varying degrees of the shame and fear of not being fully in control of themselves.

Imagine that the invader has taken over your motor centers. There you are at a party, press cameras popping away, and suddenly you know you are going to exhibit yourself and shit at the same time. You try to run, your legs won't move. Your hands, however, are moving, unzipping your fly.

And all this is within the range of modern technology. Professor

Delgado can make a subject pick something up by electric brain stimulation. No matter how hard the subject tried to resist the electronic command, he was helpless to intervene.

No doubt this good thing has come to the attention of the dirty trick department. So Brezhnev shits in the UN and Reagan exposes himself in front of a five-year-old child at a rally. Perhaps they decided to outlaw that one like the Jivaro [a tribe of headhunting Indians found mostly in Ecuador] outlawed the use of curare darts in feud killings. It's such a horrible death. And the humiliation inflicted by MC [Motor Control]. Sanction is literally a fate worse than death, a horrible maimed existence . . . madness or suicide.

It shouldn't happen to your worst enemy because the way this universe is connected, it could happen back at YOU.

Centipedes frighten me a good deal, although this is not an actual *phobia* where people are *incapacitated* by the sight of a centipede. I simply look around for something with which to combat this creature. I have a recurring nightmare where some very large poison centipede, or scorpion about this long, suddenly rushes on me while I'm looking about for something to kill it. Then I wake up screaming and kicking the bedclothes off. The last time was in Greece in August 1973. I was with my mother in a rather incestuous context. I think the ideal situation for a family is to be completely incestuous. So this is a slightly incestuous connection with my mother and I said, "Mother, I am going to kill the scorpion." It was a big thing, about this long. At this point the scorpion suddenly rushed upon me, and I had nothing to kill it with. I was looking around for a shoe or something. I woke up kicking the bedclothes off. Then I remember another dream, which is in *Exterminator,* where someone had one of these fucking things about eighteen inches long and I said, "Get away from me!" I had a snub-nosed .38 in my hand. And I said, "Get away from me with that fucking thing or I'll kill you!" This was a combination scorpion-centipede about six inches long that runs very quickly.

BOCKRIS: Have you ever had an actual run-in with a scorpion?
BURROUGHS: I've had them around and I've killed them. I've never had one try to attack me.
BOCKRIS: Have you ever come upon one, unexpectedly in bed?
BURROUGHS: In southeast Texas I found them on the wall in my room; it drove me crazy. I can't sleep if I think there's a scorpion in the room.

If I don't succeed in killing it, then it keeps me awake all night. It's an awful electric feeling. I mean the idea of one getting on me is horrible. It's something you can't empathize with at all. It's completely disgusting. They've got no feeling at all; the thought of touching one gives me the absolute horrors—all those legs! A friend of mine told me his most horrible experience in the Pacific during World War II. He was in one of those jungle hammocks with a net over it. He woke up and a six-inch-long centipede was on the side of his face pulling his cheek all out of shape. He reached up and grabbed it. He's holding this fucking thing in one hand, trying to open the zipper with the other hand! He said it's like holding a red hot wire! This thing was writhing around biting his hand, and finally he got the zipper open and threw it out.

BOCKRIS: Could we employ insects in a useful way?

BURROUGHS: I don't know any useful work for a centipede.

BOCKRIS: Couldn't they be regular assassins if well trained?

BURROUGHS: Fu Manchu used to have a poison insect routine. He put some sort of perfume on someone that would attract this venomous creature. I think one was a big red spider that he called a Red Bride.

GINSBERG: Have you ever had a dream in which you murdered somebody and the guilt was hidden and you had heavy anxiety?

BURROUGHS: Oh, sure. I've hurt somebody, sometimes they've just hidden around . . .

GINSBERG: This is an archetypal thing because I had that the other night. In this case there was an elderly woman who was a concierge who didn't like me and I was sucking up to her trying to get a room, or trying to be at home in that country, and I was afraid that she already knew that I had this secret corpse somewhere in my past I hadn't quite acknowledged to myself yet, I hadn't quite remembered, what was the crime I committed, but I knew that it was some dreadful secret that would be uncovered any minute at the tip of my tongue or hers. But meanwhile we sat and had tea while I asked her for a room, and then she looked at me and said, "By the way, how would you like to fuck me?" And I said, "Sure," because I realized I better play up to her or she would realize I had killed a woman or something . . .

BURROUGHS: How many'd you kill?

GINSBERG: Oh, just the entire race by obliterating them in my mind and not fucking them at all. Having not had sex with a woman since 1967.

BURROUGHS [*impatiently*]: That's metaphysical, purely metaphysical. [*Bored*]: You're talking about insecurity. [*Annoyed*]: What are we talking about?!

GINSBERG: I woke up then and realized it was only a dream. Then I began examining why I would have that dream unless I had some hypocrisy or some deception?

BURROUGHS: Oh, good heavens, my dear! I don't know. I always have dreams of being arrested or tried or something like that.

GINSBERG: But the dream of concealing a murder is one I've had about four or five times, colored by dread and anxiety, a spiritual, poetic Watergate, you know. So I searched: was it 1968 in my testimony at the Chicago trials I said nobody intended violence? Was it income tax evasion?

BURROUGHS: You're too spooky . . .

GINSBERG: Was it Vajrayana delights? Or what! Was it actually being gay and not making out with women and not having children?

BURROUGHS: So what?

GINSBERG: Or was it that the night before I'd read a story which had that plot?

40

ON WOMEN

DINNER WITH ANDY WARHOL AND MARCIA
RESNICK: NEW YORK 1980

BOCKRIS: Bill was married twice. Ilse Burroughs was his first wife. Like
W. H. Auden he married a woman to get her out of Nazi occupied
Europe. W. H. Auden married Thomas Mann's daughter, Elsa Mann,
right?

BURROUGHS: Refuting any imputation of anti-Semitism.

ANDY WARHOL: And she lived on the Lower East Side.

BOCKRIS: And Ilse Burroughs is still alive.

WARHOL: No, no, but Mrs. Auden lived on the Lower East Side, St.
Marks Place. God!

BURROUGHS: Mrs. Burroughs certainly does not live on the Lower East
Side! She lives in some fashionable place in Italy.

BOCKRIS: She's apparently very wealthy.

BURROUGHS: I don't see how she could be wealthy. Certainly not from
me.

MARCIA RESNICK: Did she marry you to get a green card or something?

BURROUGHS: Yes. To get away from the Nazis. She came to America
and her first job was to work for Ernst Toller. Toller was a left-wing
playwright with a certain reputation at that time. She was working as
his secretary and she always kept very regular hours, getting back at
exactly one o'clock after she'd gone out to lunch. On this day she met
an old refugee on the street, someone she knew from the old Weimar

41

days, so they had a coffee and she was delayed about ten minutes. When she got back she sat down at the typewriter, "and then," she makes a gesture, "I get it up the back of my neck and I know he is hanging up somewhere."

So she goes to the bathroom and finds Toller is hanging on the other side and manages to get him down. But he was already dead. He'd attempted suicide several times before but always arranged it so someone got there in time to turn off the gas, or call an ambulance. The old refugee did him in.

Burroughs has often been asked about his attitudes toward women. "I think anybody incapable of changing his mind is crazy," he recently answered. Although Bill generally surrounds himself with male company, there are a number of women whom he sees regularly and has a real affection for: Mary McCarthy, who lives in Paris with her diplomat husband Jim West; Susan Sontag; Normandy-based American socialite Panna O'Grady; Italian litterateur Fernanda Pivano; English editor Sonia Orwell; publishing doyen Mary Beach; and Felicity Mason, a.k.a. Anne Cummings, author of *The Love Habit: Sexual Confessions of an Older Woman* [about which William has written: *"Anne Cummings is the forerunner of the truly emancipated woman of the future, who is casual about her emancipation. Love affairs, she feels, should provide divertissement, not disillusionment. Sex is something to enjoy, a means of universal communication that bridges the generation gap."*] are all friends of many years' standing. Among his younger women friends are poet-teacher Anne Waldman and chanteuse Patti Smith. There are a number of women writers whom Bill considers highly, among them Mary McCarthy, Joan Didion, Susan Sontag, Djuna Barnes, Carson McCullers, Flannery O'Connor, Jane Bowles, Dorothy Parker, Eudora Welty, Isabelle Eberhardt and Colette.

His second wife, whom he accidentally shot and killed, was Joan Vollmer, with whom he had, according to Kerouac, Huncke and Ginsberg, an extremely close, mutually supportive and affectionate relationship.

DINNER WITH BOCKRIS-WYLIE: NEW YORK 1974

BOCKRIS-WYLIE: How'd you feel when you shot your second wife?
BURROUGHS: That was an accident. That is to say, if everyone is to be

Burroughs Heir Held
After Wife's Slaying

MEXICO CITY, Sept. 7 (INS).—William Seward Burroughs, 37, St. Louis scion of the adding machine family, was held by police today in what they described as the fatal "William Tell" shooting of his wife, Joan Vollmer Burroughs, 27, formerly of Albany, N. Y.

Burroughs, namesake of his grandfather who invented the adding machine in 1885, said he hazily remembered playing with a gun but said his wife's death was purely accidental.

The official police report said the couple visited friends last night in the apartment of John Healy of Milwaukee. Gin drinks were served, the report said, and hours later Mrs. Burroughs was shot in the forehead and died in a hospital without regaining consciousness.

Burroughs was quoted in the report as saying at the hospital he tried "to emulate William Tell" by placing a glass of gin

Disheveled William S. Burroughs, shown in Mexico City jail, says it was accidental.
(AP WIREphoto)

on his wife's head and firing at it from a distance of about two yards.

In a later interview, he denied putting a glass on his wife's head and said "if she did it, it was a joke and I certainly did not intend to shoot at it."

Burroughs and his wife arrived here three days ago en route from Ecuador to Pharr, Tex., where he maintains a home and owns a cotton field.

The dead woman was his second wife. They were married in 1946 in New York City shortly after he obtained a divorce from Mrs. Ilse Burroughs.

1, 1951.

1948. The Assembly is due to meet here again in November.

Interpreting its instruction literally, the commission will try a change of tactics at this conference. Instead of confining itself to conciliation it will take on the role of mediator and will propose specific solutions to specific problems.

TRIAL ORDERED IN KILLING

Mexican Judge Holds Burroughs in Death of Wife

MEXICO CITY, Sept. 10 (*P*)— William S. Burroughs of a prominent St. Louis family was held today for trial on a charge of fatally shooting his wife.

Judge Eduardo Urzaiz Jimenez ordered "formal prison" on a homicide charge for the 37-year-old grandson of the Burroughs adding machine inventor. That is the Mexican court preliminary to a trial.

Court officials declined to say when the next hearing would be held. Mexican law requires a decision in a criminal case within a year. Burroughs' counsel has not asked for his release in bond. The judge's order followed the hearing of two witnesses, whose testimony backed Burroughs' own story that a pistol had gone off accidentally while he was looking to see whether it was loaded.

made responsible for everything they do, you must extend responsibility beyond the level of conscious intention. I was aiming for the very tip of the glass. This gun was a very inaccurate gun, however.

BOCKRIS-WYLIE: But after you shot her did you think, "I'm being controlled by something else and that's why this happened?"

BURROUGHS: No, I thought nothing. It was too horrific. It's very complicated to tell you. It was obviously a situation precipitated by some part of myself over which I had, or perhaps have, no control. Because I remember on the day in which this occurred, I was walking down the street and suddenly I found tears streaming down my face. "What in hell is the matter? What in hell is the matter with you?" And then I took a knife to be sharpened which I had bought in Ecuador and I went back to this apartment. Because I felt so terrible, I began throwing down one drink after the other. And then this thing occurred.

BOCKRIS-WYLIE: How did it happen?

BURROUGHS: We'd been drinking for some time in this apartment. I was very drunk. I suddenly said, "It's about time for our William Tell act. Put the glass on your head." I aimed at the top of the glass, and then there was a great sort of flash.

BOCKRIS-WYLIE: How far away were you?

BURROUGHS: About eight feet.

BOCKRIS-WYLIE: What's the first thing you thought when you saw that you'd missed the glass?

BURROUGHS: Lewis Adelbert Marker was there; I said, "Call my lawyer. Get me out of this situation." I was, as the French say, *"bouleversé."* This is a terrible thing that has happened, but I gotta get my ass outta this situation. In other words, what went on in my mind was—I have shot my wife, this is a terrible thing, but I gotta be thinking about myself. It was an accident. My lawyer came to see me. Everyone's evidently overwhelmed by the situation, in tears, and he says, "Well, your wife is no longer in pain, she is dead. But don't worry, I, Señor Abogado, am going to defend you." He said, "You will not go to jail." I was in jail. "You will not stay in jail. In Mexico is no capital punishment." I knew they couldn't shoot me. "This is the district attorney," he said. "He works in my office, so do na worry." I got over to the jailhouse. That was something else. I had this fucking gypsy who was a may–or. See, every cell block in the Mexico City jail has a may–or, a guy that runs the cell block, and he said, "Well we got decent people in here and people who will pull your pants off you. I am puttin' you in with decent people. But for this, I need money." So then I was in with all these lawyers, doctors, and engineers, guilty or not guilty of various crimes. One of my great friends in the jail was a guy who had been in the diplomatic service who'd been accused of issuing fraudulent immigration papers to people. And they were all just takin' it easy. We're eating inna restaurant, we're getting oysters and everything. All of a sudden the may-or gets on to this. He says, "This prick Burroughs is getting away with something here. We're gonna send you over to the cell block and I'm gonna put you in a colony where fifteen spastics will fuck you!" So I got over to the other cell block, and I said, "Well, this can't happen to me, ya know. THIS CAN'T HAPPEN TO ME!" You get this tremendous sense of self-preservation. So I talked to the guy and I said, "Listen, I'll pay you so much, ya know, not to do these things." Then the may-or over in the other cell block finds out what I'm doin'. He says he's cooled the may-or over there. And he's really putting the pressure on. It was just at this point that I got out. My lawyer got me out. In the nick of time, because they were really puttin' the pressure on. Some guy—the may-or—came over there and said, "Listen do you wanna go in the *colonia?* This is the place where all the big bank robbers go and everyone is having big poker games. They got nice beds and all this." I said, "Man, I don't wanna sit down and spend my life in this place, I wanna get out of here!" Just at this point my lawyer got me out.

BOCKRIS-WYLIE: After you got out of jail in Mexico, did you split?

BURROUGHS: No. I split about a year later, because I had to go back every Monday by nine o'clock to check in. They could put you back in jail. All these different people who put their thumbprints on things because they couldn't write, cops and everybody, all had to be there by nine o'clock. This woman would come in and say, "Hello, boys." A teacher. A bureaucrat. Of course while I was actually in prison I had to be very careful of my reputation. I didn't want to get known as a queer or anything like that, because that can be a murderous situation. I got some great human statements from the guards. One guard said, "It's too bad when a man gets in jail because of a woman."

BOCKRIS-WYLIE: Do you go to porn flicks a lot?

BURROUGHS: Sure, sure.

BOCKRIS-WYLIE: Do you tend to get more turned on by men or women?

BURROUGHS: I've seen both, I've seen nongay and gay porn flicks. Naturally, I'm more turned on by men than women. But if you have a beautiful woman . . . I saw this one porn flick that had beautiful women in it and that sort of turned me on too. It reminded me of the old days in the whorehouses in St. Louis. I used to come down after having made it with a whore, and the madam would shove me into a little alcove because someone else was coming in. It might be a friend of my father's. Or even my father himself.

BOCKRIS-WYLIE: How much did it cost in those days?

BURROUGHS: Five dollars.

BOCKRIS-WYLIE: How long did you have?

BURROUGHS: Five dollars gave you a half hour.

* * *

Burroughs is often regarded as a misogynist. "In the words of one of the greatest misogynists, plain Mr. Jones in Conrad's *Victory:* 'Women are a perfect curse,' " he wrote in *The Job* (1968). "I think they were a basic mistake, and the whole dualistic universe evolved from this error. Women are no longer essential for reproduction. And I think American women are possibly one of the worst expressions of the female sex because they've been allowed to go further. Love is a con put down by the female sex."

DINNER WITH BOCKRIS-WYLIE AND MILES:
NEW YORK 1974

BOCKRIS-WYLIE: Why'd you get married?

BURROUGHS: It was probably a question of circumstance. I didn't get married. I had a common-law wife, which is the same actually, because the lawyer told me, "Brother, if you're living with a woman and she is known as your wife, she *is* your wife!" Legally speaking. She can get alimony. She has exactly the same rights. She was an extraordinary person, one of the more perceptive and intelligent people I've known. Joan, for example, was the first, before I was into writing, or even thinking in these areas, who said that the Mayan priests must have experienced some sort of telepathic method of control.

BOCKRIS-WYLIE: How long did you actually live with her?

BURROUGHS: Three or four years.

BOCKRIS-WYLIE: I still don't understand how you got together with your wife.

BURROUGHS: There is a certain degree of inertia. You're living with someone, you seem to be getting along with them very well, and that sets up a relationship. It wouldn't happen now. Simple inertia. I got something that is understandable to all my junkie friends, namely an ooooold lady.

BOCKRIS-WYLIE: Were you in love with your wife?

BURROUGHS: I find great difficulty in defining what being in love with someone means.

BOCKRIS-WYLIE: Take it as the point where you start to lose power.

BURROUGHS: It's a very good definition, very good definition indeed, because if you are dependent on the other person . . . No, I was never in love with her in that sense.

BOCKRIS-WYLIE: Were you ever in love with anyone?

BURROUGHS: Oh, sure, in exactly that sense.

MILES: When Bill was in London he was much more extreme. He might, for example, seriously argue that women had all come from out of space. I really don't think he would say that these days. Mind you, it wasn't a metaphor. I think he actually believed it. We had some quite nasty arguments. I felt that I had to talk to him about this because it was making me feel uncomfortable. Apart from anything else, I had to consider whether or not I could bring any girlfriends around. That's one of the main reasons I didn't spend a lot of time with Bill throughout the sixties. William actually wanted to surround himself with an all male society and succeeded in doing so, in London anyway. Except when Johnny used to bring back these strange Irish ladies. Occasionally there'd be some fat blonde Irish girl running about and William would sulk in the corner while Johnny was trying to get rid of her. I think it was Johnny's sister, but she hadn't got any clothes on and it was a very uncomfortable situation for Bill.

DINNER WITH PATTI SMITH: NEW YORK 1980

Burroughs taped a conversation with Patti Smith for *High Times* in late 1979. The transcript was too long and the magazine rejected it.

47

Patti Smith and William Burroughs. A portrait by Robert Mapplethorpe
Photo by Robert Mapplethorpe

There were, however, some interesting exchanges in it. One was about having children. Burroughs said he'd heard a lot of women say they didn't want to have children. Patti said she'd had one and expressed her personal spartan feeling about it, in that she had no desire to see the child. She hoped that her child would have enough space to develop in and be with someone who would bring it up appropriately. Bill pointed out that there was less and less space and less and less opportunity and that "the more people have in common, the more of them you can get into less space with less friction. It's a matter of identification also," he continued. "The more contact you have with someone, if it's of a positive nature, naturally the easier it is to accept their presence in a limited space." Smith felt strongly that inspiration created space. She remembered that in school she'd been told that Burroughs' work was difficult to read, but she hadn't found it difficult at all when she finally encountered it.

DINNER WITH SUSAN SONTAG AND
JOHN GIORNO: NEW YORK 1980

BOCKRIS: Susan, do you still think it's harder to be a woman in America now than it was two years ago?

SONTAG: It's harder to be a woman anywhere than it is to be a man. It's probably less hard in America than in a lot of other places.

BURROUGHS: I think it's bloody hard to be anything.

SONTAG: We all know that, but on the other hand if I were black and sitting here and you said is it harder and then I said well sure it's hard anywhere, and then somebody else said well it's hard to be anything, you might think that was rather beside the point. Of course it's hard to be anything, but then there are additional disabilities.

BURROUGHS: But when you say it's hard to be a woman, you're speaking from a woman's standpoint, right? Things that might be very hard for you might be very easy for me, and vice versa. One man's hell is another man's paradise.

BOCKRIS: When did you meet Jane Bowles?

BURROUGHS: I don't remember when I first met her. She was someone of extreme charm. It was a number of years later that I read her books and realized what an extremely talented writer she was.

Felicity Mason (a.k.a. Anne Cummings, author of The Love Habit*) holding the manuscript of* Cities of the Red Night. *Photo by Victor Bockris*

BOCKRIS: What kind of relationship did she and Paul Bowles have when you knew them?

BURROUGHS: I know nothing about their relationship. My old Uncle Willy always told me, "Never interfere in a boy and girl fight." And the less you know about the relationship between two people who are married, or who are a couple living together, the better it is. That's something to stay out of.

BOCKRIS: The gulf between the sexes is growing. Men think it's harder to be a man while women think it's harder to be a woman . . .

BURROUGHS: Such semantic difficulties here. What do you mean by *hard to be,* and who is to be the judge of this? How hard is it to be what? I think it's very hard to be a person. I don't know . . .

SONTAG: It depends for whom.

BURROUGHS: I think it's just hard to be myself. It's hard to draw breath on this bloody planet.

BOCKRIS: Auden said that he was so glad when his sex drive died because it had always been a terrible nuisance to him.

BURROUGHS: Well, if it's a terrible nuisance to you there must be some

50

conflict connected with it. "God! Thank God that's ended!" It's a terrible English thing. They have the same attitude toward life. Life is something you muddle through, and "Thank God this is over," they say when they're dying. England is very antisexual. It's very much to do with the Queen!

BOCKRIS: How were they so successful if they had those two big problems?

BURROUGHS: They didn't have anything else to do except get out and conquer—you know *Serve the Queen,* the old Whore of Windsor, she lived to a great age. Eighty-three?

JOHN GIORNO: Ninety-three.

BURROUGHS: I think it was eighty-three, because it was not long enough to occasion comment, which it would have been if she'd lived to ninety-three.

BOCKRIS: Her husband died forty years before she did.

BURROUGHS: The same is true in the western cultures and particularly true in America. Wives outlive their husbands by many years. There's hubby working away and getting fat and under all this stress and he dies of a heart attack about the age of fifty-five. She then gets the money and lives on for another thirty years, during which she goes around the world with groups of women and they have bridge clubs. There's all these old biddies, with three or four hundred thousand dollars, and they all live in the same sort of motel. My friend Kells Elvins' father died and his mother got all that money, $250,000, a hell of a lot in those days. Then she married another one and he died so there was another $300,000. So here's this old biddy, who has no habits at all, with $550,000 and she went out and established herself in some sort of condominium. They have all sorts of retirement apartments for women of fifty-five or sixty with a lot of money and they play shuffleboard.

SUGAR, ALCOHOL, & MEAT

The Dial-A-Poem Poets

Album cover by Robert Mapplethorpe

ON MEN

DINNER WITH ANDY WARHOL: NEW YORK 1980

BURROUGHS: Cocteau had this party trick that he would pull. He would lie down, take off his clothes, and come spontaneously. Could do that even in his fifties. He'd lie down there and his cock would start throbbing and he'd go off. It was some film trick that he had.

BOCKRIS: How'd he pull that off? Have you ever been able to come through total mental—

BURROUGHS: Oh, I have indeed. I've done it many times. It's just a matter of getting the sexual image so vivid that you come.

WARHOL: How old were you when you first had sex?

BURROUGHS: Sixteen. Just boarding school boys at Los Alamos Ranch School where they later made the atom bomb.

WARHOL: With who?

BURROUGHS: With this boy in the next bunk.

WARHOL: What did he do?

BURROUGHS: Mutual masturbation. But during the war this school, which was up on the mesa there thirty-seven miles north of Santa Fe, was taken over by the army. That's where they made the atom bomb. Oppenheimer [the scientist who invented the bomb] had gone out there for his health and he was staying at a dude ranch near this place and said, "Well, this is the ideal place." It seems so right and appropriate somehow that I should have gone to school there. Los Alamos

Photos by Victor Bockris

Ranch School was one of these boarding schools where everyone rode a horse. Fucking horses, I hate 'em. I had sinus trouble and I'd been going to New Mexico for my health during the summer vacations and then my family contacted the director, A. J. Connell, who was a Unitarian and believed very much in positive thinking, and I went there for two years. This took place on a sleeping porch, 1929.

WARHOL: How great! Was the sex really like an explosion?

BURROUGHS: No no . . . I don't remember it was so long ago.

WARHOL: I think I was twenty-five the first time I had sex, but the first time I knew about sex was under the stairs in Northside, Pittsburgh, and they made this funny kid suck this boy off. I never understood what it meant . . .

BURROUGHS: Made him do what?

WARHOL: Suck this boy off, but I didn't know what it meant, I was just sitting there watching when I was five years old. How did you get this kid to do it, or did he do it to you?

BURROUGHS: Oh I don't know, sort of a lot of talking back and forth . . .

TIME MAGAZINE CHECKING QUERY
NEW YORK–PARIS NOV. 15, 1962

Checking for *Time* book review *Naked Lunch* soonest Friday is Burroughs arrested and convicted for wife's accidental death in Mexico or if freed on what reasons or simply never brought to account or what. Also our lawyer advises we have possible libel problem on calling Burroughs homosexual unless we can prove it by his own word or other authority preferably in print. Unable to do so on evidence here. Can you help? [From *Time*'s morgue file on Burroughs]

REPLY PARIS–NEW YORK NOV. 16, 1962

[This is written by David Schnell, referred to in the chapter "On the Interview."]

Burroughs gives impression wife's death and events which followed very cloudy in his teeming mind. "It's all on public record," he says. "There was a hearing several days after the trial but I wasn't there when case came up for decision one or two years later. Legal system down there is very different from our own. Think they decided it was accidental, 'imprudentia criminale' they called it and there was suspended sentence I guess. Don't remember very well."

As to homosexuality, Burroughs replied, "You're perfectly free to say I write about homosexuals and homosexual character. Actually I think a writer says all he has to say in his work, that the life of the writer is usually uneventful, passing into the realm of mythology. But I don't suppose *Time* Magazine will be very satisfied with that. Really, I am not trying to be evasive. What I will say is that I doubt any writer has life apart from his work—if he's really serious about it." Maurice Girodias, of Olympia Press, says *Time* lawyers have only to read Burroughs to convince themselves he's homosexual. Wilde also had no doubts. [From *Time*'s morgue file on Burroughs]

DINNER WITH ANDY WARHOL AND ALLEN GINSBERG: NEW YORK 1980

BOCKRIS: They have this new way where you can determine the sex of your child. Apparently everyone wants a boy.

BURROUGHS: Everyone wants a boy, so we're going to have more and more boys. It's the best thing. I don't mind if we don't have any girls at all.

BOCKRIS: It could go in that direction. In South America they have the seven-year birth control pill.

BURROUGHS: It's true: a woman went down there and found that pill. When she got back she said, "Oh well, the big drug companies will be deeply interested." They didn't want to hear about it. They prefer to sell a pill every day rather than one that lasts for seven years. She was very disillusioned. It's also reversible. If she wants to have a baby before the seven years are up she takes another pill.

WARHOL: I still never understand why a boy's never had a baby.

BOCKRIS: Allen [Ginsberg] and Peter [Orlovsky] wanted to have a baby together.

WARHOL: There must be a way. You know how freaks are around all the time, I mean there has to be a freak who is going to have . . . they call a freak a genius, right, because half their brain's gone so they discover something that nobody else thinks about, like the atomic bomb. There has to be a man, there's always a freak.

BURROUGHS: There was a story that Mohammed was supposed to have been reborn from a man.

WARHOL: Who's Mohammed?

BURROUGHS: Uuuuuhhhhmmmmm, Mohammed the prophet.

WARHOL: Oh. We know a lot of waiters called Mohammad.

BOCKRIS: With all the great advances in science it should certainly be possible for a man to have a baby someday.

BURROUGHS: Why bother when you have cloning?

WARHOL: Cloning's better.

BURROUGHS: Did you read *In His Image?* What interested me were the objections from scientists. They thought it would be terrible that someone could reproduce himself. Scientists are the most stuffy, irrational people . . .

GINSBERG: I tried to put the make on this fifteen-year-old kid who is a member of gay lib up in Newcastle . . .

BURROUGHS: I don't see many alternatives.

GINSBERG: But he likes young kids. I thought he would admire me as a hero of . . .

BURROUGHS: He doesn't need an old man like yoooooouuuu.

GINSBERG: He admired me as a hero of gay lib, but not as a body to thrust in bed.

DINNER WITH BOCKRIS-WYLIE, JEFF GOLDBERG, GERARD MALANGA, PAUL GETTY, JR., ANDY WARHOL, AND ANDRE LEON-TALLEY, NEW YORK 1980

BOCKRIS-WYLIE: Gore Vidal says there's a big sexual connection between the upper classes and the lower classes. The middle class is the sexually uptight class.

BURROUGHS: I recall during the trial of Lord Montague the prosecution asked: "Lord Montague, you seem to have a predilection for associating with your social inferiors. Would you care to comment on the reason for such associations?"

"Like a spot of fun, you know."

BOCKRIS-WYLIE: This is what Frank Harris said in 1888. You go to Tangier for kief . . .

BURROUGHS: And sex.

BOCKRIS-WYLIE: What's sex like in Tangier?

BURROUGHS: It's terribly simple. The boys are poor.

BOCKRIS: Have you been having any great affairs with anyone lately?

BURROUGHS: Hmmpfh hmmpfh hmmpfh *"had any good affairs lately?"* Oh yes, every day or so. . . . It's still the same old story, a case of love and glory. . . . You can't beat it.

JEFF GOLDBERG: I've never gotten it straight; are there any aphrodisiacs?

BURROUGHS: Pot is something of an aphrodisiac. There's yohimbine, which is very definitely an aphrodisiac, it enlarges the blood vessels in the sexual organs. There are of course poppers, which do exactly the same thing, they also dilate the blood vessels. They're known as vasodilators.

GOLDBERG: Is that the common characteristic? Does dilation give you a rush?

BURROUGHS: Yes. Vessel dilation would be the common characteristic. It brings blood to the genital regions, very definitely stimulating the sexual areas.

BOCKRIS-WYLIE: Do you ever fear coming?

BURROUGHS: This is the basic fear, my dear, this is fear. Fear which is of death, which is regret.

BOCKRIS-WYLIE: Do you think if you had a sex change it would have a big influence on you?

BURROUGHS: Nothing could be further from my mind.

MALANGA: When do you fall in love? How do you know it?

BURROUGHS: I don't know exactly what *falling in love* for me is. The concept of romantic love arose in the Middle Ages. Now remember, the Arabs don't even have a word for love—that is, a word for love apart from physical attraction or sex. And this separation of love and sex is a western concept, a Christian concept. As to what falling in love means, I'm uncertain. Love; well, it means simply physical attraction and liking a person at the same time.

MALANGA: Do you believe in a power greater than yourself?

BURROUGHS: I think the self, what you call your *self*, is like the tip of an iceberg. One tenth of the ice appears above water and the rest is under water. If you could contact all your latent abilities it would be incredible! For example, everyone knows what time it is at any hour of the day or night. I can set my mind, say if I have to wake up at six o'clock. I just have to say I have to wake up at six o'clock and I will wake up right on the dot of six o'clock. I think what we think of as ourselves is a very unimportant, a very small part of our actual potential, and that this is undoubtedly part of a still larger potential. I would say that I certainly believe in powers greater than myself. I would find it difficult not to. We should talk about the most mysterious subject of all—sex. Sex is an electromagnetic phenomenon.

PAUL GETTY, JR.: I don't think many of us are aware of how serious sex really is.

BURROUGHS: It is the one natural need that can be satisfied in a dream. To what extent do you think sex consists of wanting to be someone else, to be in their body? It's a crucial factor in homosexual relationships, to be the other person.

BOCKRIS: I don't understand what you mean.

BURROUGHS: In homosexual sex you know exactly what the other person is feeling, so you are identifying with the other person completely. In heterosexual sex you have no idea what the other person is feeling.

BOCKRIS: But they're not necessarily feeling exactly what you're feeling.

BURROUGHS: No, but you can identify with them to the extent that you become them, which of course is quite impossible with heterosexual sex because you're not a woman therefore you cannot feel or know what a woman feels. My experience with the fair sex is somewhat limited, but when I was trapped in Missouri, like someone in prison who can't get a woman so they traffick with young boys, I used to go to whorehouses. The experience was not very enlightening.

BOCKRIS: You had such a strong desire to have sex you would have sex with anything or anyone you could find?

BURROUGHS: Like the guy said, I used to get a hard on if I saw two flies fucking . . .

GETTY: What about S and M?

BURROUGHS: I never had any contact with S and M except with reading and talking with a couple of people who were into it, but it did seem to me that it is so incredibly stereotyped. One relationship is the "bad boy," that's why you have to be spanked, but I don't know how anyone could go through this with a straight face, really . . . all sorts of rules. However, sex can exist in complete dissociation from someone's personality. We are very close to being able to provide anything we want sexually by electronic stimulation. It would not only be visible, but also tactile.

LEON-TALLEY: Do you think you should charge for sex?

BURROUGHS: It depends on the circumstances. You cannot generalize about these things. Who should pay who?

WARHOL: I think the girl who's standing on the street corner should pay the guy who comes up to her, because she's hot, right? The guy's not hot. She should be on easy street and pay the person for doing it to her, don't you think?

BOCKRIS: The prostitute should be supported by the city?

WARHOL: That's it. They should be hired and be paid by the city instead of going to jail.

BOCKRIS: Does paying for sex heighten the pleasure?

BURROUGHS: No. The only way it could heighten the pleasure would be if you paid in the middle of sex and this is . . .

MALANGA: Is beauty only skin deep?

BURROUGHS: What do you mean by *that?*

MALANGA: Do you stop at what appears to you on the surface, or do you go further into it in detail?

BURROUGHS: If you have a relative, comparative universe, then beauty only exists in relation to ugliness. What do you mean by beauty? You mean something is beautiful in relation to something that is ugly? The two concepts then become completely interrelated. Which is true of all other concepts. What does weakness mean? Weakness only has meaning with relation to strength, right? Weakness means that someone is stronger than you are.

MALANGA: A weakness can also be an advantage.

BURROUGHS: Perfect example.

BOCKRIS: What was the biggest change in sex in the seventies? Then we can see what it's going to be in the eighties. I think there will be less and less sex.

WARHOL: Oh no, there's more and more because there are more and more people.

BOCKRIS: Is the sex problem a population problem?

BURROUGHS: There is a relationship.

WARHOL: You're talking about entertainment sex.

BURROUGHS: Between population and . . .

WARHOL: Entertainment sex is different.

LEON-TALLEY: What is entertainment sex?

WARHOL: Entertainment sex is the S and M thing when you go down to those S and M bars and it entertains you.

BURROUGHS: It entertains *some* people.

WARHOL: What kind of people do you like?

BURROUGHS: Young boys.

LEON-TALLEY: How young do you like them?

BURROUGHS: Oh, say from fourteen to twenty-five.

LEON-TALLEY: Is it easier to have relationships with young boys, not just sex? Can you go out with them, can you have dinner with them?

BURROUGHS: In many cases, no.

LEON-TALLEY: They don't have the concentration.

BURROUGHS: But I don't require that, I don't require that at all. . . . I'm not looking for a relationship.

BOCKRIS: Don't you find it harder to get sex, though?

WARHOL: Yes, really really hard.

BURROUGHS: Harder than when?

BOCKRIS: Ten years ago when you were a young febrile personality jumping around. Don't you find it harder now?

BURROUGHS: Presumably it gets more difficult as you get older, that seems to be what they tell me.

BOCKRIS: Actually, it's easier for Bill to get more sex now than ever.

WARHOL: Yeah, because he's good looking and adorable. He's charming and he's great!

MALANGA: What's better than sex?

BURROUGHS: That's the most difficult question of all. There are a lot of things involved. You see, we have been conditioned on this planet to think that sex *is* displeasure, or pleasure, or pain. Or that sex *is* the greatest pleasure. We know also that there are pleasures that undercut sex like junk which is antisexual. What would be your answer to that question?

MALANGA: You could always channel that sexual energy into your writing.

BURROUGHS: The answer might be what sex essentially is. And that's something I don't think anyone knows much about: What is sex? Why is it pleasurable? Do you have any answer to that?

MALANGA: Pleasure can cause pain in certain instances. Or pleasure can lead to pain.

BURROUGHS: The theory, of course, is that sex is simply a relief from tension.

MALANGA: Maybe people who tend to shy away from having sex are the ones who are most susceptible to disease, cancer or various ailments.

BURROUGHS: You know the works of Wilhelm Reich. He says that cancer is essentially a disease of sexual suppression. That all cancer patients are sexually repressed. A broad statement I think.

MALANGA: Have you ever had a strong relationship with a man that wasn't sexual?

BURROUGHS: Yes, many. Depends on what you mean by strong. I've had all sorts of relationships. Business relationships to a wide extent. Intellectual relationships. I've had quite a relationship with Paul Bowles, Brion Gysin, both of which were completely nonsexual and, of course, I've had long business relationships with publishers and agents which are also social relationships. Friendship relationships with people like Terry Southern, who is a very good friend of mine.

NEW YORK CITY 1979

Terry Southern arrived at my flat at about 7:00 P.M. carrying a shopping bag full of "drug samples," given him, he said, by "a gregarious chemist—a social-climbing artist *manqué*, but a decent enough chap after his fashion." He plopped the bag down on the table. "I'm afraid you'll not find much of the old *hard stuff* amongst this lot, Vic," he continued, momentarily assuming a la-di-da British accent he presumably thought matched my own, "I just brought them along for Bill—he enjoys rooting about in these drug samples."

I reminded Terry that we were to call Bill about dinner, so he called and told Bill we'd be over in twenty minutes. I ran into the bathroom for a wash and brush-up, and almost at once, Terry was pummeling the door. "Bockris!" he yelled. "In God's great name open up! *I must pass water!*" I was not able to vacate the premises at that particular moment and told him so—whereupon I heard a good deal of stumbling about, moaning and groaning from the room next door, followed by the clatter of dishes, and running water. "Ter!" I shouted, "what are you doing?"

"Just doing the dishes," he replied.

I ran out of the bathroom a few minutes later. "It's all yours," I said, but Ter was sitting complacently on the couch, twisting up a bomber. "No, no, it's okay," he said. "I'm, uh, into something else now."

"Damnation!" I cried, with a great show of annoyance, *"You've pissed in the sink!"*

"No, no," Ter was quick to assure me, *"passed water* in the sink."

"Damnation!" I repeated testily.

"The heavy surge of bodily fluid," Ter went on in an expansive manner, "from my giant animal-like member, cleared the dishes quite handily. No need for your ranting Howie Hughes type fastidious-ness." And he lit the big funnel-shaped joint of Columbian gold.

So we did a bit of the bomber, stashed it for later, dropped in a bottle of whiskey, and headed downstairs.

A white Rolls-Royce was parked nearby and Terry tried to get in in the belief (or pretense of belief) that it was the *High Times'* company limo, laid on for the occasion. I dragged him into a nearby cab.

DINNER WITH BOCKRIS-WYLIE AND JAMES GRAUERHOLZ 1974

BOCKRIS-WYLIE: Are you jealous?

BURROUGHS: I can be, yes. I regard it as a flaw in myself. Jealousy is awful. It's the most disgusting thing. But I will tell you how you deal with this. You do absolutely nothing, just let these feelings rush through you. The point is that most people cannot see that there's anything wrong with themselves; I can. I can see that there are things terribly wrong with myself. And any sort of jealousy is certainly one of them.

BOCKRIS-WYLIE: Do you always consider yourself to blame when you're jealous?

BURROUGHS: Absolutely.

BOCKRIS-WYLIE: You don't feel that being possessive is a really good thing?

BURROUGHS: Look, I feel that you should be in control of the situation.

Bockris-Wylie, the interview team who used that name from 1973 to 1975, as they appeared when they first interviewed Burroughs in 1974. Publicity photo by Anton Perich

If you're jealous, you're not in control of the situation. That's silly.

BOCKRIS-WYLIE: Is the love you take equal to the love you make?

BURROUGHS: I'll answer that I write my love objects.

BOCKRIS-WYLIE: Is it wish fulfillment or a record of fact?

BURROUGHS: It's both. I say this: any writer who hasn't jacked off with his characters, those characters will not come alive in a sexual context. I certainly jack off with my characters. I can write sexual situations, very hot sexual situations. I don't get a hard-on, you understand. Bull-fighters do get hard-ons in the course of a bullfight. So I have been told at least, and I do in part believe it.

BOCKRIS-WYLIE: That's very different, because that's physical; with writing it's just your fingers.

BURROUGHS: No, excuse me, there is no distinction. There's an either/or concept, as if there's some distinction between . . .

BOCKRIS-WYLIE: You can't say that you attack your desk like a bull.

BURROUGHS: Didn't say I attacked my desk.

JAMES GRAUERHOLZ: Bill does attack his desk, not like a bull, but the proverbial china-shop bull; he has an incredible talent for putting things in complete disarray from which he works and makes these great things.

BOCKRIS-WYLIE: Genet says jacking off is much better than making it with someone.

65

BURROUGHS: It is, but it's also much more destructive.

BOCKRIS-WYLIE: How?

BURROUGHS: Well, when you jack off you're jacking off with imaginary sexual partners.

BOCKRIS-WYLIE: Why don't you jack off thinking of someone you made it with?

BURROUGHS: There's nothing wrong with that if there's no one around. Okay if you're alone, but if you're not alone, what then? This is bad medicine. If you have any actual sexual outlet, to jack off is a betrayal of that sexual outlet. There's nothing worse than making it with someone and thinking about someone else. It's bad and will almost always be detected. Look, now all I'm saying is something very simple. You're making it with someone, all your attention should be on them, you should not be thinking about someone else, or not jacking off to someone else, or not making it with someone else. There was a whole year or two in Tangier when I had plenty of boys. I never jacked off. Why in the hell should I?

BOCKRIS-WYLIE: Maybe because, like Genet, you decide that jacking off is free of emotional dependence and love, so that it gives you more time to get your work done.

BURROUGHS: No. No no no no no no. That is all wrong. If you have actual sexual outlets, why in the hell should you jack off? I've seen extreme forms of this. There was for example a friend in Tangier who used to have boys in, take photos of them in the nude, then send the boys away and jack off with the photos. Ain't that an image fix for ya!

BOCKRIS-WYLIE: What do you think about Genet saying that jacking off is better than making it with someone?

BURROUGHS: After all how real is a real person, or an actual sexual outlet?

BURROUGHS IN LONDON

DINNER WITH ANDY WARHOL: NEW YORK 1980

BOCKRIS: The English are very odd sexually.

WARHOL: They're really odd, but they're so sophisticated, that's why . . .

BURROUGHS: They like to be beaten with rulers and hairbrushes.

BOCKRIS: I think the English . . .

WARHOL: . . . are the sexiest people . . .

BOCKRIS: Did you ever have any really good sex in England?

WARHOL: Oh yeah, the best.

BURROUGHS: Yeeesss . . .

BOCKRIS: Didn't you know guys in London who used to throw Ping-Pong balls at naked boys?

BURROUGHS: I've known boys who've told me about various practices. There was the egg man who had to be pelted with eggs for some reason. There was another man who made his boys get into a big cage. He had a big birdcage and he would throw some bread in there and say, "Eat it!"

BOCKRIS: Did he ejaculate at the sight?

BURROUGHS: Well, I don't know about that at all. He said, "A boy has to make a living . . ."

BOCKRIS: Andy, you had the best sex in England?

Burroughs at 8 Duke Street, St. James, London, 1972. Photo by Gerard Malanga

WARHOL: No, the best was when this guy bit off this guy's nose. That was the best sex.

BURROUGHS: I heard about that.

WARHOL: Wasn't that the best sex, Bill?

BURROUGHS: Ah yes, I imagine so.

WARHOL: *The best.*

DINNER WITH MILES: LONDON 1978

MILES: In 1964 I was working in London at the ICA [Institute of Contemporary Art] and helped arrange an evening at which William himself showed up. It was a showing of Anthony Balch's film *Towers Open Fire*. Brion Gysin painted to a cut-up tape of music, radio static, and William reading from newspaper clippings. Each one involved the number 23: there'd be 23 dead in an air crash, or 23 dead in a flood, or whatever. They didn't have the movie on because it wasn't quite finished, so William went on and sat on stage in that old brown raincoat with the velvet collar, and his hat on. There was a big tape recorder next to him and a blue light was shining on him. Above him stills from the movie were being projected. William just glared at the audience and everyone felt very uncomfortable.

BURROUGHS: In the early sixties London was a very cheap, relaxed, and pleasant place to be in. You could have a very good meal in a working class restaurant for about three shillings [approximately 50¢]. It was also a very cool place on drugs at that time. The whole set was more satisfactory.

MILES: I felt very distanced from Bill. It was extremely hard to know how to relate to him and Ian [Sommerville, Burroughs' collaborator and companion at the time, since dead in a car crash on Bill's sixty-second birthday] had played it up: "William's feeling rather nervous this evening . . ." I suspect he was stoned, in some kind of cold blue silence on his own, quite apart from anything that was being projected on him. I don't think he was on H or anything like that, but he'd probably had a few joints.

BURROUGHS: I was in and out of London in the sixties. I didn't actually move there until 1966 after I'd spent 1965 in New York. The Empress Hotel, where I stayed during these early visits, was London's equivalent of the Beat Hotel in Paris and we all stayed there. It was in Earl's

70

Court just off the Old Brompton Road. One pound [approximately $3 in 1964] a day with breakfast for a very good very comfortable room.

BOCKRIS: What prompted the move to London?

BURROUGHS: Nothing in particular. I knew people there. It had been a pleasant place. It deteriorated rather shortly after that. The more positive times I had in London were in the early sixties when I was in and out. The Empress Hotel no longer exists. Nor do those cheap restaurants. So-called "cheap" restaurants are fifteen shillings now, and you can't eat it. Rents have quadrupled.

BOCKRIS: You have said, "A writer often travels intuitively to get images and scenes for something he may need thirty years later." What are your ties with the different cities that you've lived in and how have they affected your work?

BURROUGHS: The different cities I've lived in . . . well, Mexico City is one. Tangier is another; London, Paris, and New York. These are the places that I've lived in for any length of time and the influence in my work I think is very clear. Whole sections of *Naked Lunch* certainly come from Tangier. There's another section on Mexico. South America I never lived in but traveled there for about six months and that's another area of influence. Another influence is Scandinavia. I was only there for about a month and a half or something like that. The whole concept of Freeland was born there. Copenhagen. Sweden. I was only in Sweden for about two days.

BOCKRIS: I know it's difficult to say, inasmuch as writing is a magic process, but can you say anything about why going to a place suddenly has this kind of effect?

BURROUGHS: I've always noticed if you just hit a town that you've not been in before you see a lot more than the people who live there. Also, I've noticed that when you've been in a town for a while it becomes less and less stimulating and interesting. For example, my brief experience with Scandinavia, about a month and a half, most of it in Denmark, was very useful. But when I speak about locations I'm also speaking about a seemingly arbitrary decision like *the pirate camp is here,* then I later find out that indeed there *was* a pirate camp in that place. Or take my essay "Roosevelt After Inauguration" [which portrays Roosevelt as a Roman emperor]. I wrote that back in 1953. Allen Ginsberg later dug up a picture of Roosevelt at an actual toga party. That's what I'm talking about. Not necessarily the actual location.

Although there's no doubt that Paris, Tangier, London, and New York are very important locations, as are Mexico and South America.

MILES: In 1966, Paul McCartney, myself, Marianne Faithful and John Dunbar had the idea that we should bring out a monthly magazine in record form. There'd be somebody at all the good poetry readings, we'd have a few snatches of groups rehearsing, and I would be going out doing interviews for *International Times* and we could do bits of those on tape. As you can imagine, we smoked an enormous amount of dope and thought this was the greatest idea in the world. So we needed someone to operate the tape recorders and nobody knew anyone who could do this except me: Ian Sommerville knew a lot about tape recorders. We also needed a studio and Ringo had this old flat that he wasn't using in Montagu Square, a ridiculous pad with green silk wallpaper, and he said we could have that. Ian actually moved in there. I don't think he was supposed to, it was supposed to be the studio. Bill never moved in, to my knowledge, although when you went to see Ian there, Bill was usually mucking about, but he kept out of the way because he definitely had the impression that this thing was somehow to do with the Beatles and he wasn't supposed to be there.

BURROUGHS: It *was* kind of uneasy there. . . . This was when the Beatles were just getting into the possibilities of overlaying, running backwards, the full technical possibilities of the tape recorder. And Ian was a brilliant technician along those lines.

Ian met Paul McCartney and Paul put up the money for this flat which was at 34 Montagu Square. There were people like bodyguards and managers who didn't like this at all and they were always threatening to come around and take the equipment away. I saw Paul several times. The three of us talked about the possibilities of the tape recorder. He'd just come in and work on his "Eleanor Rigby." Ian recorded his rehearsals. I saw the song taking shape. Once again, not knowing much about music, I could see that he knew what he was doing. He was very pleasant and very prepossessing. Nice-looking young man, hardworking.

MILES: I recall one day when Peter Asher, Ian, and I were there. Bill was there but sort of distant and not spending much time in the room, always doing things in other rooms. Paul arrived with the acetates for "Rubber Soul." That was the first time anybody'd ever heard those; they'd just finished mixing them. We were talking about what direction rock music was going to go in, no doubt toward electronic music, but no one knew what that really meant. In those days digital technology didn't really exist. We all knew that somehow there was going to be a combination of electronics and rock that would be really exciting and that music had gone beyond the barriers of just a bunch of guys playing instruments. Bill and Paul were talking about this.

I remember another time there was a big scene at a party in which a famous English poet beat up his wife's lover. It got kind of rowdy and the police were called. They were at the door and said, "What's happening? We had a call." It was a big fancy place so they took their helmets off. Panna O'Grady, the hostess, was flustered and William was standing behind her saying, "Nothing's happening, nothing at all." He was reassuring. In fact the fight was going on upstairs. He was barring the stairway, standing at the bottom of it holding on to the banister. Fresh-faced public schoolboys who'd just arrived at the party were approaching but William was two or three stairs up and obviously wasn't going to let go. "We would like to go upstairs," they pleaded, and he would reply, "There's nothing upstairs. Nothing at all," and stare at them. But all the time you could hear the sound of ferocious fighting going on upstairs, and the sound of things being broken.

Mick Jagger arrived at that party and Allen Ginsberg asked me to introduce him, which I did. Jagger and Allen went and sat on the balcony and talked about music and chanting and breathing for a long time; I then made Allen introduce Jagger to Burroughs.

BURROUGHS: Mick gave off the impression of great energy and intelligence and a sort of special cool of knowing where his connections are going. I had admired his work, what I'd heard of it, and also I admired him because of the pressure he was under. There's someone who is idolized and yet receives shockingly rude treatment. Six cabdrivers refused to have him in the cab when he and Marianne Faithful arrived at the airport. There's something about Mick that arouses great antagonism in a certain kind of person, the cabdriver–hardhat–redneck strata throughout the world, and to be able to stand up to that and be able to maintain his equilibrium and cool, as he certainly has, is quite something.

BOCKRIS: Were you at any point in London close to the mythical swinging London scene?

BURROUGHS: No, not at all. It was going on; I wasn't involved in it except very moderately, it didn't interest me much. So-called "swinging London" seemed to occur when London, to my way of thinking, was very much on a downgrade, and I always wondered where *is* this swinging London?

BOCKRIS: A lot of people say that. Were there any English writers you had contact with?

BURROUGHS: I met Anthony Burgess in London. We went out to a number of pubs. I had been very much impressed with his novel *Clockwork Orange* and had written something for it; that was the basis of the relationship. I found him extremely charming. Very much interested in my work as I was in his. I asked him if he saw many other writers in London, he said, "No, they're all a bunch of swine."

MILES: I think William felt a crossover of literary ideas into music, but I don't think he picked up on any kind of musical ideas that he could use. He was a little bit impressed that literature had moved out of being a gentleman's pursuit and now he could actually talk to people about it. The avant garde was out in the open again, here he was talking to musicians. That side of it excited him I think, but the kind of writing that William produced in 1964, 1965, and 1966 was totally nonmarketable. It was either cut-up experiments on tape or else multi-colored collages in notebooks, which would have cost an absolute fortune to reproduce and again were noncommercial. He had some extremely lean years financially where he engaged in a lot of cerebral activities, extending cut-ups way beyond cutting up words as entities but into imagery. I think Bill was really questioning his medium. He finally came back to writing because writing was what he knew and he was, after all, as Genet said, "a man of letters."

William was very much under the spell of Brion in those days. Brion remains a significant person in William's personal history. Brion would say, "We're going to go and see the Rolling Stones. You can't possibly wear those awful clothes; we'll have to go and get some flared trousers." And there'd be William in these awful flared trousers which didn't suit him at all, designed for someone forty years younger, looking quite uncomfortable, but he would do it because Brion said so.

BOCKRIS: Burroughs moved to Flat 22, 8 Duke Street, St. James in 1967 and began to write again after a long period of tape recorder, scrapbook, and cut-up experiments that had produced no major work.

74

He completed *The Wild Boys* in August 1969 and then began to gradually slip into an isolated and unproductive existence at the beginning of the seventies.

His flat was expensive and small. Burroughs saw hardly anyone except constant companion Johnny, pictures of whom appear in the Covent Garden Edition of *Port of Saints* [London 1974], Brion Gysin, and Anthony Balch, who lived in the same building.

MILES: While he was living at Duke Street, Bill didn't communicate with people very much. He was purposely ex-directory. People would come by, students and others, the kind of guys who he would probably be very friendly with these days. He would answer the door and they'd say, "Are you William Burroughs?", and he'd say, "Yes." He would totally freeze them out, they'd get really upset and embarrassed and have to turn around and go away.

He always had Johnny. You know—*Johnny*. They were always called Johnny for some reason. But he really did get way out on a limb

Brion and William at 8 Duke Street, St. James, London, 1972. Photo by Gerard Malanga

when he was living at Duke Street. He was writing away, studying these Egyptian texts. He was happy seeing Brion and Anthony. His ideal restaurant was one which was totally empty.

BOCKRIS: Johnny's influence was ambiguous; on the one hand he was fiercely protective of Burroughs and a strong bond of affection existed between them. On the other hand, he constantly brought pimps, hustlers, and small-time gangsters to the flat.

Burroughs may have enjoyed his Dickensian view of lowlife London, but it did no good for his health when the gangsters stayed all night, paying little attention to his needs and taking advantage of his hospitality. On top of this, Johnny was not an amanuensis and Burroughs relies a lot on friends and companions to help him in the editing and retyping of his work.

A picture emerges of Burroughs in London sitting in his apartment day after day smoking cigarettes, drinking tea, looking over old pieces. He has said that he is never lonely, but admits that a novelist "needs the reader in that he hopes that some of his readers will turn into his characters. He needs them as vessels on which he writes."

Increasingly isolated, Burroughs lost contact with this audience he needed, lost his ability to write fiction, and his life became burdensome.

MILES: I think Bill felt that he hadn't written anything significant since *Nova Express* in 1964. He'd gone through a number of years of experimentation with tapes and collages and most people in the literary world had almost forgotten about him. He hadn't published anything at all and then when he did it was *The Wild Boys,* which was not greeted as the greatest novel of the century. It was not understood, in fact. And William was working in a vacuum.

BURROUGHS: On the contrary, *The Wild Boys* was an English best seller. Also produced in this period: *The Last Words of Dutch Schultz,* the Mayfair articles and *The Job, Port of Saints, Exterminator.* I would say that I was less available then, I was seeing fewer people. In Paris, we had this whole hotel where we were seeing a great number of people. In Tangier, I also used to see more people. In London, in the mid to late sixties, there weren't many people around that I wanted to see.

MILES: I think William started to wonder whether or not he was still a writer, because he was having to depend almost entirely on Brion to tell him so. He didn't see any other writers. A lot of his evenings were spent alone. When Brion was away, since he didn't want to eat by himself, he just didn't eat. It must have been a very strange and lonely period, living in his pied-à-terre, which he never dusted the entire time he was there—the dust was inches thick.

But when William was living in London, we all did regard him as a significant figure, thinker, and part of the underground scene. I remember him coming to Indica [Miles' bookshop] on Christmas Eve one day to see a poster that we'd done. He wished everyone a Merry Christmas and put up a notice saying that if anyone wished to be audited they could call him up. He was very much with scientology, but it cut him off from a lot of people.

BOCKRIS: It was in this state of malaise that Allen Ginsberg, visiting London in the summer of 1973, primarily to spend time with Burroughs, found the confrere he had seen only briefly for years. Always the organizer, Ginsberg found a solution. He knew that the City College of New York was looking for an established American writer to give a course of lectures on writing between February and May 1974. Would Burroughs like to give the lectures? It could be arranged.

Burroughs had lectured before, but never at an American university and not for a full term. He considered the proposal—inspected his life, his apartment, his checkbook, and his prospects—and decided there was nothing to be lost by taking the job. It would earn him some needed money with which he could return to London and continue . . .

Burroughs arrived in New York in January of 1974. Ginsberg introduced him to James Grauerholz, a young Kansan who had just arrived in New York. James became Williams' amanuensis-companion, and Burroughs began to give his lectures. It usually took him from six to eight hours to prepare each lecture. The course became a full-time job with two lectures a week, two office hours for consultation, and papers to be read in the evening.

GRAUERHOLZ: Soon after he arrived in New York Bill told me, "I don't know if I can still write fiction." I had only just met him at the time and I was very much in awe of him. I can't tell you how I felt when he said that; all I could say was, "Oh, man . . . don't say that." What really pulled William out of that slump was the series of public read-

William looks out his window at London, 1972. Photo by Gerard Malanga

ings he gave for virtually the first time in his life. The response he got from the lectures led to his decision to give up the London flat and remain in New York.

ANDREAS BROWN: Burroughs had gotten very paranoid in London and it was a great thing to see him come alive again. I was at the first reading he gave in New York. You could see his face change as he realized that people wanted to hear him.

BURROUGHS: If you're still there after the fear then you got the courage, baby, that's all. If you're not, then you're dead.

DINNER WITH SUSAN SONTAG: NEW YORK 1980

BURROUGHS: England has the most sordid literary scene I've ever seen. They all meet in the same pub. This guy's writing a foreword for this person. They all have to give radio programs, they *have* to do all this just in order to scrape by. They're all scratching each other's backs. "I'll write a preface for you if you give me a blurb."

BOCKRIS: Is there' an advantage for a writer to be in New York?

SONTAG: People are very isolated in New York, everybody's essentially alone here, but there's probably less hack work. I not only agree with what Bill said about the English literary scene, but I can think of hardly any writers I even admire in England. The whole thing has become so genteel and diluted. I like Ballard.

BURROUGHS: He's good.

SONTAG: It's so philistine.

BURROUGHS: Incestuous! Incestuous!

SONTAG: Writers do dissipate their talents doing television and reviewing, two things which are much less developed here. Television doesn't exist here as an outlet for any serious writer, and reviewing is a very minor occupation.

BURROUGHS: English writers have to write four reviews a week and then do several radio shows just to get by.

SONTAG: The funny thing is, they always thought that they should do it even when they didn't need the money. Virginia Woolf for instance, who certainly didn't need the money, was doing two or three reviews a week, which is an enormous amount of literary journalism. That's the sort of thing you do if you're a writer over there, you turn out this enormous amount of junk.

Album cover by James Hamilton

BURROUGHS IN
NEW YORK

BOCKRIS: You first lived in New York during the Second World War. What was the atmosphere like then?

BURROUGHS: The place was full of uniforms and there were incredible amounts of money being made in any business. You just had to run a laundry or any fucking thing and you could make a fortune, because the services were all broken down. They were pulling people off the streets to get them to work in anything. It was extraordinary. Personally, I had the distinction to be actually fired from a defense plant during the war.

I lived five months at 69 Bedford Street. That was when David Kamerrer lived around the corner at 35 Morton Street. Sixty-nine Bedford Street was on the second floor; it was a furnished apartment; it had a couch and a few chairs and a table; it had a closet, kitchen, and bathroom. Very mediocre. I lived there by myself. That was when I was working as a bartender and later as a private detective. I didn't do very much. I wasn't working most of the time. I had two jobs. I spent a great amount of time at home in the pad.

Kerouac took this word picture of an always courteous Burroughs at 69 Bedford and printed it in *The Town & the City*, Jack's first novel:

Dennison [Burroughs] had concluded his own ministrations and was punctiliously cleaning out his needle and eye-dropper with water.

"Yes, Johnson wasn't a bad sort at all," he was saying.

"Yes," said Al, daubing his bleeding scar with a piece of cotton, "he came from a good family, you know, but found it hard going to live up to their square standards, you might say."

"Well I suppose they'll take his license away from him, but he'll get another one somewhere else."

"Yes, I suppose he'll make out some way. We all have to take the bumps when they come and try to make the best of it."

They cleaned everything up, put away their pills and needles and cottons with great care, Dennison washing out glasses and spoons, Al rubbing the top of the table with a cloth, and everything was neat again. Al put on his coat and hat, and Dennison said he would accompany him downstairs.

"I've got to get a few quarts of milk at the grocery, Al, and some Benzedrine and codeine cough syrup at the drugstore, a few suppositories I want to try out, headache powders for pickup in the mornings, a few things like that, so I might as well walk with you downstairs."

Whereupon the tall cadaverous Al opened the door and said, "After you, Will."

But Dennison bowed slightly at the waist, smiling, "Please, Al, I am home here."

DINNER WITH GERARD MALANGA: NEW YORK 1974

MALANGA: Are you surprised by your life?

BURROUGHS: Yes, sometimes. If you weren't surprised by your life you wouldn't be alive. Life is surprise.

MALANGA: What does living in New York City have that no other city you've lived in has to offer?

BURROUGHS: One very important thing. Every other city I can think of is going down, getting worse, and this is not true of New York. New York is a much pleasanter place to live now than it was when I was last here for any length of time, which was in 1965. London has been going down steadily. I just got to the point where I couldn't stand it. Higher and higher prices. More and more money to buy less and less. Duller and duller. I think that is certainly unique about New York as the cycles go up and down. It's one of the most polite cities I've ever lived in. I'm very well satisfied with my decision to return here.

MALANGA: Do you attract comments from people on the street? Do people recognize you?

BURROUGHS: Much more here than they do in London. I've had quite a few very pleasant encounters with people on the street.

DINNER AT FRANKLIN STREET 1974

For the first few months Burroughs lived in a loft on Broadway. He then moved into a fourth floor walk-up loft at 77 Franklin Street. I visited him there shortly after he moved in, and wrote this account of our first evening together later on the same night:

It's a rainy Thursday evening when I step out of a cab at the corner of Broadway and Franklin streets in lower Manhattan on my way to dinner with William Burroughs.

I gaze down a line of warehouses with a haphazard mixture of small trucks and old cars parked in front of them, spot Burroughs' four story building, hurry diagonally across the street, push open the door and step into the foyer. The hall light is out and I feel cautiously for the banisters as two bottles of cold white wine clink in the crook of my arm. Warped wooden stairs lead to the top floor past a series of wall paintings.

I knock on Burroughs' green door and James lets me in. Burroughs is standing in the middle of the room. He walks toward me, hand outstretched. The loft is impeccably clean. The old wooden floors beam with polish, the bed is neatly made, all surfaces are devoid of other than essentials. A manuscript is lying on the kitchen counter next to a stack of black and white 11 x 14 prints of photographs of Burroughs by Peter Hujar just delivered. In one he is lying on the bed, head propped on hand, grinning, a silk scarf wrapped around his neck, a cheerful check jacket with graceful lapels slung over his shoulders.

As James takes my coat and hat and Burroughs busies himself putting the wine in the refrigerator, I notice that an efficient looking brand new kitchen has been installed. The loft feels warm and lived in whilst remaining concisely organized. Three small paintings by Brion Gysin decorate one wall.

Bill makes me a vodka and tonic. We all drink the same without ice, and as the conversation begins we are discussing the King of Morocco's birthday party which terrorists attacked with machine guns. .

"Can you imagine all those people angling for invitations to his birthday party and when they get there they get shot?" Bill chuckles. "I think the Belgian Ambassador was killed. Some guys were brighter, they stood behind pillars . . ."

Since settling in New York, Burroughs has taken to buying American clothes. He usually adopts attire in some way suitable to the area. He is wearing a good-looking dark green single breasted blazer with gold buttons, a pair of well-cut tan slacks and dark brown highly polished English leather boots with a regular heel. A slightly wide green tie is knotted carefully between the long straight collar of a tan shirt. Burroughs carries his outfit well, managing to look relaxed and comfortable.

"I really enjoyed your reading the other night," I tell him. "Your timing was perfect."

"I rehearse a lot for these readings, and for a long time. It's a performance," he nods.

We sit around the table by the kitchen, talking about collaborations in literature. "Conrad's done some quite remarkable books in collaboration with Ford Madox Ford which are very little read now. I'd mention *The Inheritors* and *Romance*. There are passages where he seems to be escaping from words or going beyond words, in a quite conventional, quite classical narrative form," Burroughs tells me.

Twenty minutes later dinner is ready and we carry the plates up to a low table past the curtain by the bed. Bill opens a bottle of wine, and we sit down to a delicious meal—the fish accompanied by rice and broccoli. I ask him what he thinks of Alexander Solzhenitsyn.

"Never heard of him."

"But . . ."

"Nope."

"He was on the cover of *Time*."

"Never heard of him."

"What would you do if you weren't a writer?"

"I figure I could do anything—run a corporation—but they wouldn't let me."

Over coffee Burroughs says: "Most people don't notice what's going

84

on around them. That's my principal message to writers: for God's sake, keep your eyes open."

My eyes travel to the spectacles of Burroughs as he turns and says, "Guns are a part of my life. I was brought up around them." Suddenly in the middle of the meal, he walks calmly over to a storage area behind a small walk-in closet and re-emerges carrying a toy M-16. Posting himself in the middle of the room, some six feet away from the table, he snaps the thing up to his shoulder and carefully aims at the other end of the loft. "Yep! This is what they use," he states flatly— and for a moment I get a frozen flash of him, a close-up that knocks me out of my seat.

On an average day in New York, Burroughs gets up between 9:00 and 10:00 and shaves. In a dream note made on 13th August 1975 he wrote: "Things needed. Shaving mirror. Anyone used to shave feels deterioration if he cannot." From *Retreat Diaries*. Burroughs associates shaving with civilization and throughout his travels has never grown a beard or mustache.

Then he takes a 100 milligram capsule of vitamin B1 because he believes it replaces the B1 that alcohol removes from the system. He dresses, washes last night's dishes, and eats breakfast. He likes coffee with a donut, English muffin, or angel food cake.

Around 11:00 he goes down four long flights of stairs to get his mail (5–10 pieces daily). Between 11:30 and 12:30 he putters around the loft looking at notes, writing notes, and checking through various books.

Between 12:30 and 1:00 Bill often goes out shopping for groceries or, lately, new clothes. He's usually back by 1:00, eats no lunch and writes between 1:00 and 4:00 in the afternoon.

If James Grauerholz is working with him on a manuscript or a reading, James will arrive around 4:00 in the afternoon and will stay through dinner. This happens, on the average, three times a week. They go over the work between 4:00 and 6:00 when Burroughs often relaxes, sitting in a rocking chair by the window. "It's a very beautiful sight," James says. "I'll be working at the other end of the loft. I'll look up, and there will be William just sitting perfectly still in his chair looking kind of serene."

At 6:00 P.M. Burroughs pours himself a drink. Dinner is between 7:30 and 8:30.

He has seen enough time pass. Photo by Gerard Malanga

All his life Burroughs has eaten in restaurants. Today, he shops and cooks for himself, often having friends over, or going to their places nearby for dinner. After dinner, conversation continues until 11:00 or 12:00 and then usually home or to bed. Occasionally he stays up talking till dawn.

An average Burroughs day produces six pages. Sometimes he'll write as many as fifteen. When he started *Cities of the Red Night* he produced 120 pages in two weeks. "William's very good at knowing when to leave things alone and when to go back to them. He knows when enough is enough," James reports. "Sometimes I may try to push him on something—looking at a manuscript when 600 pages have been written and saying, 'We should begin editing that'—and he'll say, 'No . . . that'll take another couple of years.' He's seen enough time pass that he knows how to pace himself."

DINNER WITH DEBBIE HARRY AND CHRIS STEIN: NEW YORK 1980

DEBBIE HARRY: Have you been to Portugal?

BURROUGHS: Yes. I have been in Lisbon once for a meal, but I don't know Portugal at all. It's strange, because it looks like no other place. I was in Lisbon. The people there don't look like any other people I ever saw, the architecture doesn't look like any other architecture. I remember in Tangier, when a Portuguese fishing boat would suddenly be blown into port on some kind of a wind, and you could spot a Portuguese sailor a block away. They're a strange, slightly uncouth-looking archaic people dressed in these odd clothes, some of them very beautiful, some of them awful-looking.

HARRY: That's also true of the Atlanteans and Druids, right?

BURROUGHS: But they were *so* distinguished. You could just look down the block and say, "There is a Portuguese man."

CHRIS STEIN: The more I travel around, the less I want to live anywhere else than New York. Bill, you live next door to where we used to live on the Bowery.

HARRY: We used to live in a haunted building.

BURROUGHS: What haunted it?

HARRY: On top of the liquor store. We had a doll factory that had employed child labor.

STEIN: When we moved into the place things went berserk, they were flying round all the time.

HARRY: Fires!

STEIN: It was a really big floor through on three floors, totally destroyed, but I found these old things in there from the forties, old plaques.

HARRY: There were bullet holes in the windows from the Mafia when they had the place.

BURROUGHS: What were these psychic phenomena that occurred? Tell me about it.

HARRY: There was an entrance that came up from street level, a narrow long staircase that was very dark, and at the top of the staircase there was a flat wall with a doorway in it, and Chris decided to paint this wall black. Suddenly there was loud knocking and he saw like a little boy.

STEIN: Flashed on a little kid. It was more like a feeling. It was more like a presence.

BURROUGHS: Did you have any impression of the child's age?

STEIN: Eight, nine.

BURROUGHS: Was there anyone in the vicinity of this whole operation that young?

STEIN: No, there were no little kids around.

BURROUGHS: Because, as you probably know about poltergeists, they almost always manifest themselves through young people.

STEIN: Our adolescent bass player was constantly having nervous breakdowns.

BURROUGHS: That's it! That's it!

STEIN: Gary was almost electrocuted.

BURROUGHS: Wow! Sounds like real poltergeists.

STEIN: I came into the room and there he was clutching this lamp. I knocked it out of his hand. He was standing there; his clothes were fried.

BURROUGHS: God! How terrible.

AT THE BUNKER

Burroughs currently lives on the Bowery in a large three-room apartment which used to be the locker room of a gymnasium. He calls it the Bunker. Going to the Bunker can be a hazardous experience, and in fact William personifies more than any other man I have ever met a person aware of the hazards surrounding him. He has recently equipped me with a cane, a tube of tear gas, and a blackjack. "I would never go out of the house without all three on me," he says pointedly.

In fact, walking down the street in a dark blue chesterfield, his homburg pulled down over one eye, a cane swinging alertly from his right hand, Bill steps right out of a Kerouac novel. . . . I was constantly struck by the similarity of Kerouac's portraits of Bill to the William who was slowly becoming revealed to me during the time I was constructing this portrait.

It wasn't until late 1975 that Burroughs found what would become his GHQ New York City. The Bunker is an elegant old red brick building. One of the first people I ever brought over to visit him was

Bockris with Chris Stein, Burroughs, and Deborah Harry at his apartment after dinner. Photo by Bobby Grossman

the British writer Christopher Isherwood, whose novels and travel books Burroughs had read and admired as well as used, and his companion the artist Don Bachardy. I turned on my tape recorder just as the cab pulled up in front of the locked iron gate of the Bunker on the chilly, deserted, windswept Bowery.

BOCKRIS [*on the street*]: A foreboding entrance. It's rather hard to get in here sometimes; it depends on whether the gate's open or not. Bill will come down and unlock the gate.

DON BACHARDY: Is that because it's a bad part of town?

BOCKRIS: I don't think that's the reason. It's a big building and they lock the gate. Bill doesn't personally lock it. [*We walk across the street to a bar half a block away. Icy wind. People wrapped in blankets leer out of doorways.*] Now this bar's perfectly safe, we'll call Bill and he'll come down. [*Open door, go into bar, loud noises of laughing, shouting, breaking glass, screams. Christopher and Don run very close behind. Voices from various conversations appear on tape: "That's my two dollars" etc.*] Is there a telephone in the bar?

BARTENDER: Nope. There's one right across the street.

CHRISTOPHER ISHERWOOD [*gleefully*]: It's so Eugene O'Neill! [*Open door into second bar. Repeat of above atmosphere. Voices drift in and out of the tape: "You and me are gonna meet tomorrow, you better believe it! When your friend ain't around. I've had enough of your shit! All your goddam 'friends!' "*]

BOCKRIS: This is part of visiting William Burroughs though, isn't it? [*On phone*]: Hi! James! We're down on the corner here . . . [*Hangs up.*] They're coming down. [*Walks out into street.*] Is it worse to be a drug addict or an alcoholic do you think?

ISHERWOOD: God, I don't know. I never tried either.

BOCKRIS: You do see more alcoholics in the world. It seems that drug addicts either die or else they don't get in such bad shape.

ISHERWOOD: I've drunk rather a lot during my life, but I never came anywhere near to being an alcoholic.

BOCKRIS: [*Burroughs' secretary, James Grauerholz, appears behind the iron door with a key. We walk up a flight of stone steps.*] I'll lead the way. [*They walk into William Burroughs' spacious apartment.*] I'll introduce everyone. [*They shake hands, nod, smile.*]

BURROUGHS: Why don't you take off your coats, gentlemen. [*All put coats in Bill's room next to his pyjamas, which are lying neatly folded on*

90

his bed, come back into living room and sit in a series of office-style orange armchairs around a large conference table that Burroughs has in the kitchen section of his apartment.]

GRAUERHOLZ: Can I get you a drink?

EVERYBODY: YES!

ISHERWOOD [*looking around*]: This is a marvelous place.

BURROUGHS: There are no windows. On the other hand, there's no noise. This whole building was a YMCA. This used to be the locker room. The man upstairs has the gymnasium and downstairs is the swimming pool. It's a furniture shop now.

BOCKRIS: Why did you move from Franklin Street to the Bunker?

BURROUGHS: I was very dissatisfied with walking up those stairs in Franklin Street; also they were putting up the rent. The "in" was John Giorno, who has a place upstairs. The landlord showed me this place. No one wanted it because it didn't have any windows. It was used for storage then. The sink was already in and the shower and toilet. I decided to take it. It was originally one space so we put up these partitions. James moved in first for about six months, and then I moved out of Franklin Street. I was trying to sell it because I'd spent a good deal of money on Franklin Street. It was in a pretty bad state when I moved in and by the time I had bought a refrigerator and put in a sink and a set of cabinets and some reflooring, it cost me $7,000. But nobody would give me anything for it, so I finally gave it to Malcolm McNeil, who lives there now. I happened to hit the market at the wrong time. Also, nobody wanted it because it was a three-story walkup. Now it's a hell of a thing to have a refrigerator brought up three flights. It costs you a lot extra.

BOCKRIS: What gave you the idea to paint the Bunker's floors white?

BURROUGHS: When I first moved in it was battleship gray and it looked dingy. It's obvious you need all the light you can get in here since there isn't any natural light and I was very pleased with the results. There is of course no view, but what kind of view did I have at Franklin Street? I had some buildings to look at. Also I have four doors between me and the outside and I have people down there in the daytime. It's pretty impregnable.

BOCKRIS: This entry via telephone system is good. No one can come knock at the door unexpectedly and bother you.

BURROUGHS: I think it's better this way. I am very comfortable here.

91

In front of the Burroughs building, New York, 1975: A portrait by Gerard Malanga. Photo by Gerard Malanga

DINNER WITH SYLVERE LOTRINGER, GERARD MALANGA, AND DEBBIE HARRY: NEW YORK 1979

SYLVERE LOTRINGER: When I visited William at the Bunker to discuss plans for the Nova Convention he struck me as totally American. The distance, the twist, the sarcastic tone were, for me, very American. His way of talking is so elaborate and at the same time so Middle American. It's only by the humor that I connect his conversation to what he writes, though the way he speaks *is* very much connected to his writing. The emphasis of his voice is very precise. He reminded me of T. S. Eliot.

BURROUGHS: Of course, when you think of it, *The Waste Land* was the first great cut-up collage.

LOTRINGER: I met T. S. Eliot once when I was in England. I will always remember his diction. He spoke, like Burroughs, as if the sentences were already written down.

MALANGA: Do you find your work makes relationships with people more difficult?

BURROUGHS: I do spend a great deal of time alone. I'm not very gregarious. I don't like parties or miscellaneous gatherings with no particular purpose. I think parties are largely a mistake. The bigger they are the more mistaken they are. We don't have such parties here. You wake up the next morning and assess the damages to your premises. I have a few close personal friends who I see regularly. I don't see a lot of people. I don't go out a lot.

HARRY: Are you a good cook?

BURROUGHS: I am reasonable, yes.

HARRY: Do you open cans or do you buy things and make them?

BURROUGHS: I cook tastily for as many as ten people.

Album cover by Les Levine

ON DRUGS

At Burroughs' apartment, Ter emptied the bag of drug samples onto Bill's big parlor table, and as I turned on the tape and fired up the bomber, Bill motioned us to fix our drinks, donned his reading glasses, and settled in for a good scrutiny of the dope labels, using a magnifying glass like a jeweler examining precious stones.

BURROUGHS: Now then, what is all this shit, Terry?

TERRY SOUTHERN: Bill, these are pharmaceutical samples, sent by the drug companies to Big Ed Fales, the friendly druggist, and to Doc Tom Adams, the writing croak. Anything that won't cook up, we'll eat. Give them good scrutiny, Bill.

BURROUGHS: Indeed I shall.

SOUTHERN: We'll get them into the old noggin one way or the other! On double alert for Demerol, Dilaudid, and the great Talwin!

BURROUGHS: *Pain*—I'm on the alert for the word pain . . . [*murmuring, as he examines the label*]: Hmm . . . yes . . . yes . . . yes, indeed . . . [*reading from a label*]: "Fluid-control that can make life livable." Well, that could apply to blood, water . . . [*reading another label*].

SOUTHERN: All our precious bodily fluids!

BURROUGHS: I'll just go through these methodically. Anything of interest I'll put to one side . . . [*makes a separate grouping*].

SOUTHERN [*getting a paper bag*]: We'll put rejects in here.

BURROUGHS [*gesture of restraint*]: I'm just picking out what *might* be of interest . . . [*examining a label*]: Here's a possible [*sets it aside*].

SOUTHERN: Now a lot of these are new synthetics, Bill—names you may not be familiar with, because they're *disguising* the heavy drug within! This could warrant some serious research, and a good article for one of the dope mags—on how the pharmaceutical companies connive to beat the FDA—you know, and get Cosonal back on the shelf! *

BURROUGHS [*scrutinizing a bottle*]: I don't really know what this one may be . . .

SOUTHERN [*enthusiastically*]: Well then, down the old gullet with it, Bill! Better safe than sorry!

BURROUGHS [*dryly*]: I think not . . .

SOUTHERN [*picks up a bottle and reads*]: "For pimples and acne" [*throws it aside in disgust*]. Now here . . . "Icktazinga" [*handing it to Bill*]: Ring a bell?

BURROUGHS [*examining it*]: "Chewable." I'm not much interested in anything *chewable* . . . [*makes a wry face*].

SOUTHERN: But they're saying, "Chew one at a time," and I'm saying, "Cook up eight!" *If One Will Chew, Eight Will Cook Up!* There's a title for you!

BOCKRIS: Here's a diuretic.

SOUTHERN: A diuretic may contain *paregoric*—and you know what *that* means!

BURROUGHS: No, no . . .

SOUTHERN: I say a diuretic is chock-a-block full of a spasm-relieving nerve-killer . . . definitely a coke-based medication!

BURROUGHS: A diuretic . . .

SOUTHERN: It'll cook right up, Bill.

BURROUGHS: . . . is something to induce *urination,* my dear—that's *all* that it is.

SOUTHERN: Is *that* all a diuretic does? Induce urine?

BURROUGHS: Yes.

SOUTHERN [*gravely*]: Well, Doctor, I suppose we're in for another damnable stint of trial-and-error.

BURROUGHS: Yes, I'm afraid so. Such are the tribulations of the legitimate drug industry.

---

* A codeine-based cough syrup sold over the counter a few years ago.

BOCKRIS: Nicotinic acid! What's that like?

BURROUGHS: That's *vitamins,* my dear.

SOUTHERN: Hold on, Doctor, it *could* be some sort of synthetic speed!

BOCKRIS: Yes, it says, "For prolonged action."

BURROUGHS [*scrutinizing yet another label*]: Pain!—look for the word "pain" . . . that's the key.

SOUTHERN: Let "pain" be our watchword!

BURROUGHS: Here we are, this could be it. [*He inspects an ancient-looking bottle with dark green label on it.*] Yes, this is the stuff. It's got a little codeine in it.

SOUTHERN: We'll have to savor it. . . . But, Bill, I hope you're not underestimating these synthetic painkillers, just because they're not labeled *heroin* or *morphine* . . .

BURROUGHS [*impatiently*]: Man, I know every synthetic . . .

SOUTHERN: No, no, legitimate drugs have gone *underground.* Everybody is picking up—it's a question of the old Miltown syndrome. I mean, they have to be very cool vis-à-vis the FDA—they can't just say, "Well, this will get you high."

BURROUGHS: Man, the FDA has to know before they can even send out a sample, believe me.

SOUTHERN [*to Bockris*]: Bill's threshold of tolerance is getting narrower.

BOCKRIS: Now here's one for hypertension—so it's a down, right?

BURROUGHS: No, hypertension is merely indicative of high blood pressure . . .

SOUTHERN: But surely it's a *down,* man, if it's antihypertension it must be a down . . .

BURROUGHS: No, it isn't.

BOCKRIS [*with another*]: Now this one could be speed. "Prolonged activity" it says.

SOUTHERN: Good!

BURROUGHS: What *kind* of activity? I'm not sure I *want* any more activity.

BOCKRIS [*reading*]: "Niacin!"

BURROUGHS: Man, don't you know what niacin is?

SOUTHERN: Down the hatch for heavy action, Bill!

BURROUGHS: You know what niacin is, don't you? It's a vitamin-B complex!

SOUTHERN: Has a bit of the old Spanish fly in it, if my guess is any good! Well, let me ask you this, Dr. Benway: do you acknowledge the existence of an attempt to pass on to a *not unsuspecting* public—*au contraire,* to an all too eagerly awaiting public—some sort of drug that they would recognize that would occlude pain?

BURROUGHS: I categorically deny this—because, you see, in order to consume a drug orally you've gotta have the FDA's approval.

SOUTHERN: Well, how did Cosonal get through?

BURROUGHS: What does it have to do with Cosonal?

SOUTHERN: Cosonal was this cough syrup—this was while you were out of the country—there was a period of about six months or more when you'd walk into a room literally ankle-deep in empty Cosonal bottles. Sick junkies were drinking fifteen or twenty bottles a day. It was 85 cents a bottle—and then the price started going up, inexplicably—before there was a scandal about it and it was taken off the market. It was chock-a-block full of codeine.

BURROUGHS: Believe me, nothing gets by the FDA. You can't put it out if they don't okay it.

SOUTHERN: Yes, but can't they okay something that will get you high without their knowing it? Something *new,* which they don't yet know is sense-deranging? *Or,* coming from yet another direction, couldn't the drug companies sell something which the patients would take without realizing they are getting high from it?

BURROUGHS: No, and I'll tell you why—in the first place, all the big companies are hand in fist with the FDA—the FDA are the *company cops,* that's exactly what they are.

SOUTHERN: I'm talking about corruption *within* the company . . .

BURROUGHS: Yes, there's corruption within, but it's more likely that it has something to do with drugs that *kill* people, rather than get them high. Occasionally they will turn up something . . . something like Milanite. Something like that can sneak through. Other things can sneak through, but then they find out they cause liver damage . . . very little sneaks through that is going to get you high . . . [*picking up a bottle*]. Now, this is the one thing we got—it contains half a grain of codeine sulfate—hardly any, but if you drank one of these bottles you might get a little buzz.

SOUTHERN: Down the gullet, Bill!

BOCKRIS: What we should do is take William out to dinner.

BURROUGHS [*ignoring this*]: You can get all the codeine you want right across the counter in France or Switzerland, but you can't get it here. [*He picks up a bottle and reads*]: "Confused, forgetful, cranky, unkempt, suspicious personality . . . Transient cerebral ischemia, inimical psychological condition for the second day in a row and they deal with underlying circulatory . . ."

BOCKRIS: I want to get straightened out. "Unkempt." I'll take one of those.

BURROUGHS: Each to his taste, as the French say, but I advise against it. [*Grumbling*]: Now here's something that goes straight in the wastepaper basket—"non-narcotic"! . . . I don't want anything non-narcotic on these premises! Heh-heh-heh.

SOUTHERN: Listen, they can say "non-narcotic," but they may have some really weird definition of narcotic, like something out of *Dracula* . . . I mean, think of the fantastic competition that must be going on between the headache-remedy people—trying to cure headaches and make you feel good.

BURROUGHS [*reading another label and tossing the bottle aside*]: Well, we

William and Terry backstage at the Nova Convention: New York 1978. Photo by Marcia Resnick

don't need any inflammatory agents for ancient arthritic conditions.
SOUTHERN: Wait! That's a *painkiller!* "Arthritis" is the word they use now for "pain," and that means *heavy codeine*, Bill!
BOCKRIS: This potion is well known to me—it's merely your friendly cough syrup with all the regular ingredients.
SOUTHERN: But it might cook up into something really sensational! You cook it up until everything disappears except the *essence,* which would be dynamite in terms of sense derangement . . .
BOCKRIS: We need an isolizer to isolize it.
SOUTHERN: No. Trial and error, trial and error . . .
BURROUGHS: We'll not go the trial-and-error route on these premises.
BOCKRIS: Shall we smoke another joint before we go out?
SOUTHERN [*opening a small metal can*]: Now this is from the Republic of Columbia—dynamo-dynamite. I'll just twist one up [*takes out pink papers*] using these clitoral pinks to give it zest.
BOCKRIS: Why don't you twist up another one? It looks like Bill might smoke that one up himself. [*Burroughs has picked up a series of newspaper clippings about murders and is acting out the various parts on the other side of the room, Terry's first joint in one hand.*] Bill, was there a lot of cocaine in Paris during Hemingway and Fitzgerald's time?
BURROUGHS: Man, there was *plenty* of cocaine and heroin. In the late 1920s it was all over the place in Europe, if you knew how to go about getting it. It was about 1/100th the price it is now.
SOUTHERN: Hemingway and Fitzgerald never mentioned it—no reference to dope . . . in their "entire collective oeuvre," so to speak. They were both heavily into the juice.
BOCKRIS: What I'm asking is, were Picasso and Gertrude Stein and Hemingway snorting coke?
SOUTHERN: No, but in Paris, where you have a large Arab population, you can turn on with hash quite openly—in the Arab cafés near the Hôtel de Ville. They have the strongest hash you can get, so they had that thing in the Gide, Baudelaire tradition . . .
BURROUGHS: You are confounding your times in this message. You got Gide and Baudelaire at the same fucking table sniffing cocaine. Why don't you throw in Villon, for Christsake!?! They all had a sniff of cocaine together! I think you're sniffing *time-travel,* baby!
SOUTHERN [*with a show of indignation*]: Doctor! I am referring to the

sustained tradition of sense-derangement among decadent frogs of the so-called Quality-Lit crowd! Baudelaire! Rimbaud! Verlaine! And the late great Andy Gide!

BURROUGHS [*adamant*]: Time-travel!

SOUTHERN: Bill's threshold of tolerance is about the width of a thai stick.

BOCKRIS: I hate Quaaludes.

BURROUGHS: You really feel logy in the morning. It's terrible stuff. I don't like them at all.

BOCKRIS: I hate that stuff—and Mandrex.

SOUTHERN: The great Mandrex! Is that the same as quay?

BOCKRIS: Stronger than quay. The English equivalent, but stronger. They use it a lot for seduction.

SOUTHERN: That's the thing about Quaaludes—chicks *love* Quaaludes—makes them less self-conscious, I suppose, about fucking. The druggist says it's a great favorite with *hookers*. With *students* and *hookers*. They must have something in common.

BURROUGHS: Intense pain.

SOUTHERN: They call them "floaters"—I guess they float above the pain.

BURROUGHS: *On* it, more likely—floating on a sea of pain!

SOUTHERN: Right again, Doctor! A. J. himself would agree!

BURROUGHS [*muttering as he examines a label*]: Sometimes I wonder about A. J. . . . remonstrated with him time and again . . . advised him to place himself exclusively in my care . . . all to no avail . . .

SOUTHERN: It's said that he has little or no regard for human life . . .

BURROUGHS: That is correct . . . except for his own, of course.

We go over to Mickey Ruskin's restaurant at One University Place for dinner.

BURROUGHS: I've reached the age where I can get a drink in Chicago without showing my ID. God man, listen to this, we walk into this bar and they demand IDs. The waitress looked at me coldly and said, "I guess *you're* all right." Were you along on that? Did you get a drink, Terry? Were you "all right"? If anyone asks for my ID I should be deeply flattered.

The cab arrives outside the restaurant. As we walk toward the door

Burroughs growls, gangster style, "I'll get you boys in, I swear." Inside, Roy Orbison is beginning to sing "Pretty Woman." The music washes over us as we take a table . . .

BOCKRIS: Terry, what do you think is the most interesting development we could have in drugs right now?

SOUTHERN: I think the first thing is price and quality control . . . the establishment of a standardization system. There would be a Dr. Benway type who would designate the criteria for the evaluation process and it would be priced according to quality. And the criteria should probably be technical—like the number of units of THC present, rather than, you know, on the basis of how much of a *rave-up* it causes any particular person . . . in other words, as nonsubjective as possible. Within that framework you will have your critics, of course. Charlatans will move in with their various hybrids. One can see it: "All right, why don't you try a little of Brand X—half the price of your usual brand." Well, that sort of thing should be against the law.

BURROUGHS: It's known as the Croakings of Experts.

BOCKRIS: We ought to call this interview the Croakings of Experts. But while you're fixing these prices, what about agricultural-support schools? We gotta have some agricultural price-support schools.

SOUTHERN: As rice is to China, so the coca bush will be to Mr. and Mrs. Undernourished U.S. of A. as a painkiller from their hunger because of the overflow—hunger will be caused by the necessity of efficient production.

BURROUGHS: Yes, it sure can ease off the pangs of hunger.

BOCKRIS: Everybody could raise his own coca bush.

BURROUGHS: It isn't all that easy; they only grow in certain climates.

BOCKRIS: If the Chinese can make steel in their backyards, I can grow coca.

SOUTHERN: Now wait a minute, you should be able to do it, Bill—you can get away with making your own booze. In fact, they have a legal . . .

BURROUGHS [*impatiently*]: We *tried* making our own booze once, and it was all so horrible everybody was *sick*.

BOCKRIS: Doesn't it seem obvious that the most salable drug of all would turn out to be the drug that would make sex better? Imagine if you could advertise and say this drug makes sex better. That's the drug that's going to sell the most, right?

102

BURROUGHS [*emphatically*]: No, I don't think so at all . . . Because the drug that's always sold the most on any market, and which will eventually replace any drug that makes sex more possible, is the drug that makes sex unnecessary, namely heroin. On an open market heroin would push marijuana right off the market, which is a fairly good sex drug. See, most people don't like sex—they want to be rid of sex. Their sex life is terrifically unsatisfactory. They have a wife who they were attracted to forty years ago, it's terrible, what do they want their sex life stimulated for? Their sex life is horrible. So heroin enables them to get rid of that drive, and that's what they really want.

SOUTHERN: Which drugs are sexually stimulating?

BURROUGHS: Marijuana.

BOCKRIS: A good mixture of coke and marijuana can sometimes work, depending on the catalyst, I guess.

BURROUGHS: I don't like coke.

BOCKRIS: No, but a small amount of it can help.

BURROUGHS: Get high on marijuana and then a couple of poppers.

BOCKRIS: Do you keep poppers next to the bed?

BURROUGHS: Well naturally, you see, all the young people do. They say the stink of amyl nitrate fills the halls of the hotels up at Bellows Falls.

BOCKRIS: Terry, which drug would you most like to have for yourself?

SOUTHERN: Cocaine is the most enjoyable drug for me—in moderation, natch, due to its price.

BOCKRIS: What would you most like to see developed?

SOUTHERN: It would depend on the good Doctor's recommendations—Dr. Benway's. It's a question of metabolism, you see.

BURROUGHS: If I were going to be a scapegoat, I would say just leave your body and go away somewhere, perhaps not even come back. It would save me a lot of trouble . . .

SOUTHERN: Hurry up, Doctor. I think a citizen's arrest should be made. I suppose you are Satan, substituting for the mad Benway. I suppose . . . [*suddenly turning to the waitress*] How would you like to be in the movies, my dear, with the mad Dr. Benway?

BOCKRIS: I don't see any reason to believe there's going to be a change in the way drugs are distributed to people.

BURROUGHS: What are you talking about?

SOUTHERN: Once the acceptance changes, then the laws will change to accommodate that fact.

William and Terry consider the future in terms of the news. Photo by
Marcia Resnick

BURROUGHS: Are you referring to what comes out of the drugstore? What are you talking about?

BOCKRIS: I'm talking about how the drugs are going to get distributed to the people who want them. How are things going to become available more easily?

BURROUGHS: My dear, that's been changing for most of my memory. It's unbelievable the degree of change.

BOCKRIS: It's still not that easy to get the drugs you want to get.

SOUTHERN: The regulation of it will happen when it suits the convenience of certain people, the same people who have the cost of a color TV set at $400 while a black and white is $55. It's an incredible discrepancy, obviously due to a conspiracy within the industry. They said, "Let's get rid of our total inventory of black and white sets before we convert exclusively to color—like the movies—let's bleed them to within an inch of their lives." And this sort of thing can be anticipated in the dope market as well. But eventually there will be some sort of regulatory body—a bureau of standards. And legalization is highly commendable on other levels as well—not the least of which is its source of revenue to the government, through taxation, to support things like public transportation systems, low-income housing, medical facilities, and so on—the same as with taxation on alcohol, tobacco, lotteries, and gambling . . . a tremendous source of revenue. The bottom line is simply that the two things—legalization and standardization of quality—should occur simultaneously. Otherwise, everyone will end up smoking catnip.

DINNER WITH PETER BEARD AND RAYMOND FOYE: NEW YORK 1978

BOCKRIS: In the future will they really be able to make drugs that do almost anything?

BURROUGHS: They're well on their way. Very soon they're going to achieve the synthesis of endorphin. It's an opiate created by the body, thirty times stronger than morphine, which they have now extracted from the brains of animals, particularly camels, who have a very high pain threshold: and they've found that it does stop acute pain and relieves the symptoms of opiate withdrawal, but it's still terribly expensive—$3,000 a dose. It's about in the state that cortisone was in

105

when it first came out. *Very* expensive. But it's a question of additional research and synthesis, although it's going to take them five years to get endorphin on the market, because the fucking FDA is really crippling any kind of research. It may well solve the whole problem of addiction, because being a natural body substance it's presumably not addicting itself.

BOCKRIS: Can we expect to have much longer life spans quite soon?

BURROUGHS: There's a very interesting book on this, *The Biological Time Bomb* by Gordon Taylor. He says that the ability to prolong life to as much as 200 years is not 100 years in the future, it's ten or fifteen years. Then there comes a question: Suppose everybody's going to live that long? Where are we gonna put 'em all? We got too many people now.

Any sort of *selective* distribution of a medication to prolong life would run into, uh, social difficulties. What he points out, essentially, is that our creaky social system cannot absorb the biologic discoveries that are on the way. We will also be able to increase intelligence by the use of certain drugs. But then who is going to receive these drugs, who is to decide?

BOCKRIS: It points toward a much more controlled society.

BURROUGHS: I don't think it does at all. A point that Leary made, which I think is quite valid, is that Washington is no longer a center of power, it's no longer a center of anything, it's a joke. It's having less and less influence on what is actually going on. There's no necessity for somebody to control all this because the indications are that they wouldn't be called on to do so.

Suppose I'm a wealthy man and I hire a bunch of scientists and they discover a longevity pill. Well, *I* decide then what to do with it. I can give it out to all my friends, or to the scientists who made it. That's what Taylor points out, that our government could not make these decisions, so they won't be called on to make them. They won't be in charge. There's no way that the government can completely monopolize all scientific discovery. So I think we are not going to get a more controlled society. Science by its nature is very difficult to monopolize, because once something is known it becomes common knowledge in scientific quarters and anybody can do it.

BOCKRIS: What's actually causing the growing acceptance of drugs?

BURROUGHS: Less ill-informed media exposure is making the biggest difference. They're going to legalize marijuana, and sooner or later they're going to come around to some form of heroin maintenance. Many people connected with drug enforcement actually think that there's no use going on trying to enforce an unenforceable law and that it's been as much of a failure as Prohibition. That would make a terrific change. It would destroy the whole black market in heroin and eliminate the necessity for the Drug Enforcement Administration.

RAYMOND FOYE: You said at a recent press conference that there were some drugs you thought they should stop manufacturing altogether—such as speed.

BURROUGHS: Sure. There's no use for it.

FOYE: No medical use.

BURROUGHS: Almost none. I've talked to doctors about this; they say there are very few cases where there's a medical indication.

Ginsberg tells Burroughs that he will smoke a joint at The Gramercy Arts Club while Burroughs, who can smell them a mile away, looks askance across the room at CIA agents. Meanwhile Mailer tells Orlovsky, our quiet American, a joke. Photo by Marcia Resnick

BOCKRIS: Is heroin a drug that should be developed and used more?

BURROUGHS: Basically there's no difference between heroin and morphine. Heroin is by volume stronger, which means that it is also qualitatively stronger. Pain that no amount of codeine will alleviate can be alleviated by morphine. There probably are conditions, like leprosy of the eye and fish poisoning, where they could pump in any amount of morphine and it wouldn't do any good. Heroin might get it. Of course heroin should be used more medically. They're thinking of legalizing the manufacture of heroin here because it's a better pain-killer than morphine and it's less nauseating. There are situations where nausea can be fatal after certain operations. In those cases heroin is a much more useful drug than morphine. It's also much more useful in terminal cancer. I've had a lifelong interest in drugs and medicine and illness. Pharmacology was a lifelong hobby. In fact, I took a year of medicine in Vienna. I decided not to go on with it because it was too long a period of study. And then I wasn't at all sure I'd like the actual practice of medicine. But I was always interested in diseases and their symptoms, poisons and drugs. Since I was thirteen years old I was reading books on pharmacology and medicine. However, sick people get on my nerves.

PETER BEARD: How did you lose your finger?

BURROUGHS: Oh . . . er . . . explosion. Blew my whole hand off. See, I nearly lost the . . .

BEARD [*looking closely at scars on Burroughs' hand*]: Oh . . . yes.

BURROUGHS: Whole hand, but I had a very good surgeon.

BEARD: And he saved the other fingers?

BURROUGHS: He saved them.

BOCKRIS: Was that a gun explosion?

BURROUGHS: No no no, it was, er . . . chemicals! Potassium chlorate and red phosphorus.

BEARD: What were you doing with it?

BURROUGHS: Chemicals! Boys! I was fourteen years old . . .

BEARD: Fabulous, just fabulous.

BURROUGHS: . . . and I was putting the top on . . .

BEARD: A Charles Addams character at large . . . playing.

BURROUGHS: Not at all, not at all. Everyone when I was a kid had these things known as chemistry sets and they had little wooden cases with very fresh hazardous chemicals in them and instructions for making powders and all sorts of things and they'd often blow up when you were putting the top on.

BOCKRIS: Did your finger actually come off right there?

BURROUGHS: Yes.

BOCKRIS: Did you feel any pain?

BURROUGHS: Oh yes I did. I felt pain about fifteen minutes later. The thing is numb for a while, but then it begins to really hurt. By the time I got to the hospital the doctors had to give me a morphine injection which they said was "almost an adult dose."

BOCKRIS: Congratulations.

BURROUGHS: Yes, indeed. I've been addicted ever since.

BOCKRIS: How did you become addicted to heroin?

BURROUGHS: My first addiction was to morphine. Addiction is a disease of exposure. By and large people become addicts who are exposed to it—doctors and nurses, for instance. People I knew at the time were using it. I took a shot, liked it, and eventually became an addict.

BOCKRIS: Weren't you aware of the dangers?

BURROUGHS: The Federal Narcotics Bureau does a grave disservice by disseminating a lot of misinformation. Most of what they say is such nonsense that I didn't believe them about addiction. I thought I could take it or leave it alone. They give out that marijuana is a harmful and habit-forming drug, and it simply isn't. They claim that you can be addicted in one shot, and that's another myth. They overestimate the physical bad effects. I just didn't believe them about anything they said.

DINNER WITH TENNESSEE WILLIAMS: NEW YORK 1976

BURROUGHS: Paul Bowles had a first edition of your book *The Angel in the Alcove*. I borrowed his copy to read. I was on junk at the time and I dripped blood all over it, and Paul was furious. It should be quite a collector's item—first edition, and with my blood all over it.

WILLIAMS: Do you ever take drugs at all anymore?

BURROUGHS: No, not that kind. I don't have a habit or anything like that.

WILLIAMS: I've always wanted to go on opium. I did try it in Bangkok. I was traveling with a professor friend of mine, and he had been in the habit of occasionally dissolving a bit in his tea, and drinking it. Anyway, he was angry at me, or confused mentally, I don't know which, and I called him one morning, as he'd gotten me this long black stick of opium, and I said, "Paul, what do I do with it?" And he said, "Just put it in the tea." So I put the whole stick in the tea. I nearly died of an OD, of course. I was puking green as your jacket, you know? And sicker than ten dogs all that day. I called in a Siamese doctor. He said, "You should be *dead.*" I said, "I feel as though if I weren't walking or stumbling about, I would be." I've always said I wanted to write under the drug, you know, like Cocteau did—all of a sudden, my head seemed like a balloon and it seemed to go right up to the ceiling. Do you ever take goofballs?

BURROUGHS: I have, but I'm not an afficionado. De Quincey reports that Coleridge had to hire somebody to keep him out of drugstores, and then he fired him the next day when the man attempted to obey his instructions. He told him, "Do you know that men have been known to drop down dead for the timely want of opium?" Very funny indeed.

WILLIAMS: It's all a big joke. Maybe a black joke, but it's a big joke.

BURROUGHS: Have you ever written film scripts?

WILLIAMS: Yes, I've written one called *One Arm,* which has been floating around, I don't know where it is. I wrote it one summer while I was taking Dr. Max Jacobson's shots. I did some of my best writing while taking these shots. I had incredible vitality under them. And I got way ahead of myself as a writer, into another dimension. I never enjoyed writing like that. You've never written on any kind of speed, have you, Bill?

BURROUGHS: Well no, I'm not a speed man at all.

WILLIAMS: I am a downer man.

BURROUGHS: I don't like either one very much.

WILLIAMS: Speed was wonderful, while I was young enough to take it; but you don't like either one now? You don't need any kind of artificial stimulant?

BURROUGHS: Well, cannabis in any form is . . .

WILLIAMS: Cannabis has the opposite effect on me. I think Paul Bowles finds it very helpful. I have tried it: *nothing.* Just stonewalled me.

110

DINNER WITH JEFF GOLDBERG AND GLENN O'BRIEN: NEW YORK 1980

BURROUGHS: I've known lots of whores. The great majority of whores are addicts and they just fuck to get money for junk.

BOCKRIS: So many girls seem to need to take Quaaludes to have sex. Would heroin relax them in the same way?

BURROUGHS: It isn't nearly as much of a knockout drug as Quaaludes. Addiction has always been endemic among whores. They're one of the most heavily addicted segments of the population. And their pimps supply them with their junk.

GOLDBERG: It's one of the most basic control situations.

BURROUGHS: Except in the nineteenth century it was very easy to score for junk anywhere before all this nonsense started. But the addicted whore is a very old syndrome: as early as the use of opiates was common. The use of opiates all through nineteenth-century England was terrific. On market days they'd have great jars of opium pills on drugstore counters and people could just go in there and buy them. It was cheaper than alcohol, and much better, so God knows how many thousands of addicts there were at that time. Nobody knew anything about it because it was legal. After it became illegal, and all through the twenties and thirties, it was restricted to the very high and the very low, to millionaires, movie stars, playboys, playgirls, and, on the other hand, criminals, whores, and thieves. You see it was cheap and easy to get. Heroin was $28 an ounce in the 1920s. Actually there was more morphine on the street rather than heroin. In the 1920s they brought in morphine. Then heroin came in in the late 1920s. Heroin is now about $9,000 an ounce, so imagine from $28 an ounce to $9,000 and junk turns out to be a model for inflation, being the most inflated item. A friend of mine, Phil White, who did time on Rikers Island in the thirties, told me the guards came in every morning with a shoebox full of heroin decks at fifty cents a deck. On one deck you could stay loaded all day and do the time standing on your head. With junk you are immune to boredom and discomfort.

GOLDBERG: Why was there this switch from the image of the habitué sipping laudanum to the dirty-needle junkie?

BURROUGHS: In the early forties, when Harry Anslinger took over, he forced the market up. As soon as the drug was illegal, naturally enforcement became a very important factor. Just as in Prohibition the fact that whiskey was illegal made it more expensive.

BOCKRIS: It seems that however much they put the price up, an addict will keep paying.

BURROUGHS: If the price gets too high they can't pay, and the prices do come down.

BOCKRIS: You mean it really gets to the point where people say forget it?

BURROUGHS: It isn't that they say forget, they just can't pay. Now there's good heroin on the street again and you can maintain a habit for $12 a day. So it does get to a point where people just cannot pay, then somebody else comes in, brings the prices down, and gets the market. In the old days the price of heroin was manipulated like any other commodity price. Someone comes into Morocco, buys up all the sugar, puts it in the warehouse and takes it off the market. There are sugar riots in Tangier. When it comes back on the market it comes back at an increased price. And they've pulled the same thing with heroin here again and again and again. It's known as a panic. Suddenly there's no heroin anywhere that can be bought and the junkies are all walking around to doctors, trying to get stuff from them, and the doctors are saying, "Get out! Get out! Get out! You're the tenth one who's been in here today. I'm a professional man! I can't service people like you!" But the panic never goes on long enough for people to really get off. It goes on for about a week and then the stuff comes back at *double* the price. You see, the sugar comes back at only a slightly increased price, and that's known as manipulation of commodity prices. A lot of people have made huge fortunes out of the poorest people by monopolizing basic commodities and holding these commodities off the market, then reintroducing them and extracting as much as the people can possibly pay.

GOLDBERG: The poppy is basically like a Third World commodity, so they're in a kind of chaotic situation.

BOCKRIS: What's the connection between the chaos in Afghanistan and Iran and the heroin coming from those sources?

BURROUGHS: It's just that most of the poppies are grown in those areas. But there is no reason for that. We have always imported our opium, we've never attempted to grow it here, but we could. Poppies can be

Burroughs comes across a variety of the yage vine in the jungle outside Macao, Columbia, in 1953. Photographer unknown

grown anywhere. There are lots of places in America that are quite suitable for growing poppies, besides which they can grow in greenhouses. The poppy is a plant that adapts itself to dry, slightly mountainous climates. I'm sure they could be grown all through the Rockies, say from about May to September, and of course cocaine plants could easily be grown in many regions as well. Opium is made from the poppy. The extraction of morphine from opium is a very simple process, and heroin is a step beyond morphine. It's a very simple chemical process, anybody can do it in a basement laboratory.

BOCKRIS: Who originally did this?

BURROUGHS: I don't know, but he should go down in history.

GOLDBERG: It was named after *heroisch,* a German word meaning strong.

BURROUGHS: There must be some chemist who actually did it, but at any rate it's a very simple formula. You order your heroin-conversion kit through *High Times,* it would look just like that [*pointing to a psilocybin mushroom incubator*], see, and you'd be tinkering around peering in to see how it was coming along, then first thing you know . . . hmmpfh hmmpfh hmmpfh . . .

GOLDBERG: When you were farming in Texas were you thinking about growing anything illegal?

BURROUGHS: Yes, I was growing marijuana down there.

BOCKRIS: I heard you were also *growin'* heroin!

BURROUGHS: It springs up outa the earth what dya gonna do? Everyone got sick! Springs up outa the earth, in little packages on a Christmas tree.

BOCKRIS: If heroin was so easy to get, why would people want opium?

BURROUGHS: It has its advantages. If you don't have a habit opium will last much longer; opium will last you hours and hours and hours. Some people like it better. There are lots of opium smokers who could have gotten heroin and didn't want it.

BOCKRIS: I understand eating majoun has the effect of twenty joints hitting you at one time.

O'BRIEN: I've smoked twenty joints sitting at the typewriter.

BURROUGHS: I wrote the whole of *Naked Lunch* on majoun and I had some great experiences. It helps you to write.

BOCKRIS: I would think so, but I just wonder how far out you go. I love these potatoes.

BURROUGHS: They are good. These are excellent sweet potatoes.

BOCKRIS: What is the principle of this potato?

BURROUGHS: Principle! Well, it's a sweet potato. It's not a yam.

BOCKRIS: Is the sweet potato a cultured thing?

BURROUGHS: Why yes.

O'BRIEN: I think this is a native American potato.

BURROUGHS: They are not at all sure whether this potato was native to the New World or whether it possibly came drifting from the Indonesian Islands in the South Pacific where the yam culture is endemic. This is also known as a yam. There was an anthropological controversy which was known as the sweet potato controversy.

114

BOCKRIS: Why isn't it more popular than it was then?

BURROUGHS [*with considerable restraint*]: Well, it's quite popular. It's very popular in the South since there are so many recipes, you know, like possum and sweet potato, fried chicken and sweet potatoes. Sweet potato pie is very popular I assure you in the southern part of the United States.

DINNER WITH SUSAN SONTAG, JEFF GOLDBERG, LOU REED, AND TENNESSEE WILLIAMS: NEW YORK 1978

BOCKRIS: You're smoking again.

SONTAG: I smoke when I go out.

BOCKRIS: A closet smoker, eh.

BURROUGHS: I stopped smoking since I last saw you.

SONTAG: Was it very hard?

BURROUGHS: No, no, and it was the best thing I ever did.

SONTAG: Did you just say that's it and you stopped?

BURROUGHS: Oh yes. This cutting down is nonsense. I read a book called *How to Stop Smoking,* followed the directions, and stopped.

GOLDBERG: Didn't you get some sort of omen?

BURROUGHS: Oh yes, I put a pack of cigarettes down on the book of breathing and when I pulled it away it pulled out the whole lung of the person on the cover. I then said: this is an omen.

SONTAG: All sexual taboos have disappeared; all taboos about drugs except nicotine have disappeared. This is the only forbidden pleasure left.

BURROUGHS: If someone wants to draw smoke down into their lungs . . . I used to do it myself for fifteen years and when I got out of there it was like stepping out of a prison. After the third day I just felt so pure. Have you ever seen people who have stopped smoking? After about a week they get an almost luminescent radiant health, and when you have experienced that you won't go back.

Lou Reed came in again and asked Bill a specific question about a scene in *Junky* where a character injects heroin with a safety pin. He couldn't see how it was done.

BURROUGHS: A lot of old junkies used to do this. You make a hole with the pin and then you put the dropper over the hole and the stuff is supposed to run in.

115

WILLIAMS: I think it's most remarkable that you avoided any commitment to drugs. Except cannabis. And you're strong enough to control it. I'm strong enough to control anything I take . . .

BURROUGHS: Old Aleister Crowley, plagiarizing from Hassan i Sabbah, said: *"Do what thou wilt* is the whole of the Law."

WILLIAMS: Regarding drugs, you mean?

BURROUGHS: Regarding anything. And then Hassan i Sabbah's last words were: "Nothing is true; everything is permitted." If you see everything as illusion, then everything is permitted. The last words of Hassan i Sabbah, the Old Man of the Mountain, the Master of the Assassins. And this was given a slightly different twist, but it's the same statement as Aleister Crowley's, "Do what you want to do is the whole of the Law."

WILLIAMS: Provided you want to do the right thing, yes.

BURROUGHS: Ah, but if you really want to do it, then it's the right thing. That's the point.

WILLIAMS: Isn't that an amoralist point of view?

BURROUGHS: Completely . . . completely.

WILLIAMS: I don't believe you're an amoralist.

BURROUGHS: Oh yes.

WILLIAMS: You do believe it?

BURROUGHS: I do what I can . . .

WILLIAMS: I don't think it's true.

BURROUGHS: We were both brought up in the Bible Belt, but it's obvious that what you want to do is, of course, eventually what you will do anyway. Sooner or later.

* * *

"If you can score for sex and drugs in a place, then you know you really made contact with the place."—*Burroughs to Steve Mass, owner of The Mudd Club*

* * *

BURROUGHS IN HOLLYWOOD

DINNER WITH ANDY WARHOL: NEW YORK 1980

BOCKRIS: Andy, Bill is a great actor, he's a natural. He could be a big star. Look at his face.

BURROUGHS: Yes I can play doctors, CIA men, and all kinds of things. I do war criminals very well.

BOCKRIS: War criminals?

WARHOL: I think you should be a dress designer.

BURROUGHS: A Nazi war criminal I could play very well.

WARHOL: I think you should be a dress designer. You gotta change your profession and become a dress designer.

BURROUGHS: Well . . . hmmm, that's not my sort of thing.

WARHOL: Actually you're the best-dressed person I've ever known.

BURROUGHS: *Really?*

WARHOL: Isn't he the best? He's always worn a tie since I've known him.

BURROUGHS: Actually I have had some acting experience. I played the Toff in *A Night at the Inn* by Dunsany. That's an old old high school show. It was the principal part, my dear, *I* was the *leeeaadd.* That was at Los Alamos.

BOCKRIS: But how could you have a play if they only had twenty-six boys?

BURROUGHS: It doesn't matter. How many people do you need for a play?

BOCKRIS: Quite a lot. Was it fun?

BURROUGHS: I was a big success.

BOCKRIS: Is that where you got bitten by the bug?

BURROUGHS: I took out my .32 revolver and laid it on the table. Do you know this play, it's a corny old thing, you can't read it. Well, this gentleman who's the Toff and I think four seamen have stolen the eye out of an idol, a ruby, and the priests of the idol have followed them. So they're holed up at this inn. The Toff has figured that he will trap the priests there and they will come in so he and his confederates can kill them. But the seamen are saying, "We're leaving, Toff, we don't see any point in staying around here. Argh! Give us the ruby!"

"Certainly, Albert."

"No hard feelings, guv'ner . . . We'll see that you get your share."

At this the Toff takes out a .32 revolver and puts it on the table and sits there. So then they all come rushing back in. *"They're here, Toff!"*

"Well, I expected them about now."

You see, one of the seamen had said he had given the priests the slip. The Toff said, "People like that, if we died they'd follow our grand-children," and this fool thinks he can give people like that the slip by running around a few streets in the town of Hull. The priests come in and then we manage to knife them one after the other while I stand as bait all through.

"What's this worth, Toff? Is it worth a thousand pounds?"

"Worth all they've got in this shop, Herbert. Just whatever we want to ask for it." Then the Toff says, "Get me some water, this whiskey is too much for my head, and I must keep it clear until our friends are safe in the cellar." So someone goes out to get the water and he comes running back in and shouts, "Toff, I don't want the ruby! Take my share back!"

So the Toff says, "What is this, Albert? What's the matter with you? Have you seen the police?"

"I don't want it, man, I'll give you my share back!"

And he says, "No more nonsense, Albert. We're all in this together. If one hangs we all hang, but this isn't a hanging matter. They had their knives."

"Take it back, Toff! Take it back! Take it back!"

118

At this point the idol walks into the room, gropes over, gets the ruby and sticks it back in its eye. Then it walks offstage and intones, "Able Seaman Albert So and So!" and he's pulled offstage, *"Aaaaahhhh!"* And finally I'm the last to go. You see all along they'd been saying, "I don't think anything happens that our Toff doesn't foresee, does it now?" And I'd always say, "Well, I don't think it often does, Albert, I don't think it often does." So as I'm being pulled offstage by this force to be killed by the idol, I turn to the audience and say, "I did not foresee it."

BOCKRIS: What exactly does a toff mean?

BURROUGHS: Listen, you don't even know the slang of your own bloody limey country! It means a toff! A toff! You know, I would say something and they would say behind my back, " 'E's such a toff." He's a member of the upper classes, that's the whole point, he knows what's what. This guy is obviously down on his luck, you see, he's working as a seaman on a merchant ship going after this ruby.

BOCKRIS: What was your next part?

BURROUGHS: I don't think I ever had another.

BOCKRIS: Any Shakespeare parts?

BURROUGHS: I don't go in too much for Shakespeare. I'm a great admirer of the immortal bard, but I can't think of a part that I could really play with any real conviction, except perhaps Casca in *Julius Caesar.*

DINNER WITH CHRISTOPHER ISHERWOOD, PAUL GETTY, JR., AND TERRY SOUTHERN: NEW YORK 1975

ISHERWOOD: I was commissioned to adapt Scott Fitzgerald's second novel, *The Beautiful and the Damned.* We really preserved the book. The dialogue was between seventy and eighty percent Fitzgerald, and everybody liked it. Then, suddenly, there was a change up in the higher office and they decided no more Fitzgerald. A bad bet! He's done for! Or something.

BOCKRIS: *Gatsby* made money. They made money before it came out, from selling rights.

BURROUGHS: I cannot believe that they made money on that film.

BOCKRIS: They broke even just through selling all sorts of rights. Is *The Last Tycoon* also a flop?

ISHERWOOD: It was better than we expected.

BOCKRIS: Did you basically enjoy it?

ISHERWOOD: Well, I, I, I mean I was a bit bored with a lot of it.

BURROUGHS: It's always been my contention that the best movies based on books are made from bad books. *The Treasure of the Sierra Madre* made a great film. The book, which I read after seeing the film, was disappointing. *Marathon Man* was a great film. The book is, well, regular, as the Spanish say, *passable*. With a second-rate or little-known book they can take the necessary liberties to make a good film. When Hollywood is faced by a classic the results are usually awful. I always thought Fitzgerald is not for the movies. His dialogue is often wooden, the plot is nothing, it's all in the prose that can't be gotten onto the screen—like the last three pages of *The Great Gatsby*.

ISHERWOOD: Oh, absolutely yes, I think it's unmakeable.

BURROUGHS: And then I can think of any number of bad or second-rate novels that would make great films.

GETTY: Have you been to Hollywood?

BURROUGHS: In 1971 Chuck Barris sent first-class plane tickets to L.A. to Terry Southern and your reporter. He was interested in seeing the script of *Naked Lunch*. A Daimler meets us at the airport. We are being driven to meet Chuck Barris and his secretary Keister.

"Yes," the driver said. "Her name really is Keister." I experienced a premonitory chill.

The place was called The Cocoanut as I recall, quite nondescript. Barris is a jock type with short-sleeved shirt and muscles bulging out, no meat on his plate, and he doesn't drink or smoke. Keister is a slender blonde with brown eyes and harlequin glasses. We give Barris the script. He will get in touch tomorrow. We are driven back to our quarters in the Hyatt on Sunset Boulevard. The next day no word from Barris. Terry is putting out feelers and they come back negative. Barris doesn't like the script. Still no word. Afternoon of the second day his office calls to invite us for dinner at his place in Malibu to discuss the script. At the appointed hour the car arrives, but it has shrunk down to a two seater. After I've been sitting on Terry's lap for an hour, the driver deposits us in front of an unlighted house with a little snigger and drives away.

"Now I can't believe Old Chuck would stand us up like this . . ."

"Terry, when your Daimler shrinks down to a two seater it is time to move on fast before they renege on paying our hotel tab."

Fortunately Terry knew some neighbors who took us in and sustained us with cheese and snacks.

"I can't believe Old Chuck . . ."

"It's ten o'clock Terry, let's call a cab. It's twenty-two miles to town."

Next morning we check out, and do you know what those cheapies had done? They had put a note on our accounts—the office assumed no responsibility for bar and restaurant charges. Can you imagine!

Discouraged, and I thought rather outrageously depleted, we took a cab to the airport. "It eluded us then . . . no matter . . . tomorrow we will run faster, stretch out our arms wider and one fine morning . . ."

SOUTHERN: I didn't tell you, Bill—I thought it might give you a coronary—but I'm getting in touch with Chuck Barris [*a Hollywood movie producer*] again for another project, but this time I'm laying out our terms very carefully, which I'll have you okay, naturally, before flying out—but it'll be a big car both ways. BIG CAR BOTH WAYS is the first thing [*pounding the table*], BIG CAR BOTH WAYS and then—definition, you know—the latest and the greatest, it's gotta have video and all sorts of sense derangements and things.

BURROUGHS: Sounds great. We want a coke budget, of course.

BOCKRIS: Ask for that hundred-thousand-dollar cocaine budget right up front.

SOUTHERN: A lot of toot up front.

BOCKRIS: Terry was telling me about somebody who got an ice cream jar full of cocaine . . .

SOUTHERN: No names, no names!

BURROUGHS: Those are the choicest presents that may be given or received. You know, a piece of opium as big as a melon. Last you for a while. You can pass at least some of it on as a legacy to your grandchildren.

HOLLYWOOD: OCTOBER 1978

On arriving in Los Angeles, I called Timothy Leary to tell him that William had come to Hollywood from Boulder to visit the film set of

Heartbeat, a movie about the triangular love affair between Jack Kerouac, Carolyn and Neal Cassady, and would be staying in a suite near mine at the Tropicana for a week.

William was initially dubious about the nature of Los Angeles, so I gave a party to introduce him to some of the people I had met out there. Leary was at the top of my list. Other guests included Christopher Isherwood, Kenneth Tynan, Paul Getty, Jr., and Tom Forcade, who spent the whole party lying on the edge of the bed with a cowboy hat over his face. Tom Forcade was a legend in the American dope scene, and a pivot between the sixties and the seventies. He owned and published *High Times,* the most successful new magazine in the United States since *Rolling Stone.* I had known him for a few months when he joined us in California. I introduced him to Burroughs and they liked each other immediately. They also had a mutual interest in guns. Tom invited Bill to come shooting with him next time they were in New York together. The Nova Convention was in preparation at the time and its financial committee desperately needed $1,500. James asked me if Tom might be approached and I said I would talk to him about arranging a meeting. During the party, James came into the bedroom and said, "We need $1,500 . . . as a loan," and explained the details. Tom listened studiously, said okay, and explained how to pick up the money from an office in New York. The party was a great success and William was soon thoroughly enjoying himself in the seedy ambiance of the Tropicana where the palm trees waft over the pool.

The next day, William, James, and I drove out to Culver City, a fittingly dilapidated Mexican area, and turned into the Universal Studios parking lot, just like in a fifties movie. We were led onto a stage set of Neal Cassady's house in the fifties—ancient copies of *Life* magazine, fifties toys and paraphernalia were scattered about. We stood around feeling conspicuous and uncertain of what we were meant to do there. Being an onlooker on a movie set is a very boring business. Everybody has something to do except you. There are no chairs to sit on so you have to just wander around and get in the way, or stand still and get in the way. And they do fifteen takes to get one minute's worth of film.

John Heard, the actor who plays Jack Kerouac in the movie, came up to William and said, "Hello, I'm Jack Kerouac." For a moment of historical illusion, that was pretty good. William shook hands politely, but there was really very little to say except "How's it going?" Heard, who was having some trouble with his role, inasmuch as Cassady always seemed to be having all the fun while Kerouac seemed uncertain and just standing there, shuffled off. When I recounted this episode to Allen Ginsberg, he said: "That sounds just like Jack." I guess Heard had got the part down pretty well. Or it had gotten him down. You can never be sure just which way is real in Hollywood.

Moments later I spotted Bill deep in animated conversation with a tall blond guy who turned out to be Nick Nolte (Neal Cassady in the film). I joined them and we discussed the unusual atmosphere created by an actor when he is playing someone who has died within recent memory. Burroughs asked if he felt any psychic contact with Cassady during the shooting of the picture and Nolte immediately replied that he had. He was sitting on a hammock in the backyard of the house they were shooting in on location. Improvising, he picked up a toy cap pistol that was lying in the grass and started playing with it, finally putting it to his temple and pretending to shoot himself as a statement of how Cassady felt at the time. When Carolyn Cassady saw the rushes the following day she said the only time she'd seen Neal sitting on the hammock in the backyard that is exactly what he had done. Nolte concluded that he "felt Neal around somewhere." They were both born on February 8.

Bill said that Kerouac always had Cassady talking a mile a minute, whereas he had driven with him for eight hours at a time without Cassady saying a word, but that his mind was always working. For example, he'd turn around and say he'd memorized the signposts for the last fifty miles. Bill said Jack and Neal were always complaining about each other. Neal said Jack was fat and stingy. Jack said Neal was trying to hustle him. Nolte reflected on some of the difficulties Heard had had with the Kerouac role. Later William told me that on numerous occasions over the next three days, he would be sitting beside Nolte and suddenly feel that he was sitting next to Cassady, at which point he would do a double take.

Before we left, Sissy Spacek, who plays Carolyn Cassady, came over, stuck out a hand, and said, "Bill, hi, Bill! My name is Sissy Spacek. I play Carolyn, Neal's wife." Bill bent slightly toward her, extended a hand, and said, "Hello." There was a pause while we stared

Bockris and Burroughs take a walk. Photo by Michael Montfort

OPPOSITE: *Burroughs waits in the sun by the Tropicana Motor Hotel swimming pool. Photo by Michael Montfort.*

124

at each other and then she said, "Well, I just wanted to say hi," and walked onto the set.

Sissy looked even greater when we arrived on the set at 12:30 the next day, for a brief photo session with Bill, during which I leafed through a very large collection of still photographs which had been taken throughout the shooting of the movie. Particularly interesting was the resemblance of Ray Starkey (who plays Allen Ginsberg) to Allen. Nick Nolte looked very much like photos of Cassady, but I noticed the resemblance really did come through the way he held his body rather than from makeup. I told Sissy Spacek, "You look like Lauren Bacall in *To Have and Have Not.*" She said she'd only just seen it, but turning to Bill said, "This is Lauren Bacall," and did a snap second imitation with her eyes and posture. Bill did another appreciative double take.

That evening we decided to dine at Lucy's El Adobe Cafe, an excellent Mexican restaurant on Melrose. We had called ahead for a reservation, but when we arrived: "No reservacion, Señor." Slipping past the maître d' one by one, we commandeered an empty table for six. It is hard to move six hungry people. The waiters looked worried, but hastily served us and we gave little thought to the people whose table we had stolen.

After the meal we got stuck running into a bunch of guys in the congested corridor that leads to the exit. Shuffling along, I found myself face to face with Jerry Brown. He looked a little tired and spaced out, as if he were waiting for a bodyguard to tell him what to do, a jacket slung over his shoulder.

"Excuse me, Mr. Brown," I said, touching his arm. "I'd like to take the opportunity to introduce you to William Burroughs."

Brown stuck out a hand and said, "Not *the* William Burroughs, the novelist, author of *Naked Lunch*?"

"The very same," replied Bill. Brown studied Burroughs intently. William seemed shy at first. Then he said, "We came out here to fight proposition six (the California antigay bill)."

Brown replied, "You'll win. The establishment is against it. Have you been in touch with Henry Miller recently?"

"No," said Bill, surprised and slightly bemused. "I haven't seen him in years."

Brown looked embarrassed. "I somehow always associate you with him," he said. Then, pointing to the table we had just vacated, he said that he'd been waiting for them to get his table ready and graciously invited us to dinner. We declined, hurried to our cars laughing.

BOCKRIS: Did you ever meet Henry Miller?

BURROUGHS: I met him at the Edinburgh Literary Conference in 1962 at a large party full of literary people all drinking sherry in the middle of the floor and he said, "So you're Burroughs." I didn't feel quite up to "Yes, maître," and to say "So you're Miller" didn't seem quite right, so I said, "A long-time admirer" and we smiled. The next time I met him he did not remember who I was but finally said, "So you're Burroughs."

Los Angeles is a charming place to visit, but *charm is a power that is hard to pinpoint,* I was thinking as I stood on the veranda outside my room the evening before departing when a spectral form glided up, a vodka and tonic (no ice) in its right hand. My eyes traveled to the spectacles of William Burroughs as he looked out over the city and said, "I will tell you about it. The sky is thin as paper. The whole place could go up in ten minutes. That's the charm of Los Angeles."

While I flew back to New York to work with Tom Forcade on some "Hollywood deals," William flew up to San Francisco where he was interviewed by Raymond Foye in a punk rock newspaper called *Search & Destroy.*

FOYE: To punk rock you are something of a major provocateur.

BURROUGHS: I am not a punk and I don't know why anybody would consider me the Godfather of Punk. How do you define punk? The only definition of the word is that it might refer to a young person who is simply called a punk because he is young, or some kind of petty criminal. In this sense some of my characters may be considered punks, but the word simply did not exist in the fifties. I suppose you could say James Dean epitomized it in *Rebel Without a Cause,* but still, what is it? I think the so-called punk movement is indeed a media creation. I did however send a letter of support to the Sex Pistols when they released "God Save the Queen" in England because I've always said that the country doesn't stand a chance until you have 20,000 people saying BUGGER THE QUEEN! And I support the Sex Pistols because this is constructive, necessary criticism of a country which is bankrupt.

FOYE: What are your feelings about "punk rock," politically, musically, or visually?

BURROUGHS: It's an interesting and important phenomenon. I am very much a fan of Patti Smith. But it's always been my feeling that you get much more if you're *there* than you can ever get with a record, because I can't get the real impact of Patti Smith and the vitality that she produces in the audience, and the whole electrical energy that's in a performance doesn't always come through on record.

FOYE: Do you think it's making a dent in the establishment?

BURROUGHS: The establishment is full of dents! I don't think there *is* an establishment anymore. I mean, who is the "establishment" in America? There *is* an establishment still in England. Which is an anachronism, but it still exists, as people still do want the queen and the royal family. And there are still these five or six hundred very rich and powerful people who really control England. That's why they can't pay anyone a living wage. By the time the people at the top get through splitting it up there isn't enough to go around. But in this country, I don't know what you'd say was the establishment.

BURROUGHS IN COLORADO

ANNE WALDMAN: I fell in love with William last summer at the Naropa Institute in Boulder, Colorado. He's such a good teacher. Meticulous. He said: "Remember, a writer has to write." He also had this squirrel he befriended and fed. Everyone reacted very well to him and he handled the situation of being there perfectly.

* * *

Colorado has decriminalized marijuana. Open smoking there is quite pleasant. We stood out in the street in front of the Hotel Boulderado with the desk clerk and smoked a good joint yesterday afternoon. Bill told me that not only were there a number of very hip places in the States outside of New York, but the trend to go to New York was reversing and people from New York were moving to places like Boulder, Eugene, Oregon, etc. Little is lacking and life is much cheaper, safer, and, in some cases, more productive. Both Bill and James feel they are getting a lot more work done out in Colorado than they ever got done in New York. Though Bill points out that he has very carefully kept out of the New York social life because it is too distracting. "I see very few people and mostly people I know very well, but I probably know more people in Boulder than I know in New York."

I meet Burroughs in the bar. He's halfway through his first Bloody Mary. He's wearing a rumpled turtleneck, a faded light blue check summer sports jacket and a pair of check trousers. A stack of his *Retreat Diaries* sits on the table on top of a manila envelope beside a copy of Arthur Koestler's *Roots of Coincidence* and Burroughs' perennial gray hat. Burroughs is shocked that Bellow won the Nobel. Burroughs is disgusted. "He just isn't a major writer," says Bill.

We decide to go upstairs to his flat in the hotel for dinner. Bill has made a delicious split pea stew which is bubbling in the pot. James is going to heat up some cutlets. There's nothing much to drink, but Bill digs up a bottle of vermouth and splashes some into my half-full glass of vodka. "There's your martini," he says. I split it with him. Best martini I ever drank.

We sit down on the couch and talk about mugging and weapons. "Oh yes," Bill says, "look to mother nature for weaponry . . . the porcupine quills . . ." He leafs through a book called *Killers of the Sea*. "Electric eels . . . a snail that shoots a poison dart . . . the ink screen of the squid . . . and so many poisons for the CIA to play about with. The poison contained in the spines of the stone fish causes intolerable agony like fire through the blood. Victims throw themselves around screaming. Morphine affords no relief. Often the victim dies of pain, quite literally tortured to death. Now if one had an immediate antidote, stone fish poison could be the perfect shortcut in interrogation.

"And consider the poison of the tiny blue ring octopus found in Australia and the South Seas. A nerve venom of unknown ingredients and unbelievable potency. Young soldier on a beach saw a small octopus two inches across of a bright blue color. He picked the creature up and it glowed an even brighter blue (the blue ring octopus lights up like neon when the creature becomes excited). A few minutes later, feeling dizzy and rightly suspecting a connection, he removed the octopus from his hand. Two tiny bruises could be seen in the skin. He collapses and is rushed to a hospital. Ninety minutes later he was dead.

"More of mother nature's nonsense: Here is a tiny creature that must prey on even smaller fish and crustaceans . . ."

"But what use does he have for a poison that can kill a big beefy

130

William Burroughs and Anne Waldman, Naropa Institute, summer 1975. Photo by Rachel Homer

marine?" I interrupted. Bill waved an admonitory finger. "Overkill. She's at it again, the old bitch . . ."

> *Reading this may save your life. If you are ever by chance in the South Seas area and you see a little blue octopus, don't say, "Oh isn't he cute" and snatch it right up or little bluie may show you just how cute he can be.*

THE FOLLOWING AFTERNOON

During the ride out of Boulder into the surrounding countryside Burroughs talked mostly about the mountains, with which he expressed an uncertain relationship. "The thing is there's nowhere to walk around here. You need streams and trees and things. All this rock"—he waved a disconsolate hand—"what are these people gonna *do?*" He chuckled, pointing out small houses nestled among rocks with no view. "It gets awfully dark and oppressive in these mountains sometimes . . ." Spotting a No Hunting sign, I ask him what animals inhabit these hills. "There are a lot of deer and they're pretty tame, they come right into Boulder sometimes. Lots of squirrels, raccoons and chipmunks."

"How about bears?"

"They wouldn't come in that close. The animals that come in close have accustomed themselves to suburban living."

When we get back from the drive it's 5:45 and we head straight for the bar. I learn that Bill is planning a trip to Guatemala where for ten dollars a day you can live in luxury and the fare is only three hundred dollars round trip. I also found out that Bill has never been particularly interested in the writings of Henry Miller and that he is intrigued by tycoons. J. Paul Getty, Jr., is a friend. "This story thing about Getty being the richest man in the world is completely wrong. The story is that while he was alive and the whole thing was running there was a lot of money, but the actual estate was not all that large. Getty was apparently a pretty decent guy. He liked to party and drank pretty heavily in his youth. In later years he was a teetotaler. He was considerate of his staff. If a man was an alcoholic or a drug addict, he would not fire him automatically but try and get him off the stuff. Hughes, on the other hand, had a reputation for being a bastard to work for. He would allow no one on his staff who drank or smoked. I've known people who've worked for rich people. There are some rich people who treat people so badly that they just can't keep a servant for more than two months." Burroughs finds this amusing. He seems pretty interested in Howard Hughes and returns to his comparison of Hughes with Beckett. Hughes was obviously afraid of people, he maintains. "He was quite a playboy up until the thirties and then this recluse thing seems to have come upon him very suddenly, where he just shut himself up and wouldn't see anyone. I think he decided he was different than other people and he didn't like other people at all. He thought they were going to come in and give him some terrible disease."

The subject turns to inflation. "In the last thirty years I've seen the subway go from a nickel to sixty cents and of course everything else has gone up too," Bill says. "In the late forties and early fifties I was living in London and Paris in relative comfort on an income of $200 a month, an allowance from my parents. Can you imagine that today? When the situation got bad in London I decided I was not going to pay for the sins of the English. All the bad kharma of the British Empire is dumping itself back onto London now. And I figured I hadn't been given the advantages of living out in India with faithful native boys at my service so why'd I have to pay for it? I split. But this inflation has been going on for years now and nobody really understands it. Prices are slightly ahead of the wages and everybody is kept in constant need by that mechanism."

We go upstairs to Bill's room where James is preparing what will turn out to be a magnificent dinner of yams, meatloaf, oyster stew soup, and broccoli. There's nothing to drink but a little of the vermouth left over from last night so I pour some for Bill and myself. "We'll make martinis in our stomachs," he says, referring to the three vodkas we'd already had in the bar. We sit back around the table while James cooks. William tells us that he had a private pilot's license some years ago and enjoyed flying small planes. Just recently a friend, Robert Fulton, piloted down from Aspen in his Cessna 195 and Bill flew some of the way back. He says that while he passed the test he could never get a commercial license because his eyes weren't good enough. He gesticulates during the detailed explanation. "The first thing you learn in flying is about stalling speeds. K.F.S., Keep Flying Speed, is the basic law of flying. You get to know what your stalling speed is so if you get close to it you know you're going to lose altitude quick. Then I had to do spins and difficult landings in small places. I was once forced to land in a cornfield. I just poured some gas into the plane and took off again," he chuckles.

Richard Elovich comes in for dinner. The conversation goes from alligators to sharks. We agree that alligator kill must be very different than shark kill. And finally on to one of Bill's favorite subjects—poisonous snakes. He knows a lot about them and gives a detailed account of which snakes are poisonous, how quickly they move, and the comparative time it takes to die. "Snakes are not as dangerous as people think because they don't really move that fast," he says. Talking about boa constrictors squeezing people to death and eating people, he says most of that is nonsense. "First of all they can't swallow a whole person; biggest thing they could swallow would be a small pig." He tells me about an incident where a man was half eaten by a crocodile and they found parts of his body in the crocodile's stomach. "Last time this guy was seen was standing waist deep in water on a rock. A few

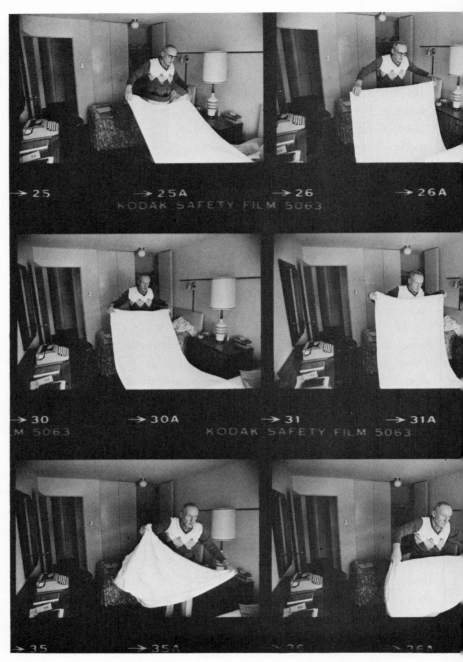

Burroughs makes his own bed, Boulder, Colorado. Photo by Michael Montfort

minutes later he has disappeared. A crocodile had dragged him under. What they do is, they drown you first or kill you under water and drag you down to the bottom, where they eat part of you and leave the rest. It takes them two weeks to digest food like that. They found a whole foot and parts of a leg; these gruesome pictures are in *Eyelids of Morning* by Peter Beard.

Discussing writing again I suggest, "Intellectualism is useless in relation to writing." James likes useless as a description. Bill agrees. "I always thought that Aldous Huxley's work was crippled by that English intellectualism he was involved in," he says. "If you actually looked at those novels they weren't so much novels as treatises, and then if you stripped them down to consider the thought behind them it wasn't particularly interesting or useful. Bloomsbury was a crippling organization, particularly for its younger members." Bill knows Francis Huxley and thinks highly of his anthropological work but thinks that he too is somewhat crippled by that particular form of British intellectualism. I ask Bill about his reading habits and what he is reading, but he is vague. He is not interested in *Roots of Coincidence* by Koestler. Someone sent it to him. "One thing I will tell you though, is if you're a black writer in this country you have got it over a white writer in the same way women writers have got it over men. There's no doubt about that." I asked Bill what he thought about the effect of worldwide news on the ability to write fiction, and he pointed out that this was not relevant because there were just as many incredible things going on and being reported in the last century and writers have always used information that comes through the news for fictionalization.

Around nine we get up to leave. James is off to his room for a short break. Bill is apparently going to read. They talk briefly about plans for the coming week. Bill has got some lectures to give. He prefers the students in Boulder to those he taught at CCNY in New York. In Boulder they're paying for these courses. In New York they were just trying to get an easy credit. "I didn't really like teaching there. This is much better, but even this I only want to do for a short time because I can't write while I'm teaching. The preparation takes too long." He is pulling material from the manuscript of his CCNY lectures. "Anything you say about writing is obviously open to complete revision three years later." His novel *Cities of the Red Night* needs another six months' work on it, he tells me, and he doesn't know when he will get an uninterrupted period in which to work on it.

For three years, Burroughs taught at the Naropa Institute and made Boulder into a kind of Headquarters West. During this period, his son, William Burroughs, Jr., was going through a delicate liver transplant operation and subsequent long-term recovery. Since Billy has recovered, Burroughs has closed down the Colorado location.

BURROUGHS: I started residing in Boulder, Colorado, when Billy became ill and I stayed there most of that winter. After that I had an apartment there which I maintained for two years, through 1978 and 1979. It then became too much of an expense. Boulder was getting to be more and more of a boom town. Prices were rising drastically. In most university towns, there's not enough housing for the students and then people are being overcharged.

William Burroughs Communications now has its headquarters in Lawrence, Kansas, where James Grauerholz, who worked closely with William in a secretarial capacity on a daily basis over the five years William spent writing *Cities of the Red Night* (which James spent the final three months editing in collaboration), has moved.

While holding the Bunker at all costs, William has since been looking for an alternative country location and considered two opportunities: to buy land in New Mexico near where some friends of his are living, or in Florida, where he was presented with a particularly intriguing opportunity which he investigated further.

136

BURROUGHS IN ITALY

DINNER WITH LEGS MCNEIL, JAMES GRAUERHOLZ,
ANDY WARHOL, AND RICHARD HELL:
NEW YORK 1980

BOCKRIS: I think Pasolini died happy.

BURROUGHS: I don't think there's any reason to believe that he died happy at all. The implication is that the boy was paid to kill him. He hit him over the head with a board with nails sticking out of it. Then when he was unconscious the kid backed the car over him. Now the boy himself, who's still in jail, has never confessed to the fact that he was paid to do this because they said, "Okay, kid, we'll take care of you; we'll get you out if you keep your fucking mouth closed." It was a political thing.

GRAUERHOLZ: He was murdered by the right?

BURROUGHS: Sure. I don't think there's much doubt about it. I talked to somebody who's a friend of Felicity Mason's, who is writing a book about this whole affair and interviewed the boy. It wasn't his lover at all, it was a pickup. There's no reason to believe there was anything pleasurable or masochistic about it. This boy hit him over the head. That was something he didn't expect at all. The boy was a hit man. Pasolini had had experience with lots of boys like that. Pasolini was a black belt karate, he could have handled that kid with one hand, but he didn't have a chance. The kid hit him over the head from behind. The kid claimed that he was horrified by the sexual demands of Pasolini. That is absolute rubbish. The boy's story did not stand up. He got life.

Indeed, he is still in jail. He's been in there for some years. So this guy that I met was writing a book about it. He had inside information; he had interviewed the boy and the lawyers and everybody connected with the case.

RICHARD HELL: Pasolini was dangerous to the right wing?

BURROUGHS: I know nothing about Italian politics, but apparently there were people who had reason to believe that and wanted him killed.

BOCKRIS: Legs, do you enjoy having dinner with Bill?

LEGS MCNEIL: He's a lot of fun at parties and a heck of a nice guy, but I like the dinners Bill gives inside the Bunker best. They always have a little quiet desperation about them. . . .

WARHOL: Who do you think has a good walk?

BURROUGHS: I've got a pretty good walk. One foot goes right straight after the other. They don't turn out. Tomorrow I'm leaving to talk on the unconscious at an international conference of psychoanalysts in Milan. I'm saying there isn't an unconscious. I'm going to talk about the fact that although Freud was one of the first to observe some of the psychological damage caused by the capitalist ethic and the whole industrial revolution, he never got beyond this ethic himself, being an academic. While he saw the importance of lateral thinking he never thought it could be used constructively. The unconscious was a hell of a lot more unconscious in his day than it is now. In the nineteenth century sex was unmentionable and in consequence it became unthinkable to many people. The unconscious, then, is not a fixed entity, but varies from person to person, culture to culture, and epoch to epoch. I will suggest that the unconscious may be physiologically located in the nondominant brain hemisphere and cite Julian Jaynes. Freud saw the unconscious as undesirable and formulated the aim of therapy: "Where Id was there shall Ego be." Julian Jaynes stresses the importance of the nondominant brain hemisphere, which performs a number of useful—in fact essential—functions, among which are space perception. If the right brain hemisphere is damaged in an accident the simplest space problem becomes very difficult. So it isn't a question of territorial war, but rather of trying to harmonize the two brain hemispheres. I'm announcing it at the conference as something called "hemispheric therapy."

BOCKRIS: And what exactly is that?

BURROUGHS: Harmonizing the two brain hemispheres. Instead of being

138

Burroughs in edge of jungle before going on a jaguar hunt, South America, 1953. Photographer unknown

in conflict they are complementing each other. If you get rid of your unconscious, your whole right brain hemisphere, as happens sometimes in accidents, you're terribly handicapped. There are all sorts of things you can't do. For example [*draws on a paper napkin a series of O's and X's*] it would be very difficult to say which was the next one in sequence if your right brain was damaged. You wouldn't know.

BOCKRIS: Were you invited to speak about whatever you wanted to speak about?

BURROUGHS: No. The whole conference is on this subject, they wanted me to speak to it. They asked me: "Have you got something to say or read?" I answered yes. So they said, "Oh, but we thought you said you never read Freud." "On the contrary," I told them, "I have read practically everything that Freud ever wrote." About twelve volumes. So I'm very well acquainted with this whole theory.

BOCKRIS: When did you read Freud?

BURROUGHS: About thirty-five, forty years ago.

BOCKRIS: What was your reaction to it when you read it?

BURROUGHS: It's obvious that the whole thing is riddled with errors and a lot of these errors are inseparable from the social configuration. For example, hysteria has almost ceased to exist as such. This is when someone faced with difficult circumstances, say like taking an examination, becomes quite genuinely sick. He doesn't know what he's doing, and he doesn't realize that he's doing it to himself; if he did he wouldn't be able to do it. Hysterics produce quite genuine symptoms. This illness called hysteria was common in Freud's day, whereas it's rare at the present time, or confined to backward places like Ireland and Portugal. Take hysterical paralysis: people are paralyzed for long periods and it's simply hysteria. You just have to say the right words or get them to say the right words and bingo they're cured, like people cured of paralysis at Lourdes. They were suffering from hysterical paralysis so they get up out of their wheelchairs and walk, but they were never organically paralyzed to begin with.

BOCKRIS: Is this a scientific conference? What kind of people are they inviting?

BURROUGHS: Psychoanalysts. It's a psychoanalysts' convention, but I don't think I will be the only nonpsychoanalyst there. There'll be people from all over the place, mostly Europeans, and a lot of them, oddly enough, are Marxists.

BOCKRIS: That's not so odd for Italy is it?

BURROUGHS: It's not odd for Italy, but I don't see any connection between psychoanalysis and Marxism.

BOCKRIS: Freud better look out for his rep!

BURROUGHS: Oh well, his reputation's been bandied around a great deal and he is now being increasingly seen in more perspective as an innovator and a pioneer. He was a therapist. His patients were middle-class nineteenth-century Viennese. It's hard for us to imagine the extent to which sexual subjects were taboo and unmentionable. This is back in the nineteenth century, and I think he had more women patients than men. Many of his female patients had symptoms that were obviously the result of sexual repression. I'm going to cite Julian Jaynes, Dunne's *Experiment with Time,* and Korzybski's *General Semantics.* I am skeptical of the whole concept of "mental illness." Wherever there is "mental illness" there is physical illness. I had a cousin; at the age of thirty-eight he was a square citizen, started having these bizarre hallucinations—his leg was on fire, all kinds of things like that so the doctors gave him a neurological once-over, very sloppy as it turns out, and said there was no sign of organic illness, therefore he had a psychosis, right, schizophrenia. So they were analyzing him on the couch and in the course of this he died of a brain tumor. Well, that was sloppiness on their part. I would have said, if you don't turn something up keep looking, because there's something there. There's no reason for a square stockbroker at the age of thirty-eight to suddenly exhibit these symptoms. And they were saying, "Why would he be thinking all this?" and looking for childhood traumas. He was vomiting and they said, "Oh, this is a psychosomatic symptom." The next thing you know he was dead of a brain tumor.

BOCKRIS: Was there a particular point at which you turned away from this psychiatric approach?

BURROUGHS: It's not a specific approach; there was just a particular point when more evidence turned up relating to precise brain areas. I think analysis is a very antiquated approach. In fact, I've seen people who've been in psychoanalysis for five years and weren't getting any better, and I said this is a bunch of shit.

BILL'S 66th BIRTHDAY DINNER AT THE BUNKER, FEBRUARY 5, 1980

BURROUGHS: I just got back from Milan. The guy who organized it, Professor Verdiglione, is a lay analyst. Verdiglione is a practicing psychoanalyst; he has his own publishing company, with branches in France and Italy, and he's written a number of books on language and the unconscious, a small fat man, but with great authority. This convention is the third one he's organized. He'd gotten a big building around a courtyard called the Palace of the Orphans, which used to be an orphanage back in the Middle Ages and was now being used to house the participants. The rooms were reasonable, small but with a bath. He says to me in the afternoon, "Mr. Burroughs, so and so is giving a talk in ten minutes. You will be on the platform." It's not an invitation, it's an order. I said, "Well, I have to go up to my room." He said, "You are coming back." Anyway, I gave my talk on Freud and the unconscious at nine o'clock in the morning the day after I arrived. They were trying to translate it into both French and Italian because a lot of people there were French, and at this rate it would have taken the rest of the day. So Verdiglione said, "Let Burroughs read it in English and then you give a summary." They did. It was impossible to tell if anyone understood anything I said or not. Then I was drafted to be on the platform with this other guy, a Frenchman named Alain Fournier, whose talk had nothing to do with the unconscious; he was just going on about the rape of Cambodia, the invasion of Afghanistan, in other words the non-Communist left, Mary McCarthy's camp. He was calling for a boycott on the Olympic Games. I was sitting there all this time and people were taking pictures. Then there was a big lead in the newspapers the following day: THE UNCONSCIOUS SAYS NO TO MOSCOW.

BOCKRIS: For the rest of the conference did you listen to everybody else's talks?

BURROUGHS: There's no point, I can't understand it, it's all in French and Italian.

BOCKRIS: What do you think his interest in you was?

BURROUGHS: PR obviously. He wants as many "name" people as possible at his conference. The more such people he gets, the more important the conference is. Anyway, in the afternoon I was supposed to take part in a roundtable discussion including questions and answers with the audience in all languages. This started at 2:30 and I had some appointments to do interviews about 4:00. At 4:30 I said, "Well, I've got to see these journalists," so I left the platform. Meanwhile, the roundtable went on until seven.

BOCKRIS: Is Italy very tense politically?

BURROUGHS: I felt no tension.

BOCKRIS: Did you get much of an impression of Milan?

BURROUGHS: Nothing. Pretty blank. I saw the Cathedral and the famous Gallery. The weather was cold and rainy.

BOCKRIS: What did you do in the evenings?

BURROUGHS: The first evening I had dinner with Verdiglione, the second evening I had dinner with Sr. Pini, the third evening I sulked in my room. This was the evening after I missed my plane. I went down and got a sandwich at the bar and went back up to my room and read a mystery story. And the next day I just got up and said goodbye.

BOCKRIS: Did people come up to you and respond; did anyone say anything about it?

BURROUGHS: Some Englishman who understood it got up and said it was an interesting talk, but he had some questions he wanted to ask and I never understood his questions; he went on and on. People who get up and want to ask questions want to make a statement. You see it doesn't matter at all. The thing is that Mr. Burroughs is there and they will probably publish something in the paper. The press was there and took a lot of pictures, that's it. It wasn't a question of anyone understanding what I was saying. This kind of conference is like nothing I've ever seen before because it's not a conference. I thought a psychoanalytic conference would be actual psychoanalysts, most of them would be medical doctors, and fifty or sixty of them. Instead, I find most of them aren't psychoanalysts at all, or aren't there to talk about psychoanalysis, and there are three or four hundred people milling around, some of whom have paid to attend the lectures. It's unlike anything else I've ever seen, but they have such things in America. Steven Lowe's father belongs to the Order of the Flying Morticians and they have conferences, so there's nothing phony about it, it's just cultural analysis created out of nowhere, using psychoanalysis as a springboard . . .

THE NOVA CONVENTION

Produced by John Giorno, James Grauerholtz & Sylvere Lotringer
A Giorno Poetry Systems Presentation, in association with the Entermedia Theater, the Department of French & Italian of New York University, & Semiotext(e)

Stage Director: Joe LoGiudice; *Stage Manager:* Rebecca Christensen;
Sound Designer: Bobby Bielecki; *Lighting Designer:* Jan Kroeze; *Publicity:* Jeff Goldberg

This event was made possible in part by support from Poets & Writers, Inc., which is funded by the New York Council on the Arts. Special thanks to the late Tom Forcade.

Thanks for help from Joanne Akalaitis, Julia Aaron, Tom Bishop, Victor Bockris, Burt Britton, Francois Bucher, Tom Carey, Feint Type, Steve Hamilton, Edna Kapp, Marc Kramer, Francois Lagarde, Steven Lowe, Stewart Meyer, Tina Freeman, Andi Ostrowe, David Prentice, Jim Quinlan, Nancy Morgan, Mickey Ruskin, Greg Schifrin, Alan Schwab, James Sherry, Paul Sinclaire, Jeanette Watson, Joe Asaro, David Secter, and countless others.

Thursday, November 30, 1978
Reception at La Maison Francais, New York University, 5-7 PM.
Booksigning party for William Burroughs & Brion Gysin in honor of the publication of *The Third Mind* by Viking Press, at Books & Co., 7-10 PM, Opening an exhibition of Burroughs & Gysin collaborations, manuscripts & artwork, Dec. 1-30.
Cinevirus Film Showing, Schimmel Auditorium, Tisch Hall, N.Y.U., 7-11 PM: Anthony Balch, Michael Oblowitz, Bruce Conners, Eric Mitchell, Kathryn Bigelow, Seth Tillett, Tina Lhotski, Michael McClard, Amos Poe, Marc Olmstead, Steven Lowe, & Kathy Acker reading *Blood & Guts In High School.*
LE PLAN K: *The Penny Arcade Peep-Show,* Westbeth Theater Center, Nov. 30-Dec. 15, 8 PM.

Friday, December 1, 1978
PANEL at N.Y.U.'s Schimmel Auditorium, 4-7 PM: Maurice Girodias, John Calder, Richard Seaver, Serge Grunberg, Jurgen Ploog, & Gerard-George Lemaire.
PERFORMANCES, Entermedia Theater, 8:30 PM, 96: Laurie Anderson & Julia Heyward; The BBC Project Theater Co. performing *A.J.'s Annual Party* from *Naked Lunch,* adapted & directed by Don Sanders; Anne Waldman. Merce Cunningham & John Cage in "A Dialogue"; Ed Sanders premiere of the Bardic Pulse Lyre; Allen Ginsberg & Peter Orlovsky.
NO WAVE ROCK CONCERT, Irving Plaza, midnight: B-52's, Suicide, Stimulators.
Party at The Mudd Club, midnight.

Saturday, December 2, 1978
CONVERSATIONS, Entermedia Theater, 1-4 PM, 92: William S. Burroughs, Brion Gysin, Timothy Leary, Les Levine, Robert Anton Wilson.
Film Showing, Entermedia Theater, 4-6 PM: *Towers Open Fire & The Cut-Ups* by Anthony Balch.
PERFORMANCES, Entermedia Theater, 8:30 PM, 96: Terry Southern, Philip Glass, Brion Gysin, John Giorno, Frank Zappa, William S. Burroughs, & Patti Smith.
Party at Kipling's Last Resort, midnight.
NO WAVE ROCK CONCERT, Irving Plaza, midnight: B-52's, Suicide, Walter Stedding, Robert Fripp, Chris Stein, & Debbie Harry.

Centerfold Nova Convention Album by James Hamilton

NEW YORK CITY CLOSE-UPS

DINNER AT JOHN GIORNO'S: NEW YEARS EVE
1979-1980

BOCKRIS: Which is your nearest supermarket?

BURROUGHS: The Pioneer. It's sloppy and it's dirty and there are all these old biddies with their baskets and their cigarettes all in the corner of their mouths jamming the aisles and hovering around, but it's the only supermarket within twenty blocks. You meet all sorts of people there. I meet Mike Goldberg, John Giorno and various people from the neighborhood at the check-out desk. Once I saw this young man with a beard and our eyes met and I said, "Well, how do you do?" And he said, "I know you but you don't know me," and I said, "Well, happy New Year." I know all the cashiers. If they're feeling really good, if it's a really jolly day, they might say thank you. But it's a great day if you can elicit a thank you out of the clerks at the Pioneer. It's just that they don't care. To a customer in Boulder it's unthinkable that a clerk wouldn't say, "Hi there! Hi there! Hi there!" and then go on to "Thank you. Come again. Happy New Year! Have a good day!" But this doesn't happen at the Pioneer in New York. It does happen, though, in the drugstore. I'm well known in the drugstore. I go in there and gab with the pharmacist, who's a gabby old guy anyway. Buying vitamins and talking about his experience with vitamins. They've got their own special vitamin pill, which contains everything that you need. "If you take one like this," he says, "it's like a drop in the rain bucket every day, and it can head off an awful lot because there are all these things you need you're not getting. Things like zinc." Are you getting enough zinc? Horrible results of zinc deficiency. All your teeth fall out for starters. So, it's on that basis. They always have anything I want. I wanted to buy a special kind of glue. You wouldn't think you'd buy it in a drugstore, but they had it: Duco cement. They have a special kind of ball-point pen that only costs 59 cents, the only kind I use; they have stationery; it's one of those drugstores that does everything. And his wife is very much of a theatrical Spanish Dolores type, fairly good looking, a middle-aged woman who's had a lot of sorrow but has great dignity and a great presence. She says, "Oh, why didn't you say the usual, Mr. Burroughs?" Her husband was much older than she was. He was the one who told me that vitamin E gave him diarrhea. He died shortly after that and I never saw him again. But then she, who I presume was his wife, was around with the armband for a while, and she also has either a daughter or sister who looks like her but is not young enough to be her child, sort of a heavy-set woman with a mustache. It's a whole family. A new pharmacist appeared and what the relation between him and her is at this point I don't know. He knows everyone in the neighborhood. For example he'll advise someone: "You need glasses. You're entitled to them on your social security." He's always instructing someone, telling them to do this or that. "I can give you this and charge you more for it, but I can give you the same product and charge you less." It's also a news exchange. There'd been a mugging and there was a report. Some woman got beaten up and she's at the counter and they're all commiserating and saying "two black boys." And the Patrone, grandiose and sad in a Latin way, experienced woman said, "Yes, those are the ones, those are the ones . . ." She's got quite a lot of style; she's a real actress in the classical manner, still beautiful and still sort of trembling on the verge. . . . There's a whole French novel right there on The Last Adventure: She gets taken by some Puerto Rican boy and the old pharmacist, mad with jealousy, comes in and kills them both. He's an old character, that guy.

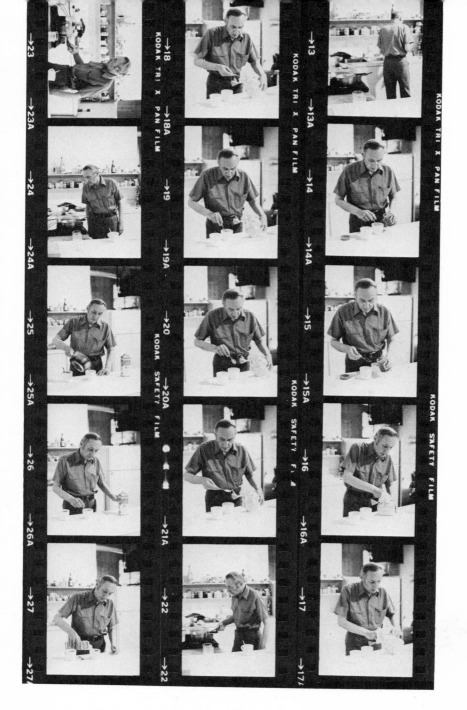

Burroughs making coffee at Franklin Street, New York City, 1974. Photo by Gerard Malanga

DINNER WITH PETER BEARD AND BOCKRIS-WYLIE: NEW YORK 1976

BEARD: If I were a cabdriver I'd have a weapon for sure.

BURROUGHS: Personally it would give me a great feeling if faced by muggers to pull out a gun on them.

BEARD: I'd like to blast them.

BURROUGHS: I don't mean shoot them. I'd give them a chance. I'd say: "You better get out of here quick."

BOCKRIS-WYLIE: I love that story you told about the guy on the Bowery who said he had a gun in his pocket . . .

BEARD: You never know how many guys are just around the corner backing him up.

BURROUGHS: He didn't have fuckall backing him up, he was just all alone there trying to get smart.

BOCKRIS-WYLIE: Do you think you'd be good in a situation defending yourself?

BURROUGHS: I've always been good in those situations.

BOCKRIS-WYLIE: Has anyone ever tried to kill you?

BURROUGHS: People have attacked me. I beat the other person hands down. He's causing me trouble, I said, *"Don't like ya and I don't know ya and now my God I'm gonna show ya!"* That's from *The Wild Party*, written in 1922. On the few occasions in which I've been attacked physically I won hands down.

BOCKRIS-WYLIE: Do you think that's because you want to stay alive more than the person who's attacking you?

BURROUGHS: Exactly. It was like the original situation in the subway. This guy says, "Okay you guys, ya been in my pockets, we're goin' downtown." And the Sailor hit him and he fell down, but he was still hanging on to the Sailor and the Sailor said, "Get this mooch offa me." So I hit him once in the jaw and kicked him once in the ribs. The rib smashed. Because I hadda get outta that, man. I hadda get out of that situation.

BOCKRIS-WYLIE: Have you ever been really scared that you would die in a situation where you were attacked?

BURROUGHS: I can't say that I have. There was a situation in Tangier where I was talking to some boys out in front of the house and this nutty shoeshine boy comes up and says, "You fuckin' queer." I said something, and he hit me across the face with his shoeshine box. So I pulled the old elbow on him. There's no strength needed in fighting, no strength needed at all. Just threw an elbow across his face and brought it back and he ran away to a big lot and hit me with a stone.

BOCKRIS-WYLIE: What'd you do then?

BURROUGHS: Nothing, because he could run faster than I could. I remember one CIA man in Tangier who got in an altercation with a shoeshine boy. He slapped the shoeshine boy, the shoeshine boy grabbed a piece of glass and the CIA man kicked him in the nuts and the boy ran off screaming. He was the ugliest American of them all . . .

NIGHT OF THE WHITE PILLS

I got to the Bunker around 6:30. Howard was there also. We had drinks and a light, pleasant dinner which Bill cooked and served. I was still feeling pretty ropy from being ill and Bill seemed a bit out of it himself. We drank a bit too much. I've noticed recently that Bill isn't getting drunk very often. But this night we continued to drink more vodka after dinner. I was telling Bill that I didn't know what to do and he said, "Do nothing." He said, "Most of these problems are very simple. People think they're very complicated but they're not—just do nothing." He said, "If one man refuses to believe in all this crap, that liberates everyone from it."

Howard produced a handful of small white pills which he said were Swedish and very good, suggesting we all take some.

"What are they?" Bill asked.

"I don't know. I have no idea," Howard replied, "but this friend gave them to me and said they were great."

"I ain't takin' nothing if I don't know what it is," Bill said. "Why don't you take some and we'll see what happens to you?"

Howard agreed, and took two of the pills. When they'd been in his system for an hour and a half he was able to report that he felt quite good—"drowsy eyelids—maybe some kind of synthetic opiate." Bill swallowed two of the pills. Half an hour later I noticed that there was only one pill left, so I took it. I remember looking at my watch. It was 11:30 and I said to myself, "You really ought to go." I was supposed to be at the Mudd Club at 10:00. The next thing I remember is looking at my watch and it was 6:30 A.M., I was sitting straight up in the same chair I'd been sitting in so I presumed I hadn't moved. William was standing over by the sink washing a saucepan. "Bill wha . . . what's happening?" I stuttered. "What are you doing?"

"Oh, nothing," he replied vaguely. "I'm just checking things out, seeing what's going on."

I asked Bill if I could stay over because, even though at the time I felt all right, I basically knew something was wrong, so I stayed over on intuition. I went into the bathroom and washed up. Bill showed me where the blankets for the spare bed were kept, made sure I had everything I needed, and we both went to bed around 7:00 A.M. I heard Bill moving around about noon. After a while he came in to see how I was. I was sick and couldn't get out of bed. I asked him if it would be all right if I stayed in bed for the day. He said, "Of course" and basically left me alone between noon and 6:00. He made one attempt to entertain me when he came in to show me the handful of pellets he'd dug out of the phone book in the orgone box in the cupboard. I couldn't make out what he was talking about. "Don't you remember?" he said. "I was firing the air pistol off last night. Look, I'll show you . . ." and he led me into the cupboard, opened up the orgone box, and there was a heavily peppered telephone book.

Around 4:00 in the afternoon someone who was writing a dissertation on him came by. At 6:00 Bill came in. "What you need is the hair of the dog."

"What do you mean?"

"A drink," he said. Funnily enough I really felt like one, so, getting up slowly, I dressed and we met again at the conference table twenty four hours after we'd originally sat down to cocktails the previous evening. "Everything's back to normal," I said.

"Yes, everything's back to normal." Bill gave me a vodka and tonic and said, "I'll make you some Jewish penicillin." I ate my chicken soup and went home to bed.

———

ALLEN GINSBERG TEARGASSED BY
WILLIAM BURROUGHS

Miles was visiting New York. I called William up and suggested the three of us get together. We arranged a date. We arrived at Bill's place almost exactly on the dot of 6:00, taking a pint of vodka and some extra tonic water with us. William seemed in fine fettle as he met us to unlock the gate. We went upstairs. Soon John Giorno joined us. We talked about the White Gorilla of which William had seen pictures in *National Geographic*. He remarked that *National Geographic* provided the perfect CIA front: "Well, our man has been in the area for twenty years and he knows all about it. Anything you need, ask *our man.*"

The facts about our night on white pills were beginning to come into focus. According to John, we had paid him a visit around 3:00 A.M. that night. I passed out into his lap every ten minutes, but John would always lift me back up, at which point I'd come to. William, on the other hand, talked loquaciously. Neither Bill nor I have any memory of this visit.

The phone rang. Knowing how much Bill dislikes talking on the telephone, I answered. It was Terry Southern calling to announce his imminent arrival in New York. It rang again. This time, it was Allen trying to get in. I went down to open the gates. It was while I was downstairs that, according to Miles, William put his teargas gun on the table and started explaining how it works. Miles' girlfriend, Rosemary, said she didn't believe it was as powerful as Bill claimed and, to make his point, Bill said, "Look, I'll show you," turned away from her and pointed it out into the room. "Careful, Bill, this is a closed space!" John shouted as William fired. By the time Allen and I came upstairs, John, Miles, Rosemary, and Bill were convulsed in coughing fits. At first Allen and I couldn't tell what was going on, but then Allen said, "What is that?" and everybody tried to gurgle something out in between coughing and laughter. We heard: "Tear gas! Tear gas! Bill teargassed us!"

William had certainly made his point. We all went into the small room next door where Bill keeps his phones and files and found the air in there significantly clearer. Allen was slightly peeved: "Well, Bill doesn't seem to be taking this very seriously." William was trying to keep a straight face while being immensely amused as he ran around the Bunker waving a handkerchief in a feeble attempt to clear the air. It took an hour. When we finally sat down to dinner, William was still more amused than anybody else. "It's so chic to be teargassed by William Burroughs just as you're sitting down to be his guest for dinner," I said to Allen, and he had to agree, chuckling over the incident for the first time now.

FRIDAY NIGHT

"Hello, old boy," Bill murmured through the iron gates as I approached from across the street. "See, we got a new lock."

"Why?" I asked.

"Somebody broke the old one." As we walked upstairs I said, "It's good of you to see me at such short notice." I had just called an hour earlier.

"Not at all, not at all." Bill was clearly spending the evening alone. When I went in there was a paperback on the table turned upside down and open about halfway through. He was making a small meal in a saucepan on the stove. He offered me some, although there was only enough for one. I declined on the grounds that I had a later dinner appointment.

We sat down. I started drinking vodka quickly. We had a very pleasant two hours together. William remembered a story that Robert Duncan had told him. Apparently one day Burroughs was supposed to be walking along the Seine with Beckett discussing the efficacy of random murder. Beckett questioned Burroughs' points, upon which William pulled out a gun, whirled, and picked off a passing Paris clocharde. He disposed of the body in the Seine and Beckett was convinced. "I rather like to hear that kind of story," William laughed, "and I do nothing at all to discourage them. In fact, the people who repeat these stories might find the same thing happening to themselves, *you see,*" and he slapped the table emphatically.

William told me that Gregory Corso broke the front door when it wouldn't open at his command and that Mike Goldberg, who lives upstairs, was very upset and shouted at him. Burroughs agreed with Mike. "My reputation in the building has been affected by the event. It's always like this with Gregory," he complained. "Wherever he goes it's always *cops* and everything. The last thing I want is *cops* coming around. These two policemen came up here and asked if they could come in and I said, 'Well, no, I'm sorry, you haven't got a warrant, but I will bring the people responsible to the door, you see.' That's when Gregory got into the screaming match with Mike Goldberg."

I left a copy of my *Birthday Book on Bill* for Allen. "I advise you to have one beer and nurse it," Bill said. Just as we reached the bottom of the stairs, Mike Goldberg and his wife were coming in. "Oh, thank you for the new door, Mr. Burroughs," they said. Bill smiled politely. "I hope your reputation hasn't suffered too much," I whispered.

"Oh well, it's not all *that* bad," he muttered, sheepishly amused.

THE ORDER OF THE GREY GENTLEMEN

Dinner at John Giorno's with William. There was Bill, sitting in a medieval wooden armchair, nursing a vodka and tonic in front of a low, round, Moroccan table. "Hello, my dear," he said, extending a hand, smiling. John's apartment is furnished in medieval Moroccan Moslem chic. A whole lamb was being roasted in his fireplace. It was the beginning of summer. William looked like Graham Greene in Panama.

This was the evening of the formation of the Order of the Grey Gentlemen. It was all Bill's idea. "A bunch of chaps should meet at one chap's apartment and have a drink and a joint and hit up some coke. Then they go out on a mugger hunt with two or three companions and just stand around subways." He pointed out that the Grey Gentlemen would have to always be impeccably dressed and approach the matter in classical fashion. The Grey Gentlemen, for example, carry only canes and Mace.

"If you saw someone being molested," William continued, "you'd just casually stroll over and laconically, but at the same time with an authoritative air, say, 'My good woman, is this man *bothering* you?' And then you take this mugger and give his arm a good twisting and that'd be a warning." Bill got worked up at this point. He was snarling and strangling his napkin. "So that if you see a mugger a second time, see, it's *onto the tracks* . . . And the Grey Gentlemen always leave their card.

153

(From left) Adam, Stewart, Howard, Bill, David, Udo, at the Bunker on Bill's sixty-sixth birthday. Photo by Victor Bockris

"Of course, they have a relationship with the Inspector. 'Well, Burroughs, we can't overlook too many more *bodies,* you know. Listen . . . this is the last time I'm warning you . . .' and the Grey Gentlemen smile politely. . . ."

At one point during Bill's detailed description of various raids that would happen, our relationship with the Red Berets, how the police would react, etc., I developed a scenario where we could rip off the jewels in Upper East Side restaurants. Burroughs leaped up and strode vigorously across the room.

"What we gonna do that for? We're after muggers, man! You suddenly got us all set up as a gang of Raffles jewel thieves! This is an affront to the Grey Gentlemen!" And he whipped out his handkerchief as if it were a switchblade. John stepped between us. I humbly apologized, realizing my waywardness.

"Well, that's all right, but watch your step," Bill mumbled, fixing himself a short drink. Then we decided there'd be a showdown and one of the "Gentlemen" gets killed. This would be for the movie version. "Somebody may get killed but it's not gonna be me," said Bill, getting up and moving again.

"Well, Bill, it would make more sense to the audience if the older man got killed . . ."

"Nobody's going to get killed! Why should anyone get killed? There's not going to be any showdown! We're just gonna go out on a mugger hunt . . ."

WINTER NIGHT

Since returning to New York William has gradually equipped himself with a small arsenal of weapons that includes a cane, a tube of teargas, which can be released in an assailant's face by depression of a plunger and is particularly effective in subway situations, and a blackjack. "I never go out of the house without all three on me," he says pointedly. "I don't feel dressed without them."

It was a bitterly cold, icy December night as I ran up the Bowery from the phone box on the corner of Canal Street to the gates of the Bunker where William was waiting concernedly.

"If I'd known it was like this I wouldn't have asked you out," were his first words as he opened the metal gates. He was wearing a jaunty tweed jacket, brown suede shoes, light brown pants, shirt, tie and sweater. "I went out today," he said on the way upstairs. "It's on days like this that you really [*opening the front door and ushering me in*] get to appreciate the Bunker. All the heat you can use."

"I wouldn't put a dog out on a day like this."

"Well, I thought, 'I'll take my scarf I guess,' but Jesus when I got out there!"

"Have you ever met Robbe-Grillet?"

"No. I saw one of his films."

"*Last Year at Marienbad?*"

"No, it wasn't *Last Year at Marienbad,* but it was very good, full of details of eating and things like that."

"I wondered if you'd like to meet him."

"Oh, well . . ." I could sense he wasn't that interested.

"The thing is, I don't know if Robbe-Grillet can speak English."

"All the more reason for me not to meet him."

"In that case there would be no point," I agreed.

Bill looked up from where he was rolling a joint and said, *"J'aime beaucoup votre livre, Moussieur."*

"Oui," I said. "I will tell him. He is very pleased."

"Yes. Tell him that I think he is a great artist and an excellent writer."

"Oui. Monsieur Burroughs dit que . . ."

"Yes, and then he whips out a book he purchased just ten minutes before our meeting and asks me to sign it, saying he has been a fan and read all my work for years. No, no, I really think such meetings are of little value."

DINNER WITH FRED JORDAN: NEW YORK 1980

BURROUGHS: It's a funny thing that's never really been analyzed, the linguistic ability seems to be something special almost like a card sense that some people have and some just don't have. I don't have it at all, I just can't learn a language.

FRED JORDAN: You're lucky, because that makes you very strong in your native tongue.

BURROUGHS: Not at all. James Joyce was a brilliant linguist, my dear. Suddenly I've taken refuge with Shaw. I knew this guy who was a very good linguist with the CIA and he said in learning to speak Arabic he'd get this actual ache all through his throat and lungs, just like somebody riding who hasn't sat on a horse in years. He had to use entirely different muscles. It comes easily to children. When I was in Mexico, shopkeepers would turn to my little kid who was four years old and say, "What did your father say?" And the boy would tell him in Spanish.

BACK AT THE BUNKER

I noticed a wrapped Christmas gift (unmistakably a cane) standing next to William's cane by the wall. On a previous visit he had told me that he was planning to buy me a cane for Christmas and ascertained my height to make sure that it was the correct length. We returned to the conference table and continued talking. A few minutes later Bill said, "Victor, I have a Christmas present and I'm going to give it to

156

you now. I don't agree with all this waiting around for the exact day, it's Christmas now, it's a Christmas present," and he walked into the bedroom.

I got up and walked to the middle of the room so that I would be in an advantageous position to formally receive my cane. When Bill came back into the living room he advanced and presented the cane sideways, like a sword on a pillow. I ripped the wrapping off, and saw that it was a replica of his cane. I started swinging it around and Bill launched into his new theory about the Caneraisers and how we were going to encourage a view of the cane as a weapon and see if we couldn't get a commission from this shop he was dealing with if we started everyone buying canes. "See, it's definitely a weapon that you are allowed to carry," he pointed out. Then he went into the bedroom, got his cane, and we stood around brandishing canes and practicing cane maneuvers. At one point I got the handle of my cane stuck around the lower part of his leg at the moment that he got the handle of his cane stuck around the bottom of my leg, and we paused, embarrassed. "Oh . . . *excuse* me."

"Bill, do you ever drink whiskey?"

"I used to, but I rather lost the taste for it."

"When you were living in London?"

"Yes. I got a call today from someone at Rolling Stone records inviting me to Keith Richard's birthday party tonight."

"Let's go!"

"I told them 'Thank you very much, but I can't make it.' "

"Bill! Why?"

"They said they'd send a car and everything to go somewhere out in the country. I thought it was very kind but I am very reclusive and not much of a partygoer."

"Keith likes you very much . . ."

"I like him too."

"Mick would be there. It'd be nice for you to see them again; it's been a long time."

"I know, but . . ." and he wandered off into the other room.

The next day Bill felt ill. He was ill for four days. I spoke with him on the phone daily. He did sound depressed. James called from Kansas, concerned about these depressions. "Bill has these feelings of being trapped in his body and not really wanting to be alive at all sometimes and I sympathize with him, but it's no good him just sitting there and not doing anything."

Burroughs does tend to withdraw into these periods where he will sit around the Bunker talking about going on mugger hunts and practicing with his various weapons. On the other hand he just called this afternoon to invite me over for dinner tomorrow with Allen and Peter and said he was going to Mickey's tonight with Ted Morgan. Udo was going to drop by in the late afternoon, so he seems to be fairly active.

I took my friend Damita over for dinner on Monday, the 24th. She gave Bill a small cannon for Christmas and I gave him a St. Laurent shirt. Howard was there. We had a pleasant dinner. Bill's liking Damita reflects a change from the problems Miles had when he took his girlfriends to dinner at Bill's in the early seventies in London.

In fact, William seems in better shape than any time since I've known him. He's flourishing in the afterglow of finishing *Cities of the Red Night* and continues to write essays, work on a new novel tentatively entitled *The Place of Dead Roads,* and prepare a series of European lectures and readings with vigor and confidence, still striding, as Kerouac had him, like an insane German philologist in exile.

DINNER WITH ALLEN GINSBERG: NEW YORK 1980

BURROUGHS: Did you read about those young scoundrels who terrorized a train? We must get our cane brigade organized.

BOCKRIS: Bill and I have organized a cane fighters group. Everyone has a cane like this and we're going to go on the subways. Three or four of us in the evening.

GINSBERG: New York City, 1980—the Cane Brigade! On my block everyone is armed with a staff or cane.

BURROUGHS: These are great, terrifically effective weapons.

BOCKRIS: There are many things you can do.

BURROUGHS: I'm ordering a blackjack for you.

BOCKRIS: When did you start actually cooking for yourself?

BURROUGHS: When I came back to America. When I was in Europe it wasn't necessary to cook because there were so many cheap restaurants. When I came back here it became obvious that eating out was absolutely ridiculous.

158

The Caneraisers! Photo by Raymond Foye

BOCKRIS: You turned to cooking in your sixties as a new art form.

BURROUGHS: A new form of saving money is what it amounted to.

BOCKRIS: Did you hear about the guy who got a weekend pass from the mental hospital and went straight home and killed his wife? He said it was God's justice.

BURROUGHS: Whatever happened to God's justice? I am convinced that God exists and God is one asshole.

BOCKRIS: If you were terminally ill in such a way that you couldn't do anything about it, or caught in an impossible situation, would you take your own life?

BURROUGHS: The only rational reason for people to carry cyanide around is if they are agents and facing torture if captured. I don't know how you suddenly find yourself in an impossible situation just walking around the streets that calls for cyanide. I mean the same way with terminal illness. It isn't something that just leaps upon you. Sort of "Jesus! I don't even have time to get my cyanide out!"

BOCKRIS: What is your position on suicide?

BURROUGHS: Suicide, according to the Dudjom, is very very bad karmically. Unless it's an impossible situation. Naturally it's logical to kill yourself to avoid torture, which is a much worse karmic situation because it could leave you crippled psychically, but committing suicide for no good reason seems to me a very very bad move. In the first place, if you were actually able, if you were in a position of mastery, you would be able to leave your body, you would be able to die at will, as some people do apparently. The master chooses when he will die. If you're in that situation, fine, but if you're not in that situation, by committing suicide you're sure to make your situation worse.

LUNCH WITH THE TIME MACHINE

A European artist named Kowalski had called me through Timothy Baum and asked to arrange a meeting with William, to whom he wanted to show his time machine. He had discovered and invented a machine that can reverse the voice at the same moment it releases itself so that you hear yourself, through a set of headphones, talking backward and forward at the same time. He thought Burroughs would be interested. He was. We made an appointment to meet at the Ronald

Feldman Gallery, East Sixty-third Street, at 12:30. When I arrived, William was already there in a three-piece suit and his green felt hat. We spent twenty minutes looking at, talking about, and playing with this machine which is constructed inside a small metal suitcase. The suitcase is plugged into two speakers and a microphone. You can speak into the microphone and over a set of headphones hear yourself talking forward in one ear and backward in another. If you think about it, it sounds impossible. To reverse sound is easy but how is it possible to hear your words reversed at the exact moment you speak them?

Timothy had invited us out to lunch. Although Bill had told me on the phone the previous day, "That's very nice of him, but I don't think I have time for lunch as well," he now turned to me, in response to Timothy's repeated invitation, and said, "Victor, what do you think? Shall we have a bite of lunch?" I, of course, agreed, and so we walked around the corner to a small Greek restaurant. We ordered some food and two bottles of retsina. William drank ice water. "This man is a priest. He will not touch alcohol," Timothy explained to the waiter.

After lunch, we headed toward Books & Company. As we strode up Madison Avenue I asked Bill about a puzzling sexual dream I'd had a few nights before.

"Yes, this is well known," he said. "This is a visit by the succubus. Of course, you know about it."

"I don't know anything at all about that. Please tell me."

"What! You don't know about the succubus and incubus? My dear, this is well-known endemic folklore—household words in medieval times, I fancy."

"Yes, but what is it?"

"The Demon Lover, my dear! The one who descends upon you!" At that moment Timothy descended upon us and our conversation broke off. Before we got to the bookstore I had a chance to ask him one more question. "Does the person who comes have anything to do with sending themselves? Are they at all aware of it?"

"Not much solid evidence of this. People don't like to talk about it, but it happens more frequently than one would suppose."

"Has it happened to you?"

"Of course. Many times."

He could give me no more information about it, nor leads. "The sources are scattered," he said, "but I will give you one piece of advice: don't let whoever is bothering you know about it, because they might feel they have some kind of power over you."

BURROUGHS AT THE FACTORY

A week later, William and I arrived at Andy Warhol's Studio, The Factory, at 6:00 P.M. A young man wearing a red shirt and blond mustache answered the door and we walked in. William immediately commented on how large the place was. A beautiful girl was slouching behind Ronnie's desk. I crossed to the windows facing onto Union Square, took off my coat, and put my briefcase on the radiator. William followed, taking off his coat. I turned, took it from him, and placed it with his hat and cane on an art deco armchair in a grouping of art deco pieces. I walked into Vincent Fremont's office and he was on the telephone. "I'm here with Mr. Burroughs," I said.

"Who are you?" he asked. "Do I know you from somewhere?" I made a face and he said, "I'll go and find Andy."

"Could you turn the lights on in the conference room?"

"No, we're cutting down on electricity."

I motioned to Bill and he followed us into the conference room. "Ronnie's got that music on loud again."

"Ask him to turn it down," I replied, thinking about my tape. Vincent went down the corridor. Bill and I looked through the bottles and he chose to stick with Smirnoff as opposed to trying Wyborowa, which I recommended. I ran back into the main office to get my tape recorder and came back as William was pouring some vodka into a glass. Andy entered. He was wearing an open-necked red, white, and yellow plaid shirt, jeans and cowboy boots, carrying a small Sony tape recorder, turned on, and a miniature 35 mm Minox with flash attachment.

WARHOL: Gee, you're all alone.

BOCKRIS: Bill's not alone. I'm with him.

WARHOL: Oh, you are. What do you think about people wearing earrings?

BURROUGHS: I don't know. I guess it's sort of their business, Andy. I don't have any strong feelings about it one way or the other.

BOCKRIS: You never wore one yourself?

162

BURROUGHS: Oooohhh, good heavens no! It's not my style.

BOCKRIS: You know, Bill never had long hair or a mustache or anything like that in his whole life.

BURROUGHS: I did try once to grow a mustache and it came out in all different colors and straggly; it didn't work. It was all itchy. I hated it. I've got a barber down on Canal Street. They give me a straight cut like you see here. I don't go in for McSweeney because there isn't too much to be done with my hair anyway.

WARHOL: I have terrible spots, I . . . I . . . my skin . . .

BURROUGHS: Did you ever grow a beard?

WARHOL: No, my skin is so bad I have splotches all over it. I don't know, nerves I guess.

BOCKRIS: We're spreading this thing about all men should carry canes.

WARHOL: That's a very good idea. I'm going to carry one. I used to carry a teargas gun. Taylor Mead gave me one, but you're not allowed to carry it.

BURROUGHS: I don't feel dressed without my teargas gun. I usually just carry the teargas and a cane.

WARHOL: What kind of cane?

BURROUGHS [*showing him*]: You see, there're all sorts of things you can do with a cane. I sent away for a book on cane fighting. I plan to start a cane store. It's an art, like fencing.

WARHOL: Listen, I'm going to get one, I think it's great!

BURROUGHS: This one only cost $10 and it's nice to walk with, I like the feeling.

WARHOL: It's a good shape too. It's fat enough; it feels sexy.

BURROUGHS: I also use it to quell dogs. In Boulder I used to carry this against dogs and one day I went out without my cane and by God if a dog didn't bite me. But I would prefer one made of metal with iron piping inside a wooden case.

WARHOL [*as we walk through The Factory looking at paintings*]: You're looking so good. Do you really take care of yourself?

BURROUGHS: Oh yes, I do. I have some special abdominal exercises that I do for five or ten minutes every day and it's very effective indeed.

BOCKRIS: One of the biggest problems for writers is that they sit all day.

BURROUGHS: Basically, they have to do a certain amount of sitting in order to get anything done. [*He spots a stuffed lion John Reinhold sent*

Photo by Robert Mapplethorpe

from Africa for Andy's birthday.] Look at this lion! I had a friend who was killed by a lion in a nightclub. The lion was asleep in a cage and Terry went into the cage and threw a flashlight in the lion's face and it leapt on him. He was DOA at the Reynosa, Mexico, Red Cross. He had a crushed chest, a broken neck, and a fractured skull. It just jumped on him and killed him. Can you imagine anyone waking up a sleeping lion with a flashlight? The Mexican waiter went into the cage and tried to get it off him with a chair and he couldn't. The lion dragged Terry into a corner. At this point the bartender came vaulting over the bar with a .45 and he went in and killed the lion, but Terry was dead. It's a funny thing. About a month before Terry annoyed that lion we were in Corpus Christi and we built Terry up as Tiger Terry, this punch-drunk fighter, and Terry goes into a spit and shuffle act. Yeah, *Tiger* Terry . . .

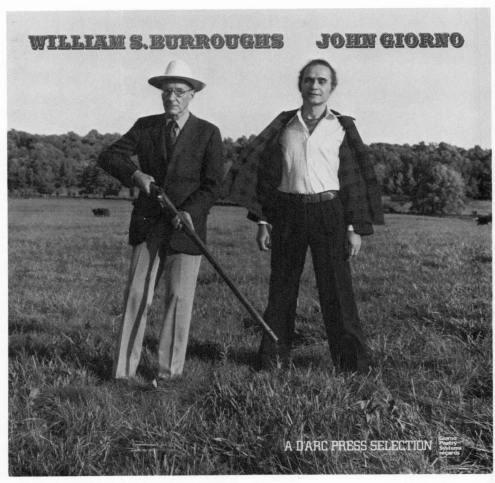

Album cover by Les Levine

ON POLITICS

DINNER WITH DEBBIE HARRY: 1980

BURROUGHS: Do you remember that great scene in *The Day of the Jackal* when De Gaulle got through because of a time fuckup? Machine-gun bullets have shattered the glass and he gets out of the car, brushing glass off himself, and says, *"Encore une fois?"* Really magnificent. "Once again." He was a completely fearless man. The people who protected De Gaulle were professionals, they knew their business. And the people who were supposed to be protecting Kennedy didn't know their business, obviously. A good bodyguard knows there's something wrong before it happens.

HARRY: We've had bodyguards. They do go on instinct a lot.

BURROUGHS: And of course if the trouble is coming from real professionals with guns it's serious. That was what De Gaulle was up against. He wasn't up against nuts, he was up against professional soldiers who knew all about the use of weapons and had access to every kind of weapon, so his bodyguard had to handle real pros.

HARRY: They work with the police, too. That's one of the things that Kennedy suffered from, because his own echelon was so separated from everyone else, it's as if he went into enemy territory. There was no cooperation between his people and the police.

BURROUGHS: Of course it has all the earmarks of a CIA and Mafia job combined. There are all these stories about Santo Trafficante. Santo

Trafficante! What a character. Imagine anybody being called Saint Trafficker! Saint Pusher! The story goes that somebody said, "What are we gonna do if Kennedy gets elected?" So Trafficante said, "He isn't gonna get elected he's going to be hit." So Kennedy had contracts out on him apparently from several sources. Nixon is a man who had the morals of a private detective. He had no basic integrity. Kennedy did. There were some things that he might actually balk at. But where would Nixon draw the line? [*Dogs are heard barking out the window.*] Oh, those howling dogs! I'm an antidog man, I love cats.

DINNER WITH SUSAN SONTAG: NEW YORK 1980

BOCKRIS: You were at medical school for a year in Vienna in 1937. Did you feel as if the whole place was going to blow?
BURROUGHS: They knew that Hitler was going to move in.
BOCKRIS: How did people react to Hitler as a media figure?
BURROUGHS: Lots of people in America were pro-Hitler; and not only the rich people. The whole Yorkville section of New York was pro-Hitler; whole sections of Chicago were pro-Hitler.
BOCKRIS: What did they find so attractive about him?
BURROUGHS: He was a leader whose hands weren't tied. We are governed by people whose hands are tied. "Well, I'd like to do something about it . . . *but my hands are tied.*"
SONTAG: Do you have a feeling that people are afraid of war?
BURROUGHS: Excuse me, there's such a difference that people can't really realize what a nuclear war means.
SONTAG: I've heard people say it's all right this time, I'm over age I won't be drafted.
BURROUGHS: I could say that myself—about being drafted—but that don't mean shit.
SONTAG: Because for America war means going over there. And casualties also have been small.
BURROUGHS: Americans are terribly naïve about what Edwin Arlington Robinson called "the merciless old verities." In his poem "Cassandra." You remember:

> Are we to pay for what we have
> With all we are

> And will you never have eyes
> To see the world the way it is?

We've never encountered them, we've never been invaded, we've never been occupied or even bombed. We're speaking in the Atomic Age. In World War I people actually used to take a bomb and drop it out the plane by hand. The pilots used to shoot at each other with pistols from their planes. Now this just shows you what a splendid thing technology is. It took them five hundred years to get the idea that a cannonball could explode on contact. Once they got that idea it developed into the atom bomb in a very short time. The cartridge rifle didn't appear in America until after the Civil War. We can orient ourselves by comparing technologies. This shows us where an artifact is, what is wrong with it, and how far it has to go. Take a bow. Nothing much wrong with it and it may well have reached the limit of effectiveness for a weapon using springs or elastic energy to propel a dart or other projectile. It can't go much further. Now look at this artifact. A flintlock pistol. What is wrong with it? Just about everything: length of time needed to load, high incidence of misfire, wind and rain can render weapons useless, black powder is dangerous to transport and store. It has this far to go. Here is the most modern machine-gun pistol, and here are some special models like the Darlick. Never hit the open market, but we may be approaching the limit with arms and projectiles propelled by explosive charge. So you can see by useful comparison the technology that is not yet finished. And we can see the human organism as an artifact, ask what is wrong with it, and how far it has to go. I wonder if anyone at this table would be alive, say, if we were all living a hundred years ago. I've had appendicitis. I've had malaria, I've had several infections checked by penicillin that might well have been fatal. Malaria is an absolutely crippling disease.

BOCKRIS: I don't understand how people can continue being involved in politics. It doesn't really seem to make any difference who wins, they always do the same thing anyway.

BURROUGHS: It makes a hell of a lot of difference, my dear. Do you realize how narrowly a fascist takeover in this country was headed off by Watergate? They all said as much quite frankly in all their boring memoirs. It is *extremely* important to keep track of these things, and remember.

BOCKRIS: Having to keep track of what's going on seems like a very tiresome thing to do.

SONTAG: But sometimes your life is at stake.

BURROUGHS: Your life *is* at stake, believe me. I knew people in that period. I remember the terrorism of the late sixties. People framed for pot. There was a time when Sinclair went to jail for ten years for one joint. It means your life to keep track of these things. Coming back to America from before Watergate and after Watergate is like coming back to Russia before and after Stalin. When I came back to this country in 1964 my luggage was pulled apart. Huncke was told at that time that the FBI had got a list of people they were out to get.

SONTAG: It was very easy to get into trouble in the fifties and early sixties. I remember the fifties as absolutely terrifying. People threw away books that were so innocent. I'm not talking about Marx, I'm talking about Ruth Benedict, John Dewey. People were hiding these most innocent liberal books because they'd be misconstrued. You can't imagine! People would throw away Tolstoy and Dostoevsky in the early fifties because they were afraid that they would be accused of reading Russian writers. This is a time, in the early fifties, when you could not write in red ink on a government form when you came into this country. You can write in purple ink, you can write in green ink or yellow ink, but you can't write in red ink. This is a time when a team called the Cincinnati Reds had to change its name. That fear went on through the fifties and early sixties. Then something happened in the sixties which we still feel works. However, one wonders if even these things are now possibly revocable as opposed to irrevocable.

BOCKRIS: I imagine that everything is revocable.

BURROUGHS: Yes. Revocable and have been experimentally revoked or suspended.

SONTAG: Sure. It's fifteen years for us, that's a long time, it's roughly the mid-sixties to now. It's a very long time, so it seems like forever.

BURROUGHS: No, you see that's just part of the sales talk—the price of your freedom here. You got it pretty easy, nobody's busting into *your* apartment at three in the morning, are they? Well, then don't worry about what they're doing in South Korea and places like that. It's like the standard of living. Are you content to achieve your higher standard of living at the expense of people all over the world who've got a lower standard of living? Most Americans would say yes. Now we ask the question, are you content to enjoy your political freedom at the expense of people who are less free? I think they would also say yes. I think the CIA is precisely dedicated to getting a yes on both questions. Yes. Yes. Yes. Give up my standard of living!? NEVER!

DINNER WITH ALLEN GINSBERG: NEW YORK 1976

GINSBERG: The thing I remember most that changed my 1940's mind and determined my own attitude was sitting around with Burroughs and his wife, Joan, listening to the radio as Harry Truman's voice came over in his inaugural speech—and Joan sniffing down her nose and saying, "His tone of voice and his prose are like a haberdasher's." And: "What kind of president is that?" She was making fun of Truman's prose style—a sort of catty putdown attitude.

It was the first time I'd ever heard anyone presume to criticize the president of the United States on account of his *mind;* in those days it wasn't done. You assumed that everything was one big dumb mind in every direction, rather than that there might be isolated points of humorous perception. It never occurred to you that the whole nation might be comprised of democratic individuals with perceptions superior to the official perceptions of the government. I don't think anybody can imagine what it was like in those days. It was a state of conditioned brainwash in which the emotional authority of the government was unquestioned. And I'm wondering: is this a hallucination on my part by hindsight? Maybe it wasn't so; maybe it was just some cranky notion that we had. Because I suppose there were all sorts of right wingers saying, "Roosevelt and unions!"—including Kerouac's father. What was surprising was that Burroughs was actually so much in agreement with conservative thought at the time. There was a vulgarity in the government that he objected to, and underneath that was some apprehension that vulgarity was somewhat sinister—that it might result in blowing up an atomic bomb. The main point is that the material the artists of the forties were dealing with was absolutely truthful and socially perceptive, and yet it seemed so off the wall compared to what was being printed, that the idea of material like this [*Naked Lunch, On the Road*] being in *The New York Times* or brought out by some respectable publisher seemed like some coup taking place

171

in a teahead's revery. Like—wouldn't it be great if the Beatles got back together in the White House, or wouldn't it be great if Jimmy Carter and Brezhnev got together naked in a stadium and fought out the cold war with socks full of shit!

DINNER AT THE BUNKER WITH ALLEN GINSBERG, PETER ORLOVSKY, AND JOHN GIORNO: NEW YORK 1979

GINSBERG [*whispering*]: Burroughs and I don't talk anymore. We sit around and chide each other. I'm afraid to open my mouth. [*Bill sits down at head of table. On his right, Allen looks up.*] I might say something too radical. I had a thought about your opinion about the Shah.

BURROUGHS: What about it?

GINSBERG: It doesn't make too much sense if Kissinger and Rockefeller provoked the Mullah to get better prices for oil—because Kissinger, *besides* being the oil representative, also has to have some sense of the sanity of the United States and not get us into a war, and this situation is really too dangerous. They might have done it to damage the relations between Iran and the United States, to make them worse.

BURROUGHS: You still haven't sold me Khomeini.

GINSBERG: I'm not trying to sell you Khomeini, however, I do approve of the effect of the idea of Iran declaring its independence from U.S. tyranny and reacting emotionally, saying, what the hell has been going on for twenty years? Although the way they've chosen to dramatize it does break the skin of sane intellectual relations.

PETER ORLOVSKY: Allen, Allen, the chicken is here, it's out and it's going to get cold.

GINSBERG: Let's eat.

ORLOVSKY: What time do you want to eat, Bill?

GINSBERG: NOW!

BURROUGHS: Well, no . . . what! Let's wait ten minutes. Have a drink . . . The Russians don't make any bones about democracy. That's why they're always one up on us.

GINSBERG [*drinking vodka and tonic*]: Right, right. Now we had Iran in the palm of our hands, we got it in 1953 and we totally fucked it up, so then fucking them up means there's some equivalent fuckup in our consciousness.

BURROUGHS: Russia doesn't just sit around waiting for us to make a mess. Now one reason . . . you say for the goodness of democracy . . .

GINSBERG: I didn't say give them democracy, I just said we fucked them up.

BURROUGHS: Now [*authoritatively*] hold on a minute! One of the big reasons that democracy wouldn't work there is because of the fucking mullahs. There are 183,000 mullahs, reactionary as priests in Ireland, sitting on the land and afraid that the land will be taken away from them and they will lose their power.

GINSBERG: Okay, so the difficulty was with land reform.

BURROUGHS: That's *one* difficulty.

GINSBERG: Okay. But let me talk to that for a moment. Aside from the Mullah, the issue here is land and the Shah may or may not have tried to make some land reform.

BURROUGHS: *He did.*

GINSBERG: *But,* but the basic approach was so heavy in capital investment in industry—overindustrialization, including nuclear—that what actually happened was that the agricultural land diminished enormously between when he took over and when he was done; so that before, Iran used to provide its own food to a great extent, and by the time he was done, they were totally dependent on the outside world for food. Because he was investing all his money in military, atomic, and upper-class luxuries and not taking care of the agriculture. If he had been a fascist or a dictator and taken care of the agriculture it would be forgiveable and he could have outflanked the mullahs, but he didn't do that, he did just the opposite, which is like a classic American thing of making an industrial monoculture with the oil and neglecting and fucking up everything else.

BURROUGHS: No, my whole point was that it's not a simple matter to just produce democracy by saying Abracadabra.

GINSBERG: I would have settled this argument for a dictatorship that was agrarian.

BURROUGHS: . . . and then I would say *again* that one of the big stumbling blocks were the mullahs themselves. They are *always* going to be a source of trouble.

GINSBERG: Well, apparently he didn't solve the problem, he only exacerbated it fifteen years ago by killing the Mullah's father or something, remember?

BURROUGHS: I don't know anything about this one, but there are 180,000 of these fuckers in Iran. It's not just this one, it's the whole system.

GINSBERG: Well, this policy, as he [the Shah] did it, only escalated domestic instability by destroying the local agriculture, totally offending the mullahs, and driving Iran into the arms of Russia.

BURROUGHS: Maybe they're all undercover Communists! I wouldn't be at all surprised if they turned out to be super-Communists!

GINSBERG: The National Committee on Labor [now Fusion Party], the right-wing-left-wing-fake, the right-wing secret agent group, says that it's a Rockefeller-Communist conspiracy, they mean it begins with Russia!

BOCKRIS: What is the overall effect of putting the hostages on trial?

GINSBERG: From an American point of view they've done us an enormous favor, I think, by making us confront what we actually did. It's investigating what we did for twenty-five years, the unacknowledged, unrepented guilt: just as in the Vietnam War, which we evaded; [guilt] for the CIA which we evaded, for the FBI, which we evaded. And they say, you're *not* going to evade it with Iran! You've been in here fucking around for twenty-five years, it's time that you faced yourself. That's at least the most sane statement of their position. Before November 1979, mass America did not know the Shah had his money in the Rockefeller banks, and didn't realize how close Rockefeller and Kissinger . . .

BURROUGHS: This whole thing is also useful in that it serves an educational purpose. The man in the street now knows something about Iran, what absolutely fucked-up people they are. Khomeini never heard of Beethoven! "Islam is everything," he says. Now, if the mullahs haven't for generations been keeping people in poverty and abysimial ignorance to their own advantage . . .

BOCKRIS: Abysmal . . .

BURROUGHS: Abysmal.

GINSBERG: Abyssinian!

BURROUGHS: Abyssinian ignorance, yes, to their own advantage is exactly what's been going on. They're the most reactionary people in the country.

GINSBERG: You were saying the other night that you thought Rock-

Burroughs in NO METRIC T-*shirt and English country cap.* The Gangster Look. *Photo by Victor Bockris*

efeller and Kissinger were not stupid, that I assumed that anybody who had different opinions from me was just stupid, which I think they are, but that they were not stupid, so that they *knew* when they maneuvered to get the Shah here that it would create a great crisis, and so the question was, what was their motive in doing it, what were their plans?

BURROUGHS: I don't know what their motive would be, but I think they must have had some idea, because the idea now is—we told you so. See, the experts, the old Iranian hands . . .

GINSBERG: First of all, the Rockefeller-Kissinger motive might have been to swing the clock back to patriotic-chauvinistic-hysterical-pro-CIA.

BURROUGHS: To some extent . . .

GINSBERG: And also they abandoned any attempt that Mondale was framing to control the CIA the other day. They increased the budget to what?

ORLOVSKY: In 1981 it's going to be 155 or 158 million and it was only 130 million last year. They've banned gay people from coming into the country . . .

BURROUGHS: Now *wait a minute*. This is not at all connected.

GINSBERG: I think it's all related as a grand master plan by the Committee on Present Danger, headed by Norman Podhoretz and Irving Kristol, the whole thing, to roll back the sixties at the verge of the eighties!

BURROUGHS [*patiently*]: In the first place, nothing in the modern world succeeds like failure. In other words, the whole Iran thing is a great failure in America and now they're saying it's necessary to keep the CIA because they fucked things up so much. Look at Nasser. Every time he started a war and won it in record time, he was in that much more solid.

GINSBERG: Nasser was?

BURROUGHS [*icily*]: Yes.

GINSBERG [*confused*]: Every time he lost or won?

BURROUGHS [*screaming*]: *Every time he lost! Did he ever win a war?* [*Testily*]: What war did he ever win?

GINSBERG: No, you said every time he *won* a war he was more solid. I was just saying that . . .

BURROUGHS: LOST a war. By *losing*. It's a sort of reversal of the fear of victory.

GINSBERG: Pyrrhic victory. [*Burroughs sighs audibly.*] I'm a very learned, bookish person.

BURROUGHS: Arrrggghhhh . . .

DINNER WITH GLENN O'BRIEN, ANDRE LEON-TALLEY, ANDY WARHOL, AND ALLEN GINSBERG: NEW YORK 1980

BOCKRIS: Up at the Natural History Museum there is a woman studying the international roach population, spending nights with them, and doing very close-up portraits of them. She obviously knows what's going on, whatever it is. These roaches are widespread and venomously effective.

BURROUGHS: Widespread they are, yes.

BOCKRIS: They're brave and aggressive creatures, because what chance do they stand against you when they come out?

O'BRIEN: Some of them are smart, some of them learn to jump at the right time.

BURROUGHS: Some of them have wings.

BOCKRIS: You stated flatly that all waterbugs had wings.

BURROUGHS: As far as I know, although they may undergo various cycles.

O'BRIEN: They eat plastic.

BURROUGHS: Yes. They eat glue, they eat the bindings out of your books.

BOCKRIS: We're closer to roaches than almost anything else in New York and we don't know anything about them, their habits.

BURROUGHS: I think you're a bleeding heart do-gooder; you think we should get to know more about roaches. I doubt it, frankly.

BOCKRIS: It's axiomatic where you're fighting a war the more you know about your opponent the better chance you have of winning.

BURROUGHS: That I agree with entirely. But all you need to know about killing roaches can be learned in one afternoon. I went out with an old exterminator and I learned it all in one afternoon. They're pretty easy to get rid of. The exterminator guarantees to get rid of them for thirty dollars and if the roaches come back he'll come back for nothing. They're much more efficient in controlling roaches now than they used to be when I was working as an exterminator.

LEON-TALLEY: Can you tell me the sex life of a roach?

BURROUGHS: I don't know about that, but I do know how to get rid of them. I'd have to look around and analyze the case, see. They get under sinks; if there's linoleum they'll get under that, they'll get in the kitchen cabinets and any kind of woodwork.

LEON-TALLEY: How do you keep them out of the kitchen cabinets where you have your best china and silverware and all that?

WARHOL: Well, they can be with the best china; it's the best food you don't want them to be with.

BURROUGHS: Take it out and spray it.

WARHOL: No, spray it and serve the people with the spray on it. That's what you do.

BURROUGHS: You spy out where they are and then you spray there and they come running out, and you soon find out where they are. You have to have a feel for it.

LEON-TALLEY: But they're so big and ugly.

BURROUGHS: Well, now you're speaking about waterbugs.

WARHOL: But I used to come home and I used to be so glad to find a little roach there to talk to I just . . . it was so great to have . . . at least somebody was there to greet you at home, right? And then they just go away. They're great. I couldn't step on them. Do you step on them?

BURROUGHS: Oh no—God, man! I either have a sprayer . . . Well, occasionally I get a waterbug in my place. There's something called Tat with a thin tube coming out from the nozzle and it makes this fine spray. If you see a waterbug you can just . . .

WARHOL: You don't have any roaches in your new place?

BURROUGHS: Very rarely. I got rid of them all.

BOCKRIS: But didn't you have a slight bedbug problem?

BURROUGHS: I got a bomb and put it under the mattress under where the springs are, that's where they get to, and I got rid of them . . .

BOCKRIS: Much of your work has been extremely condemning of the planet as a whole. Are you feeling any differently about that?

BURROUGHS: As far as the whole cycle of overpopulation and pollution, there is such flagrant bad management, what's being done about it is very inadequate, and that's only one problem. Then there is proliferation of nuclear weapons, which is also a pollution problem; the problem of the whole economic system . . . It's taking more and more to buy less and less. This is worldwide, it's not confined to Western culture. Whether there's any way of solving these problems, that's another matter. Frankly, I doubt that much will be done. Pollution has been going on a long time, but there comes a point where you reach saturation. In terms of any possible hope or solution, I agree with Timothy Leary—the only possibilities are in space. In a recent talk he gave about space stations, he said, "When a place gets full to this extent, that is a sign that it's been successful and it's time to move." He said, consider these space stations. We'll have the longevity pill; you can live 500, 600, 700 years.

He's offering, it seems to me, the two most important things—immortality and space. He also points out that real space programs will be developed by private capital, which would be one of the best defenses of private capital, doing something really useful with their money. It seems to be a possibility within the range of modern technology. These would support rather small groups of people, and apparently one could select the setting, so there'd be worlds for bisexual vegetarians and Anita Bryant!

BOCKRIS: There seems to be a limited amount of money to spend on space.

BURROUGHS: We're very near a certain point where money doesn't mean anything anyway. They say: How much money is this going to cost? This is really a totally meaningless concept. Money determines less and less our reality. Money is not a constant factor, it's simply a process dependent entirely on acceptance for its existence. We already see situations without money, and I think that we're coming closer and closer to it.

As for Communism, it's a reactive formation derived from capitalism. For this reason it's less flexible and has a lower survival potential. The days of laissez-faire capitalism are completely dead, and the assumptions of nineteenth-century Communism are equally dead, because they were based on laissez-faire capitalism. While there's hardly a trace of it left in capitalist countries, Communism is still reacting to something that's been dead for over a hundred years.

And the present-day Communist clings to these outmoded concepts, refusing to acknowledge the contradictions and failures of the Marxist system. Communism doesn't have any capacity to change. Capitalism is flexible, and it's changing all the time, and it's changed immeasurably. Communists apparently are still asserting that they are not changing, they're following the same Marxist principles. We don't have any principles. It's an advantage.

BOCKRIS: From the perspective of your life and work through the forties, fifties, sixties, and seventies, are you surprised at the state America and Americans are in now?

BURROUGHS: I'd say it's about as easy a place to live in as you can find, and it's a hell of a lot better than I would have expected. It looked like it was going to develop into a repressive police state, but then that didn't happen. One of the big turning points was unquestionably Watergate. What are Americans? We've got everything from sharecroppers to atomic physicists here, and there's certainly no uniformity in their thought processes. There's very little they have in common. In fact, Americans, should we say, have less in common than any other nationality. There are so many group and occupational differences.

BOCKRIS: Are you in favor of state, as opposed to national, government?

BURROUGHS: Nothing has come from the federal government except trouble and expense: Prohibition; this whole nonsense of trying to control drugs. The FDA is really crippling any kind of research. It's going to take them five years to get this endorphin on the market because of the FDA, and they're working hand in hand with the big drug companies. They're really company cops for the big drug companies. So the less interference from federal bureaucracy the better. They're always passing laws that affect states that have completely different problems from the eastern seaboard, these states should be allowed leeway to solve their own problems.

GINSBERG: Everywhere I go giving poetry readings I meet young people who picked up on Burroughs' vibration, whether from the point of view of heavy-metal psyche, or police state paranoiac comedy, or terminal psychological withdrawal symptoms from civilization, or space-age back-to-the-wallism. Mainly, however, it's his factual, shrewd, stoic, healthily cynical view of governments, bureaus, bureaucrats, politics, egotism, and . . . "chance operation."

I think he played a major role in either catalyzing or expressing the change of consciousness that overcame the United States in the last two decades, which resulted in disillusionment on the part of the general public with self-mystifying government. That was the first theme I picked up from him back in the forties—his contempt for the trappings of authoritarianism and his humor in seeing through military-police uniforms to the hairy cancerous body-corpse inside. And that leads later on to his cynicism about the outward forms and trappings of ego itself.

BURROUGHS: If you are asking me what the individual can do right now, in a political sense, I'd have to say he can't do all that much. Speaking for myself, I am more concerned with the transformation of the individual, which to me is much more important than the so-called political revolution.

ON PSYCHIC SEX

If I had a talking picture of you
I'd play it everytime I felt blue
I'd give ten shows a day
And a midnite matinee
If I had a talking picture
    of you.
    —A Song from the Twenties

During the period that I was seeing a great deal of William in New York, I began to have some extremely intense, what appeared to me to be sexual, hallucinations. I decided that he was the only person whom I could safely approach on this matter and told him what had happened to me on a recent morning.

BOCKRIS: I woke up around 5:00 A.M. and lay on my side looking out the window. I knew I was awake because I remember looking at my watch, thinking that I had woken up early. The next instant I was aware of a body, reclining on its side, descending upon me from approximately two feet above the bed. I immediately recognized and accepted the presence of a girl about whom I'd been having the most intense sexual fantasies morning and night for three months. Confused, I initially thought she'd come over to see me and wondered how she had gotten in. Then I realized that this "wasn't really her," but whatever it was, here *she* was and my strong sexual desire for her was being fulfilled. The creature's presence was extremely delicate and I realized that I must move slowly and calmly, making no sudden lunges, or she would evaporate. Now what was that?

Bill first expressed surprise again at my ignorance about such a visitation, explaining that this was clearly "a visit by the demon lover, my

---

181

Damita Richter in a psychic photo. Note wound in right-hand side below newspaper. This does not appear on the negative. Photo by Victor Bockris

dear!" He ran an exasperated hand through his thinning hair as he adjusted his spectacles in preparation for explaining the phenomenon to me. Bill always takes on an air of complete amazement when he comes upon the comparative ignorance of the majority of his companions. He has read omnivorously since he was a young child and attended all sorts of universities, and medical schools, doing graduate work in anthropology, and published papers in medical journals. The breadth and depth of his knowledge is remarkable, as is his ability to talk informatively about any subject ranging from the succubus to the sweet potato! "No," said I, "I don't know anything about this, Bill. What is a succubus?"

BURROUGHS: My dear, according to the dictionary, a succubus is "a female demon supposed to descend upon and have sexual intercourse with a man while he sleeps." In the male form it is called an incubus. Basically, it's any form of "other being" who visits a human sexually. It may come in the body of a person you recognize, as in your account, or in an unrecognizable human or other form. Sometimes you can feel it, but it's invisible. However, all these visits are exclusively sexual.

BOCKRIS: I've never heard anything about this. It was such a startling experience for me that I really want to find out all about it.

BURROUGHS: Much has been written about these creatures, but only in scattered sources. There is no single definitive work on them, although they continue to visit us regularly today as they have throughout history. See, most people don't want to talk about it because they think you'll think they're bananas. I've spoken to many people about it who didn't know what the hell I was talking about. It's the same thing with journeys out of the body. We urgently need explorers who are willing to investigate these uncharted possibilities and at least consider taking a positive attitude toward sex with other beings. There is Robert Monroe, who wrote in 1971 a bestseller called *Journeys Out of the Body*. He's an American businessman in his sixties who lives in Virginia. Monroe did a series of experiments in which he seemed, on the edge of sleep, to leave his body and go to other places. On some of these journeys he met people with whom he had sexual encounters. In a chapter called "Sex in the Second State," he describes some sexual contacts he had.

Now, in my opinion, in attempting to delineate the physical feelings of these sexual encounters, Monroe constructs the most objective modern description of sex with a succubus: "If the opposite charged poles of two stationary electric images could 'feel' as the unlike ends approach one another," he writes, "they would 'need' to come together. There is no barrier that can restrain it. The need increases progressively with nearness. At a given point of nearness, the need is compelling; very close, it is all-encompassing; beyond a given point in nearness, the attraction need exerts tremendous pull and the two unlikes rush together and envelop one another.

"The sexual action-reaction in the physical seems a pale imitation or a feeble attempt to duplicate the very intimate form of communion and communication in the second state. The act itself is an immobile rigid state of shock where the two truly intermingle, not just at a surface level and at one or two specific body parts, but in full dimension, atom for atom, throughout the entire second body. In an immediate moment there is a mind-shaking interflow of electrons, one to another, unbalanced charges become equalized, peaceful contented balance is restored, and each is revitalized. All this happens in an instant, yet an eternity passes by. Afterwards, there is a calm serene separation."

Monroe concludes that we are missing our real sexual opportunities: "We continue to evaluate sexuality as good or bad strictly in terms of inhibitions, restrictions and social structure." And he chastises the Freudians' sexual-dream-fantasies-caused-by-early-sex-repression theory as an easy way out. He calls it "a mislabeling to avoid facing uncharted possibilities."

BOCKRIS: But why are these possibilities so uncharted?

BURROUGHS: In view of the similarities in descriptions about the experience of having sex with an incubus or succubus—the magnetic attraction, moving together, overwhelming orgasm, and gratification with balance restored—plus a vast amount of religious, psychic, and psychiatric writings reporting similar activities over thousands of years, which I'll give you some pointers on later, it would seem unreasonable to flatly deny, as many people do, that these things do exist in some way. But many people are still embarrassed to talk about their experiences with them, and none of the current interpretations even attempt to explain the very intimate sexual form of communion and communication you've described in your experience, or Monroe describes in his. I think we have to attempt to relate to these beings from a more balanced and objective point of view than the dogmas of authority allow. As I see it, an incubus or succubus can be harmless, or it can be destructive. Like any sexual situation, the danger depends on how you handle it. Not to control such a situation can undoubtedly lead to negative effects, but we need not adopt the uniformly negative opinions of the church, psychics and psychiatrists that these are necessarily evil or dangerous beings. *All sex is potentially dangerous.* In the early cave paintings, for example, we see the animals on the wall killed after having sex, and many sexual myths involve one or both persons being killed. Our sexual feelings make us vulnerable. How many people have been ruined by a sexual partner? Sex does provide a point of invasion and the incubi and succubi simply make us intensely aware of this.

BOCKRIS: How dangerous do you think these creatures are?

BURROUGHS: Certain things are clear to me: I would say that people who are visited by someone they want to fuck in the form of an incubus or succubus usually stop having sex with the body of the desired person. The obsession itself would seem to become more important and desirable. The magnetic nature of the sexual attraction between these beings and their subjects interferes with other physical sexual forces. Any strong sexual hallucination I have had has cut down on my actual sexual experience, and has proven to be quite destructive from that point of view. Secondly, I believe it is wise not to let the person who has visited you in the form of a succubus know about it because they may realize the power they have over you and use it. Thirdly, anyone attempting to make contact with a succubus should know that they are apt to be a nuisance, difficult to get rid of, and can be exhausting if they get out of control. A succubus *can be* a good servant. He or she is always a bad master.

BOCKRIS: How would you sum that up?

BURROUGHS: Any aspect of relating to them is clearly one of degree. At what point does the fantasy become more than a fantasy? When does the ventriloquist's dummy start talking on its own? When does a cancer cell become a separate and immutable process?

BOCKRIS: People seem not to know about this phenomenon. What kind of documentation has there actually been?

BURROUGHS: This phenomenon has been going on since the beginning of time. "Adam was having sexual intercourse with Lillith, Adam's first wife and the Princess who presided over these demons known as succubi, for 130 years before the creation of Eve." That's a direct quote from Lewis Spence's 1960 *Encyclopedia of Occultism*. This Lillith character is known as "the Queen of the Succubi" because she was the first succubus. Of course the Immaculate Conception is an incubus legend. Remember: "The Angel came in unto Mary and said 'Hail thou that art highly favored, the Lord is with thee. Blessed art thou among women.' " Then he told her not to be afraid, she was such a favorite of God she would soon have his son. She said, " 'How? I haven't had sex with anyone.' " And (I'm quoting from Luke, Chapter 1): "The Angel answered and said unto her, 'The Holy Ghost shall come upon thee.' " Now, in this case the Holy Ghost is an incubus. You'll find that people's attitudes toward these things change, but their visits remain constant. We know that the Greeks also had gods and goddesses who occasionally came down on humans. In the story of Leda and the Swan, Zeus descended as a swan.

BOCKRIS: Surely in more modern times there must have been some scientific investigation of the phenomenon?

BURROUGHS: Yes, the next thing was the interpretation of the nine-teenth-century rationalists—Freud and his ilk. They came along and flatly rejected the whole idea of demonic invasion. So they dismissed the corporeal conception of incubi, saying they were simply creations of the subject's mind, or hallucinations. It's a basic postulate of Freud-ian psychiatry that all voices, hallucinations, are of endogenous origin and that these hallucinations of sexual beings were caused by severe sexual repression in infancy. So they were considered to be, and still are considered by many psychiatrists, a form of illness.

BOCKRIS: What do the psychics have to say about it?

BURROUGHS: Their most articulate spokeswoman, Dion Fortune, who was a leading member of the London-based psychic Society of Inner Light, identifies the succubus in her book *Psychic Self Defense* [1930]: "The psychic is of the opinion that the lustful imaginings of men's hearts do indeed produce artificial elementals and that these elementals are something more than subjective images and have an objective eth-eric existence." Now, although she was an adept explorer into the occult and wrote at great length about it through her adult life, Dion Fortune's attitudes toward sex were still bound by the period she lived in, so she was always outraged by the lewd sexual approach of these creatures.

BOCKRIS: Everybody is in agreement that these beings, or whatever one wants to call them, have a negative effect.

BURROUGHS: Yes. But here we have to ask ourselves just how much more objective are scientists on this matter than priests. I suggested to a psychiatrist for example that witchcraft may have foundations in fact. "NO! The witch is an hysteric and the victim is a paranoid!" he screamed. "As a scientist, I must believe this." Scientists turn out to be as emotional about their dogma as medieval ecclesiastics. If we are going to investigate incubi and succubi seriously, I really feel that we must begin by admitting that psychiatrists have no more objective proof that they come from our imaginations than priests have that they come from the devil. So in a sense we are completing a full circle, coming back to re-examining the basic positions the ecclesiastics took. If some of us are willing to consider, or at least examine, the old concepts of demonic possession and visitation, we may do so with the scientific equipment necessary to investigate the matter more precisely. For example, we may be able to throw some light on this mystery if we can learn anything from recent sexual research on the brain. We have only just become aware of the brain's being the primary erotic zone in humans. The brain is divided in two halves called the right brain and the left brain. All the speech areas are located in the left brain. The areas in the right brain that correspond to the speech areas in the left brain don't have any apparent function, but many people still hear voices in the right brain, and these are voices that they cannot control. Consider this: the most individual thing about anyone is their voice. If you are listening to someone, that person's voice is inside your head. It has to some extent invaded and occupied your brain. Consequently, while you are listening to someone else speak, you are suspending your identity to make room for theirs. So voices coming through the right brain that cannot be turned off have a special power. Consider what could happen if the voice of somebody you loved or lusted after suddenly came on in the right brain and said, for example, "Hello. It's me." It would be able to exert a tremendous amount of authority, and possibly create visual hallucinations of desired sexual objects, like itself. So these unknown voices of sexual beings coming in through the right brain *could* be the auditory basis of incubi/succubi experiences. This is merely a suggestion. Perhaps it is a matter of to what degree the particular voice gets a hold on you.

BOCKRIS: But if these voices are creating visual sexual images, and so are in fact capable of creating these other beings, do they come from inside our minds, as scientists believe, or are they of extraneous origin? Everyone who masturbates creates pictures of someone else. But where do we get the original pictures to fixate on and become sexually excited by? What creates our sexual excitement?

BURROUGHS: Following my suggestion on the auditory origin of succubi visitations, it could be that the origins of sexual excitement are in, or come through, the right brain. If this were true, the extremely beautiful and sensitive erotic zone of the ear would provide the point of sexual invasion in the human. Yeats used this image of invasion through the ear describing the Immaculate Conception in a poem called "The Mother of God": "The threefold terror of love/A fallen flare,/Through the hollow of an ear;/Wings beating about the room . . ." I think that's very good. But if we have located the origins of these images in the nondominant brain hemisphere, I am still wondering whether they came from somewhere else before they arrived there. The whole question really steps across into the realm of science fiction. Particularly when we consider the possibility of electronic brain stimulation we could create an incubus or succubus of our choice at will, which would lead to the development of the Electronic Whorehouse, where anyone could get satisfied without the encumbrance of another physical body. You'd simply plug in your desire. Sex is physics. If anyone could push a button and receive an incubus or succubus, I believe that most people would prefer a phantom partner to the all-too-dreary real thing. Many of us might eagerly choose to break our conditioning by having sex with other beings if it were possible, particularly since they can make near-perfect sex partners, providing the hottest sex, disappearing immediately after their function is fulfilled, leaving the subject satisfied and gratified, presenting no practical problems and making no remarks or complaints. The Electronic Whorehouse would expand, everyone would be providing a landing point for a succubus, which, being of a parasitical nature, does need an individual human to attach itself to in order to establish habitation, and more and more of them would land, until everyone would be jacking off alone in a private toilet, crooning: "I'm a fool/but aren't we all/each night it seems/ that in my dreams/my darling comes to call."

BOCKRIS: And sex would become completely illusory at last?

BURROUGHS: We can only speculate as to what further relations with these beings might lead to, my dear. You see, the bodies of incubi and succubi are much less dense than the human body, and this is greatly to their advantage in space travel. Don't forget, it is our bodies which must be weightless to go into space. Now, we make the connections with incubi and succubi in some form of dream state. So I postulate that dreams may be a form of preparation, and in fact training, for travel in space. It's possible then that, being of a parasitical nature, the rarefied form of these beings is dependent on contact with the denser human form in order to exist.

BOCKRIS: Are you suggesting that we collaborate with them in some way which would in fact benefit the future of our travel in space?

BURROUGHS: Well, I simply believe that we should pay a great deal of attention to, and develop a much better understanding of, our relations with incubi and succubi. We can hardly afford to ignore their possible danger or use. If we reject a relationship with them, we may be placing our chances of survival in jeopardy. If we don't dream, we may die.

Centerfold John Giorno Poetry Systems Album by Les Levine

ON THE INTERVIEW

I remember sitting up in John Giorno's apartment with Bill after he'd been interviewed for two hours for a big rock magazine and was incensed at having been asked questions like, "What do you think the state of the morality of the country is at the moment, Mr. Burroughs?" He proceeded to develop an idea for the electrical device that could rip out an interviewer's throat and have it on the floor before the first question was out of his mouth. He kept getting up and snarling, "Why don't you tell *me* what the state of the gay situation in the world is today, Victor," thwacking a cardboard box with his black steel Cobra. He stood there looking morose. "How can you *answer* such questions?"

DINNER WITH ANDY WARHOL AND GERARD MALANGA: NEW YORK 1980

BOCKRIS: Talking about interviews recently, Frank Zappa said that he didn't think questions were a particularly intelligent form of communication.

BURROUGHS: There's something wrong with the whole interview format. It's supposed to be asking the questions that all the readers and fans would like to know the answers to. *"Mr. Zappa, do you feel that you've got some kind of a message for young people that you're trying to put down, and what would you say that message was?"*

BOCKRIS: And they say, "Well, you have a reputation for living a rather unusual life, Mr. Burroughs. Do you feel that you're a good example to the youth?"

BURROUGHS: They can't be quite *that* explicit or I would end the interview right there.

BOCKRIS: What was the original concept of the interview and when did the interview begin?

BURROUGHS: It pretty much came in with newspapers, which are not very old, see, they didn't begin to mean anything until around the nineteenth century. People would come around to interview Billy the Kid, who killed twenty-one men. He actually gave an interview in jail after he'd been sentenced to death, and that was when he made his sensational escape. Somebody planted a gun for him. It was never quite found out what happened, but he killed his two guards. The interview was very dull. They said, "Well, how did you get into this life? You're considered to be an outlaw," and he said, "Well you know . . ." He was born in Brooklyn. He killed his first man at the age of twelve. Somebody was manhandling his mother and he grabbed a knife and stuck it in the guy's back. So they asked him, "When did you kill your first man?" And he told the story about how he came west and started working for one of the state cattle companies as a hired gun.

They used to interview people for much less reason than we do now. People would be in the headlines who were absolute nobodies. They didn't have anything like this Iranian crisis. Television burned down whole areas as potential fictional material. The Vietnam War is considered poison so far as fictional material and film are concerned. Did you see *Apocalypse Now?*

WARHOL: Oh yes, I liked some of the beginning. I thought Marlon Brando's scenes ruined everything.

BURROUGHS: I would say these scenes were overambitious and didn't come across. Perhaps the filmmakers were not quite sure what they were doing. The way I read it, Andy, is this: The CIA has a time travel project. Using Conrad's *Heart of Darkness* as a peg to hang it on, a landing field you might say, the Colonel was in a very sensitive area, which is why he had to be terminated with extreme prejudice, he had been indulging in *extreme experience,* and had set up a romantic nineteenth-century time capsule. All those shots of heads and good-looking corpses hanging from trees all so quaint like a postcard: Death by a Hundred Cuts in the Market Place of Peking sent by some languid Etonian to a friend in Capri. "Having fine time, wish you were here." Time travel is an actual possibility, in fact a *hot project.* The CIA doesn't want any offbeaters mucking about with this *sensitive* shit.

Television with immediate film coverage of events is quite new. The extent to which fictional areas may be burned down by TV coverage is difficult to ascertain. No successful novels on the 1968 student riots in Paris, very few on the Vietnam War. I think people feel that they have already seen it on television and they don't want to read about it. There are always exceptions. *Trinity* on the Irish thing was a big best seller. It got terrific coverage on the Belfast riots when I was in London. A car with a bomb in it set off by the bomb disposal squad. BOOM! And pieces of bodies being swept up into body bags after a bomb went off in a pub. And that's a powerful sight. And these kids, thirteen, fourteen years old, romping through the wreckage like little sprites. Thirty of them suddenly erupt around a corner and start throwing rocks at the police, then skitter away yipping like foxes. Roving bands of stone-throwing youths. They shot them with rubber bullets.

BOCKRIS: Perhaps the interview is really a dead form. That's what I'm wondering.

BURROUGHS: The interview stands exactly where it did a hundred years ago and serves exactly the same purpose. What's the difference between someone going out to interview Billy the Kid approximately a hundred years ago and Frank Zappa today? It's very unsatisfactory. What are they trying to get? *"When did you kill your first man?"* *"Now let's see . . ."*

MALANGA: Do people tend to love you for who you are or what you do?

BURROUGHS: *That* is a very difficult question. Say with a stranger—someone I don't know. Often they have a picture—an image—that they have projected on me which may have nothing to do with me at all. Whether it's the media or their impression of me they've gathered from my writing, anyone, I think, *will* tend to have a certain image imposed on them which may not have anything to do with what is actually there. I also feel that for a writer to be a novelist, he doesn't have, by nature of his profession, a clear-cut image of himself or a clear-cut image in general. If he cultivates his image too much his work will suffer. For example, a perfect case in point is Hemingway. His determination to act out what I might call the least interesting aspects of his own work. And to do everything that his characters could do and do it well limited and eventually crippled his work, down to shooting and fishing and all that. I feel that his work suffered from that. So, finally you get the image of Papa Hemingway which took over more and more. I think *The Snows of Kilimanjaro* is one of the best stories in the English language on the subject of death. In his later years the image of Papa Hemingway took over—struggling with some noble marlin, dropping a wildebeest sweet and clean with a spine shot at three hundred yards, fucking the beautiful young Countess across the river and into the trees. Now off on another silly safari, his image led him to Kilimanjaro, the scene of his classic sellout. In a light plane crash near Kilimanjaro, Hemingway suffered brain damage as Papa butted his way out.

Involvement with his own image can be fatal to a writer. Was it Yeats who said every man must choose at some point between his life and his work? Artists usually choose the work, and compromises are usually unfortunate. Hemingway's life posed a deadly threat to Hemingway as a writer, moving in a wildebeest at a time. "I have just fired a shot!" said Baudelaire turning from an 1870 barricade, intoxicated by his accomplishment. "Ah yes, the artist so longs to be a man of action." "To fire a least *one* shot is it not?" Stein lifts his hand from Lord Jim.

BOCKRIS: Can you remember when you gave your first interview?

BURROUGHS: One of the early interviews was by *Life, Time,* and *Fortune.* See, they sensed that there was something here with this whole Beat Generation and sent a team around to meet me and Brion just after the publication of *Naked Lunch* in Paris in 1959. They were really creepy . . . I felt like I was at lunch with the *Time* police, putting down a con, old and tired as their namesake: "Mr. Burroughs, I have an intuition about you . . . I see you a few years from now on Madison Avenue . . . $20,000 per year . . . life in all its rich variety . . . Have an Old Gold.

"Twenty thousand a year," they said. "Now what do you think about that?" I said, "Cheap bastards." But in those days that was a lot of money. In those days I had two hundred dollars a month, which was sent to me by my parents, and I had more money than I do now. I was the rich man in the hotel. So creepy stuff like that and really heavy, heavy, one takin' pictures and one tellin' you all these stories about the reason trained lions react to blank cartridges is that they train the lion by shooting a blank cartridge pistol into his eyes, and that's why the lion reacts reliably to the report. . . . Schnell and Dean.

BOCKRIS: Schnell and Dean!

BURROUGHS: Schnell and Dean. And the first thing that Schnell said was, "Have an Old Gold, Mr. Burroughs."

BOCKRIS: He did not, Bill!

BURROUGHS: Yes he did. I remember it exactly. He was playing the soft cop. It was goddamn great, you know—"just like a cop to smoke Old Golds, somehow."

BOCKRIS: It was Hauser and O'Brien [*the Narcotics police in* Naked Lunch].

BURROUGHS: Oh man, did they know my books. He knew my books practically by heart. He said it was the greatest book since *Moby Dick,* maybe a greater book. Oh, he was a real fan. And then they were both very offbeat people, see. Schnell weighed two hundred and thirty pounds, about six foot one, built like a wrestler, and he had been a wrestler and a bouncer and was quite a literate man too. And Dean was a crackerjack photographer. They'd been picked to interest me and I spent several days with these people and subsequently I've seen Dean in Paris. Schnell, man, I later picked up the *Reader's Digest* and there was Schnell's account of how he had almost died from penicillin. He had a penicillin allergy and he had a cough and he took a lozenge which had a tiny amount of penicillin. His wife happened to come home as he'd just about had it. They get him over to the hospital and he's barely making it, and all the symptoms of death that he describes are exactly the symptoms described in the Tibetan Book of the Dead. Like intense heat, freezing cold, and then a feeling of explosion. He had all these symptoms. He was a very interesting man. I'd like to see him again. I'd like to see both of them again. Loomis Dean and David Schnell.

BOCKRIS: Next time you get interviewed you should make it up to keep the interviewer happy. Say, "I like to go out to a nightclub and get really high and come back about three o'clock in the morning, drink a bottle of brandy and work until midday, then I like to eat a really big lunch, have sex and pass out. I wake up about seven or eight in the evening, my pet gazelle runs by, I take a sauna and my servant Juan comes in and gives me a massage."

BURROUGHS: I've been tempted to do that, but I'll tell you, it can bounce back like *Our Man in Havana*. Suddenly your man Juan there wants his salary and the IRS immediately says, "Well he isn't living like that off what he's declared." Another thing you always have to think about—giving out lies of affluence. Lies of affluence are the most dangerous. You'll have the IRS auditing you, you'll have a lot of people asking you for money.

BOCKRIS: How could you end a bad interview?

BURROUGHS: If I were going to end an interview I'd just say, "Look, I just don't think we're communicating. I don't see any point in continuing. I'm sorry, uh, go home and do your homework and come back."

LOOKING FOR IAN

Thursday, August 21, 1975
With Paul Bowles and Ian. Showed them how I could fly. Tried to teach Ian, who was wearing heavy grey lumpy tweed suit. He couldn't. In plane 30,000 up. They showed me map of landing place. I would fly, they take plane down.

Warm place behind a pine tree. . . .
                                   —Dream Note from Burroughs' *Retreat Diaries*

Ian Sommerville was a young Englishman with whom Burroughs lived and worked for a few years in London in the mid-sixties. He died in a car crash in England on February 5, 1976, a few years after they had separated, on William's sixty-second birthday. Nobody knows who was driving or what caused the accident.

One evening William asks me to come by at 6:00. He will have to go out at 7:30 with Carl A. to a seance.

"A seance!?"

William has been trying to make contact with Ian and another man called Spence who died violently on Burroughs' sixty-fifth birthday.

"Yes, Carl knows this medium and I'm trying to get in touch with these two friends of mine."

Carl comes over. He appears slightly nervous on seeing me until I reassure him that I'm just stopping by for a drink.

The following week Bill visited His Holiness the Dudjom Rinpoche (a Tibetan Buddhist monk) through the auspices of the monk's social secretary, John Giorno, to seek out the same information. The Dudjom specializes in locating people who have died and informing the interested party as to their well-being.

BURROUGHS: One man was killed by robbers. They called in a rinpoche and he said he couldn't find him. So then they called the Dudjom and he said, "Well, the trouble is he doesn't know he's dead yet. It happened so suddenly." "Rinpoche" means His Holiness. It's simply a title. They have a center on the East Side. It's in a townhouse with several floors; the Dudjom Rinpoche lives there with his two sons, and John stays on the top floor. Another flat on the top floor is now occupied by a visiting lama. John arranges the Dudjom's appointments and helps take care of his daily needs.

BOCKRIS: Are these attempts to contact dead friends something new?

BURROUGHS: I haven't attempted it before because I've never had any reliable sources. The Dudjom is much more exact in his information than this medium.

BOCKRIS: Do you have any kind of definition of what death is?

BURROUGHS: No. [*Impatiently*]: Read The Tibetan Book of the Dead.

"There is nothing to fear."
—Burroughs to Ginsberg, *Yage Letters*

The subject turns to Hitler's use of amphetamines. "Well, I dunno," Burroughs opines, "Hitler was an excellent marksman. He would be walking along and a guy used to say, 'Throw up a snowball!' They would throw it up. Hitler hauls out his Walther and blam the snowball goes apart in the air. . . . One thing for sure, no one on speed could do that."

Suddenly, in the middle of dinner, Burroughs is walking quietly over to a storage area behind a small walk-in closet. He re-emerges carrying a model of an M-16, walks into the middle of the room some six feet away from the table, and posts himself in a shooting stance. He snaps the gun up to his shoulder, aims at the other end of the loft: "Yep! This is what they use," he announces in a pallid monotone. And for a split-second I get a close up of William Burroughs that knocks me out of my seat.

"Not many writers can survive being burnt alive like Burroughs has. His consequent irony gives his writing an essential distance. For me, Burroughs writes from a distance beyond death," says Sylvere Lotringer, professor of French Literature at Columbia University, where Burroughs is taught in French, not English.

One night after a reading, four or five of us accompany William to a

Ian Sommerville, London, 1962. Photographer unknown

bar. In a good mood, he loosens up quickly and starts telling stories. "My Uncle Ivy used to be Hitler's PR man for the Do Business With Germany campaign in the late thirties. He had many conversations with Hitler and he once said, 'Hitler told me, "I haven't got anything against the Jews." ' Old Ivy died four months after *that* conversation . . . of a *brainnn* tumor, you could feel the fuzziness in his voice."

When Burroughs returned to New York, he had been out of the States for so long his audience had dwindled, and a lot of people thought that, like Kerouac, he had simply died. Others point out that he seems extremely concerned with death, talking and writing about it all the time. "Intellectually concerned," agrees Grauerholz, "but not personally. He's in good health, his teeth are in better condition than mine will be when I'm sixty-two, and he hasn't put on any weight, as you can see. But yes, the drugs did take a lot out of him; his system has had to pay."

"I may or may not have ten years," Burroughs has recently written.

Allen Ginsberg tells this story about a dinner in London in 1973. "One night Burroughs and I went to have dinner with Sonia Orwell and the conversation went on and on in that British manner, you know—light and polite—until I said, 'Let's *talk* about something!' And Sonia Orwell said, 'Oh, you know Mr. Ginsberg is so American, always wanting to discuss something serious.' Burroughs leaned forward and said, '*Well . . . let's* discuss something serious. Let's talk about death.' "

* * *

FRIDAY NIGHT, DECEMBER 31, 1979

I had been invited for dinner with William and Stewart Meyer by John Giorno. I arrived at the Bunker at 6:30 and proceeded to John's quarters on the third floor. The others were already there. Vodka and tonics were passed around. William had cooked up a batch of majoun in the afternoon and he, John, and Stewart had all eaten some of it. Stewart suggested that I might like some. Bill said, "Perhaps Victor would prefer to wait until after dinner and have it with his dessert." John hardly said a word during the dinner because the effect of the majoun was so strong he couldn't speak. (Majoun is a fudge cooked up with marijuana or hashish in it. Each wafer contains an extremely potent dose.) When you eat a piece of majoun you receive the equivalent effect of smoking twenty joints at the same time.

BOCKRIS: It seems very fitting that we should meet on this night. Do you think it's going to be a crazy night?

BURROUGHS: Something's bound to happen in Times Square. There're always atrocities in Times Square on New Year's Eve.

BOCKRIS: Did you see those three grinning youths who were arrested for stabbing people on the subways? There was a big picture of them today, quite good-looking. Were you patrolling the streets at all today?

BURROUGHS: Yes, I was up at the bank on Union Square. But they're not going up against a very sympathetic court this time. The sentiment is running high against these young criminals; no matter what their age is, I think they'll get a good stiff sentence. They're trying juveniles as adults these days and they can get sent away. They don't get off with this family-court business anymore. They should have a special tough group for these particular strata of criminal. For attempted robbery with violence we have a minimum of five years and treat 'em right, *teach 'em!* I'm sure New Year's Eve in Times Square will take its toll. Let's have a little bet.

BOCKRIS: We'll each put up ten dollars.

BURROUGHS: I'll put up ten.

BOCKRIS: Everyone put ten dollars in the kitty and when the reports come through whoever guesses nearest to the correct number wins the pot, right?

BURROUGHS: I WANT A DEATH!

200

MEYER: Actually there'll be a lot of violence possibly without a death.

BOCKRIS: I got forty dollars tonight.

MEYER: We'll all be checking out the paper tomorrow. Are we actually going to call the police department to discover the number?

BURROUGHS: No, we'll accept the newspapers. What else can we do. Well, of course [*chuckling*], if you can scrape up an unreported death . . .

* * *

A few hours later, around 10:30, Udo Breger, who picks up the evening's story in a report he later sent me, arrived at Giorno's as I was leaving.

UDO BREGER: It is an exceptionally warm soft winter night when we stroll down the Bowery to celebrate New Year's Eve. Crossing Prince Street there is Victor already on his way to the next party. All in black. Tight fitting coat. Black woolen cap drawn over his face. Walking stick and little far away eyes. He spins on the spot, bye bye, is off. John Giorno comes downstairs to open up the gate. Soon we're upstairs and among the first guests of this New Year's celebration. John's studio is spacious, a lot of green around, all kinds of plants and small trees. William Burroughs is present, Allen Ginsberg and Fernanda Pivano, his Italian translator from Milan. Angel-eyed Herbert Huncke and Louis Cartwright, Anne Waldman, Lucien Carr and friends. Carl Laszlo and Michael from Basel, accompanied by myself, *Soft Need* editor Udo Breger. Michael is rather silent and smiles. Carl is very excited about being invited to this party. There are a lot of drinks and a cold buffet. Flashbulbs pop constantly.

It's just about eleven o'clock. The party is in full swing when everyone suddenly freezes on the spot. Painstruck, Carl has got a piece of meat in the wrong pipe. He can't breathe and fights it in convulsions. All the guests are struck with terror. If nobody acts right away this man might die.

Louis Cartwright is the first one to act, then Michael instinctively does what's suggested on posters in the restaurants of Chinatown for "Choking Victims." He folds his arms tightly around Carl's waist and pulls back hard. Finally the piece of meat has moved up or down, and this two-minute incident that seemed to last an eternity is over. Carl breathes again and finds some courteous words of excuse.

Carl asks if he could lie down for a while. On the way out to the other apartment downstairs Michael says: "One more minute and I would have cut your throat open to make you breathe."

Very slowly the conversation picks up again. What kind of curse could it have been that brought Death so close?

* * *

Here is a piece of prose, taken from *Ah Pook Is Here*, that Burroughs often performs at readings:

> At this point I put some questions to control. A word about this control. Some years ago in London I contacted two computer programmers who purported to represent something that called itself CONTROL, allegedly from the planet Venus. CONTROL will answer any questions for one dollar. You give your question to the programmers who feed it into a computer some way and out comes the answer. So these are the actual questions that I sent in with my dollars and the answers I got back from CONTROL whoever or whatever CONTROL may or may not be.
>
> QUESTION: If CONTROL's control is absolute why does CONTROL need to control?
>
> ANSWER: CONTROL NEEDS TIME.
>
> Exactly—CONTROL needs time in which to exercise control just as DEATH needs time in which to kill. If DEATH killed everyone at birth or CONTROL installed electrodes in their brains at birth there would be no time left in which to kill or control.
>
> QUESTION: Is CONTROL controlled by its need to control?
>
> ANSWER: Yes.
>
> QUESTION: Why does CONTROL need "HUMANS" as you call them? (Your knowledge of the local dialects leaves literacy to be desired.)
>
> ANSWER: Wait.
>
> Wait. Time. A landing field. The Mayans understood this very well. Mr. Hart does not. He thinks in terms of losers and winners. He will be a winner. He will take it all.

* * *

BREGER: A little while later Carl comes upstairs. He feels a lot better but is still concerned about a scene he might have created. We imagine headlines in the New York papers: "Drugs, Demons and Death at Poets' Party." He lights his cigar, the cigar which he had been holding in his hand all the time. Frightening Death away with its cold smell?

Midnight 1980. A new decade. Champagne, I Ching. William throws the coins, three subway tokens. Anne Waldman reads the combination and John Giorno draws the lines. Allen Ginsberg opens the book and reads: "Anagram 12, Stagnation. The worst will happen at this very moment . . ."

* * *

THREE DAYS LATER BILL AND I VISIT ANDY WARHOL AT THE FACTORY

WARHOL: Have you been having more fun in the eighties than you had in the seventies?

BURROUGHS: It's a little hard to say. We will see. *Qui vivra, verra*, as the French say, who lives will see.

BOCKRIS: Tell Andy what happened on New Year's Eve.

BURROUGHS: One of the guests nearly choked to death on a piece of meat. But everyone knew what to do. It's been publicized so much. It's supposed to pop right up. They tried that and it wasn't working, and then one young man with great presence of mind gave him a hug here, and it went down instead of popping out.

WARHOL: How long did this take? Five minutes?

BURROUGHS: Even less than that, three or four minutes. You could be dead in five. Allen Ginsberg was about to call an ambulance. I said there's no use, there isn't time. He collapsed onto the couch, saying *"Ich sterbe!"* I'm dying. He said later that he was trying to tell people to do this but they were doing it already. They knew it wasn't a heart attack. So when this guy hugged him around the chest he said, *"Besser."* I know a man who choked to death on Lobster Newburg.

* * *

The following day I visited Bill at the Bunker and told him about a dream Damita had the night before. She was stabbed in the chest with a screwdriver at the Mudd Club. At the hospital she noticed a paper stating that a baby girl had been born to Damita Richter. Under where it said the name of the baby's father was printed "William Burroughs." I had been having a lot of psychic experiences with Damita and always found William fascinating on the subject. Although I wasn't sure how he would respond to this dream I felt an urgent necessity to relate it to him. And indeed, as usual, his interpretation made me think again. "That's very interesting," he said, "because I went to see the Dudjorr again yesterday. He told me that Spence is all right but Ian is in bad shape, he's stuck in the second level of hell because he can't get reborn again."

William never tries to impress his opinions or attitudes on you he simply opens doors to previously unrevealed possibilities. We were once discussing dreams, I insisting naively that there were obvious differences between dreams and reality. "How would you define the difference?" said Bill.

"In dreams, if somebody hits you you don't have a bruise in the morning."

"Oh don't you? That's not true *at all*, my dear. I've woken up with a black eye."

The day after we had this conversation Damita woke up with two

Carl Lazlo (bottom left-hand corner) minutes before he almost choked to death on a piece of meat, New Year's Eve, 1979, with Burroughs, Udo Breger, and Ginsberg in the background. Photo by Louis Cartwright

bruised knees. It's really true. Burroughs seeps into you. When junkies
kick they say, "I'm gonna chill out with a little Burroughs."

DINNER WITH TENNESSEE WILLIAMS:
NEW YORK 1977

WILLIAMS: I think we all die, sooner or later. I prefer to postpone the
event.
BURROUGHS: Yes, there is that consideration.
WILLIAMS: I've always been terrified of death.
BURROUGHS: Why?
WILLIAMS: I'm not sure. I say that, and yet I'm not sure. How about
you?
BURROUGHS: One of my students once asked me if I believed in the
afterlife and I said, "How do you know you're not already dead?"
BOCKRIS: Do you experience your own death?
BURROUGHS: Of course.
BOCKRIS: Is it possible to point out in your writing where your death is
reflected?
BURROUGHS: I would say in every sentence. I took a serum in Mexico
which is supposed to make you live to be one hundred and thirty-five. I
found it to work out very well for me.
BOCKRIS: Would you like to live on and on without being able to move?
BURROUGHS: Ah, you are talking about Tithonus, my dear, longevity
and the so-called Catch-22: *You will live indefinitely but you will not be
able to move.*

* * *

I left the Bunker and walked home, mulling over the significance of
the many psychic connections that seemed to extend between myself
and Damita and wondered again if Ian Sommerville had been reborn
in her dream through some complex extension of Bill's abilities to
relate through me to her. *Secret Mullings About Bill.* There was a lot of
smoke coming out of a vacant building a block away from the gates of
the Bunker. Two black men were standing around looking vaguely at
the burning building. One of them said, "I wonder if there's anybody
in there." On impulse I went in. It was an old house, wreckage lay
about, the fire was coming in increasingly large flames from a room far

in the back. I walked through the house to the back and looked in through an open door. A bed was on fire. Nobody was on it. And I heard a voice I never heard say, "I was once in a room with another person who set the mattress on fire." And echoing in my memory: "I WANT A DEATH!"

WITH BECKETT
IN BERLIN

DINNER WITH CHRISTOPHER ISHERWOOD:
NEW YORK 1976

BURROUGHS: My first visit to Berlin was two months ago. I'd never seen it before. I went there for a reading with Allen Ginsberg and Susan Sontag. I saw the Wall. The area between the East and the West is populated by thousands of rabbits. And we also went to see Beckett, who was living in the Academy of Art Building. He was in Berlin to direct one of his plays.

ISHERWOOD: Has Beckett been directing his plays for a long time?

BURROUGHS: Beckett almost always directs his plays. He feels he's the only one competent to do it. According to his English publisher, John Calder, he's really a brilliant director. I've never seen what he's directed. Allen Ginsberg, Susan Sontag, Professor Hollerer, Fred Jordan, and your reporter, through the mediation of John Calder, were granted a short audience, or visit, with Beckett at the Berlin Academy of Art. We went to see him about 5:30 in the afternoon. He received us graciously in his rooms overlooking the Tiergarten. We had brought along some liquor. The large duplex apartment was very austerely furnished. The conversation was polite and desultory. It was a very decorous meeting.

BOCKRIS: Does Beckett like a drink?

BURROUGHS: I think he had a drink of what we had, yes. I know Beckett's reputation as a recluse. Often this means—as in the case of

Isherwood hams it up with Burroughs at the Bunker, during their first meeting, winter 1976. Photo by Gerard Malanga

Howard Hughes—fear of other people. This is certainly not at all true of Beckett. He seems simply to inhabit a realm where other people are not particularly necessary. He obviously hasn't any need to relate to anyone. This is immediately obvious. It's just where he's at, where he's written himself into, this rather strange inhuman position, but that's the way he is. He's polite, but it's obvious he wants you out of there in about twenty minutes. His manner was cool and precise. He was very thin, very trim, dressed in a turtleneck sweater and a sports jacket. Beckett seemed in very good health. He is seventy but looks much younger. We stayed twenty minutes. It was time to go—shook hands, said goodbye.

DINNER WITH SUSAN SONTAG AND
MAURICE GIRODIAS: NEW YORK 1980

BOCKRIS: Were you at that famous meeting with Beckett in Berlin?

SONTAG: I was indeed. Why has it become a "famous meeting"?

BOCKRIS: William has told me the story so many times and I was intrigued to see how accurate his account is.

SONTAG: Beckett is probably the only person I ever really wanted to meet in the adult part of my life. I was very pleased to be in his presence. I felt and feel a general reverence for him.

BOCKRIS: How long were you with him for?

SONTAG: We were there for about [*turning inquisitively to Burroughs*] . . .

BOCKRIS: No, don't ask him. It's your account I want to hear.

SONTAG: It seemed very long, too long. When you were with Beckett you felt you didn't really want to take up too much of his time, that he had better ways of using his time than being with us. It all started like this: we were staying in this picturesque hotel in Berlin and Allen Ginsberg said, "We're going to see Beckett, c'mon," and I said, "Oh, William and you are going, I don't want to butt in," and he said, "No, c'mon, c'mon," and we went. We knocked on the door of this beautiful atelier with great double height ceilings, very white. This beautiful, very thin man who tilts forward when he stands answered the door. He was alone. Everything was very clean and bare and white. I actually had seen him the day before on the grounds of the theater of the Akademie Der Kunst. Beckett comes to Berlin because he knows his privacy will be respected. He received us in a very courtly way and we sat at a very big long table. He waited for us to talk. Allen was, as usual, very forthcoming and did a great deal of talking. He did manage to draw Beckett out asking him about Joyce. That was somehow deeply embarrassing to me. Then we talked about singing, and Beckett and Allen began to sing while I was getting more and more embarrassed.

BOCKRIS: Bill says Beckett made you feel as if you would be welcome to leave as soon as you could.

SONTAG: He didn't actually throw us out.

BURROUGHS: Oh, the hell he didn't! See, I have an entirely different slant on the whole thing. In the first place, John Calder said, "Bring along some liquor," which we did. I know that Beckett considers other people different from him and he doesn't really like to see them. He's got nothing particular against them being there, it's just that there are limits to how long he can stand being with people. So I figured that about twenty minutes would be enough. Someone brought up the fact that my son was due for transplants, and Beckett talked about the problem of rejection, about which he'd read an article. I don't remember this singing episode at all. You see Susan says it seemed long, it seemed to me extremely short. Soon after we got there, and the talk about transplants, everybody looked at their watch, and it was very obviously time to go. We'd only brought along a pint and it had disappeared by that time.

SONTAG: Allen said, "What was it like to be with Joyce? I understand Joyce had a beautiful voice, and that he liked to sing." Allen did some kind of "OM" and Beckett said, "Yes, indeed he had a beautiful voice," and I kept thinking what a beautiful voice *he* had. I had seen Beckett before in a café in Paris, but I had never heard him speak and I was struck by the Irish accent. After more than half a century in France he has a very pure speech which is unmarked by living abroad. I know hardly anybody who's younger than Beckett, who has spent a great deal of time abroad who hasn't in some way adjusted his or her speech to living abroad. There's always a kind of deliberateness or an accommodation to the fact that even when you speak your own language you're speaking to people whose first language it's not and Beckett didn't seem in any way like someone who has lived most of his life in a country that was not the country of his original speech. He has a beautiful Irish musical voice. I don't remember that he made us feel we had to go, but I think we all felt we couldn't stay very long.

BURROUGHS: I talked to a number of people about the art of psychic bouncing, of psychically getting rid of someone. One way is to see their image, fix it clearly in your mind, then you put it firmly outside the door, and I saw an able practitioner do it once in Paris. This guy suddenly said, "Oh, Jeez, I'm gonna have to go." He could hardly get out of the room.

BOCKRIS: Did you feel that psychic push? That Beckett had "placed" *you* outside the room?

BURROUGHS: Everybody *knew* that they weren't supposed to stay very long. I think it was ten minutes after six that we got out of there.

SONTAG: I know people who claim to feel extremely comfortable with Beckett.

BURROUGHS: I was at a previous meeting with him in Paris in 1959 in which there was quite a bit of antagonism between us.

BOCKRIS: How did that happen?

MAURICE GIRODIAS: I had the idea to arrange a dinner between Burroughs and Beckett with myself as the host in the thirteenth-century cavernous cellars of my Brazilian nightclub. There were also a couple of lesbians, and Iris Owens, who is always very lively and quick-witted. Neither of them said a word the whole evening.

BURROUGHS: I'd evolved the cut-ups, which Beckett didn't approve of at all.

SONTAG: Is he familiar with your work?

BURROUGHS: Oh yes. He gave me one of the greatest compliments that I ever heard. Someone asked him, "What do you think of Burroughs?" and he said—grudgingly—"Well, he's a writer."

SONTAG: High praise indeed.

BURROUGHS: I esteemed it very highly. Someone who really knows about writing, or say about medicine says, "Well, he's a doctor. He gets in the operating room and he knows what he's doing."

SONTAG: But at the same time you thought he was hostile to some of your procedures?

BURROUGHS: Yes, he was, and we talked about that very briefly when we first came in during the Berlin visit. He remembered perfectly the occasion.

SONTAG: Do you think he reads much?

BURROUGHS: I would doubt it. Beckett is someone who needs no input as such. To me it's a very relaxed feeling to be around someone who doesn't need me for anything and wouldn't care if I died right there the next minute. Most people have to get themselves needed or noticed. I don't have that feeling at all. But there's no point in being there, because he has no desire or need to see people.

BOCKRIS: How did you feel when you left that meeting?

SONTAG: I was very glad I had seen him. I was more interested just to see what he looks like, if he was as good-looking as he is in photos.

BURROUGHS: He looked very well and in very good shape. Beckett is about seventy-five. He's very thin and his face looks quite youthful. It's really almost an Irish streetboy face. We got up and left, the visit had been, as I say, very cordial, decorous . . .

SONTAG: More decorous than cordial I would say. It was a weightless experience, because it's true, nothing happened.

BURROUGHS: Nothing happened at all.

SONTAG: I remember that Allen was carrying on like a puppy. Beckett responded. He's curiously passive, and if someone had been very aggressive and pushy he probably would have responded to that, but if no one wants to do that he's not going to help it in any way, it's really up to you, isn't it?

BOCKRIS Do you think you'll ever see him again?

SONTAG: No.

BOCKRIS: Why not?

SONTAG: Why?

BURROUGHS: There's no likelihood that I will ever see him again.

SONTAG: It's interesting when you say that he doesn't need any input. That's true. There are no references in his work, nothing that appears from outside.

BURROUGHS: Because most writers do. For example, I get a lot from reading, I get a lot from newspapers, but with Beckett it's all inside, I don't think he needs that sort of thing at all.

SONTAG: I wonder if he has many books. I would think not.

BURROUGHS: I didn't see any while we were there, but those of course were temporary quarters.

SONTAG: People who are involved in books always manage, even on a trip, to accumulate some.

BURROUGHS: That's true. I saw no books.

212

DINNER WITH FRED JORDAN: NEW YORK 1980

JORDAN: You wrote a piece about the visit to Sam Beckett in Berlin.

BURROUGHS: I didn't write anything. This is getting to be the local Rashomon. Everyone has a completely different story.

JORDAN: Sam was in Berlin at the time, rehearsing *Endgame* in German. John Calder was in Berlin at the same time and I had lunch with John, Susan and Allen. I think you were there too.

BURROUGHS: When Allen asked Susan bluntly if she was dying of cancer?

JORDAN: Yes. Allen turned to Susan and said "You've got cancer, right? How you doin'?" and she said, "Okay." "How's your love life?" "Very good," said Susan, "I'm getting more propositions than ever." John Calder wanted to meet me the next day at five. I told John that I couldn't because I was seeing Beckett. Allen then turned to me and said, "You're seeing Sam? Can I come along?" "Sure," I said, "why not?" And Susan said, "Oh, I've always wanted to see Beckett." "Come along," I said, and before we knew it there were six of us going to see Beckett. The following afternoon when Sam opened the door to all these people he looked a bit surprised. I remember Allen talking to him about whether Joyce wrote songs, and Sam's answer to be that he did. Allen asked Beckett, "Can you sing one for us?" Do you remember when he sang that song, which turned out to be an English version of a Schubert song?

BOCKRIS: How long were you there?

JORDAN: For an hour.

BURROUGHS: Do you remember anything else that Beckett said, or anyone said?

JORDAN: Allen kept the conversation up with questions about Joyce. He then asked Beckett what he was doing in Berlin. Allen was the most active interlocutor, but it was getting darker and darker, and there was no light in the room.

BOCKRIS: Why no light?

JORDAN: There was a light, but Beckett didn't turn it on.

BURROUGHS: Quite a signal, I think. Do you remember any direct exchanges between Beckett and Susan Sontag?

JORDAN: Afterward she said he was the sexiest man she had ever met. I don't remember any exchange between them.

BURROUGHS: I think this is a terribly interesting exercise. A number of people saw someone on a sort of momentous occasion and each has a different version of what happened.

JORDAN: Do you remember how he was dressed?

BURROUGHS: He had on a turtleneck sweater, a very hard flat kind of tweed sports jacket, it looked thorn-resistant, not the furry kind, and some kind of slacks. On his feet I have an impression of sandals.

JORDAN: Had you known him before you saw him in Berlin?

BURROUGHS: I met Beckett once in Girodias' restaurant in Paris.

JORDAN: Was that the time when, apparently, you explained to Beckett the cut-up method and he responded by saying, "But, but that's plumbing, that's not writing!"

BURROUGHS: Oh, yes, he was quite upset by the whole thing. "You're using other people's words!" he said at one point. I said, "Well, the formula of one physicist is after all available to anybody in the profession." When I saw him in Berlin I reminded him that "I think we've met before, Mr. Beckett." And he said, "Yes, in Maurice Girodias' restaurant," and I said, "Yes, as a matter of fact I remember it very well." That was my opening exchange.

BOCKRIS: Had the Paris meeting been standoffish, had the conversation dribbled to a close?

BURROUGHS: John said we were both really pretty much drunk at that point, so it just trailed off into amnesia . . .

DINNER WITH LOU REED: NEW YORK 1978

In our last dinner with Lou Reed, he confronted Burroughs with the rumor that he was purported to be a very cold person, capable of murder. He asked Bill if he had any comments.

BURROUGHS [short silence]: I neither deny nor confirm these rumors, Lou. It doesn't do any good to deny them anyway. Last week Robert Duncan told me a story. According to him, I was walking along the banks of the Seine with Beckett in Paris discussing random and vicarious murder and Beckett said, "If it's random it's not murder." I said, "Sam" (as I suppose I would address him if I were walking along the banks of the Seine with Beckett—never having walked anywhere with him I don't know), "this is not correct at all and I will prove it to you," at which point I am supposed to have pulled out a pistol and shot

214

a passing clocharde, throwing her body into the Seine. Then Sam and I walked on.

Lou asked Bill if Beckett had actually worked for Joyce as a secretary.

BURROUGHS: He did for a while, yes. In fact it is obvious that *Watt* is all about his apprenticeship to Joyce. It was an apprenticeship more than anything else—the master telling the pupil how to do it—but he had to handle a good deal of typing and secretarial work too.

Lou asked if Bill thought a pupil could do better work than his teacher.

BURROUGHS: In this case, I believe so. I think the whole body of Beckett's work is wider in scope than Joyce's.

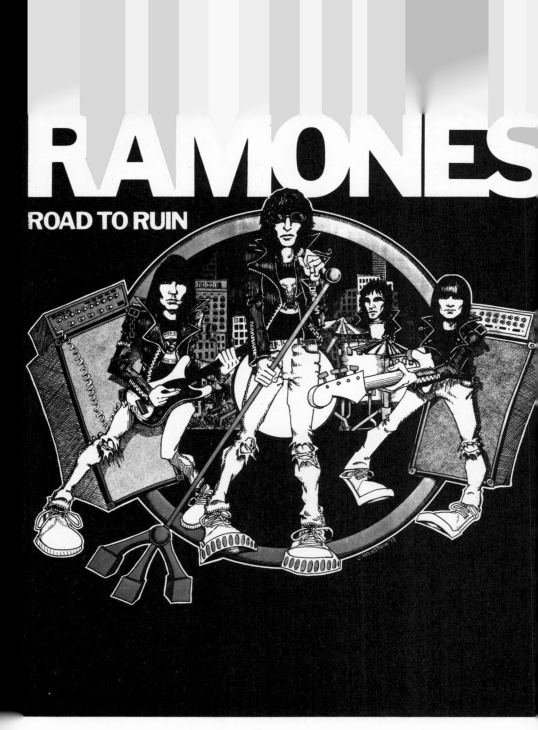

Publicity poster by John Holmstrom

NOTHING TO THINK ABOUT: WILLIAM BURROUGHS AND THE ROLLING STONES

DINNER WITH BILL WYMAN AND PETER COOK: NEW YORK 1974

Burroughs arrived promptly at 8:00 P.M.—he has never been late for an appointment in the six years that I've known him—accompanied by James Grauerholz. "What would you like to drink?" I asked.

"Two fingers of Scotch, no ice, and a dash of water," Burroughs replied. I poured myself a gin and tonic. "A summer drink," he murmured as if accompanied by ghosts. We began discussing the concept of the interview and how it could be improved upon. I told him about my best conversations with Muhammad Ali and Salvador Dali. Burroughs seemed interested. Looking across the room directly at me, he said, "Have you considered cutting up the tapes?"

"What do you mean?"

"It's very simple. Take three tape recorders and place them beside each other. Turn on the third so it is recording. Then run a section of your Ali tape. Stop it randomly, turning the Dali tape on at the same time. See where the Ali and Dali conversations intersect when you play back the results on the third tape recorder. Repeat the process indefinitely. You will be surprised by the results."

It soon became evident that Bill Wyman was going to be late and I was getting nervous, trying to keep up the conversation in between making frantic phone calls to locate him. I could see that Burroughs was becoming slightly annoyed and would soon make motions to leave.

217

If I had known how much this kind of thing annoys him I would have apologized and offered to drive him home, but I pretended not to notice and we kept chatting about inconsequential things.

At 10:30, Wyman, his wife Ingrid, and publicist Anni Ivil entered the apartment. Introductions were made, but William remained seated in his armchair while Bill settled into a corner of the couch across the room so that it was not easy to maintain a conversation.

I moved them over to a table in the hall where a large buffet dinner was laid out and said, "You're both interested in science fiction; that should give you something to talk about."

"Oh, really," said Burroughs. "Who do you like?"

"Asimov, Bradbury . . ." Wyman began.

"Oh," he sniffed, "that's not very good," and strode back to the citadel of his armchair.

As Peter Cook entered the front door with a girl I jumped up and dashed into the foyer yelling, "Judy! Judy!" (the name of a recent

Bill and Lou after their first meeting at the Bunker, New York, 1978. Photo by Victor Bockris

wife). Unfortunately, although the girl looked very much like Judy, it was only a carbon copy. Burroughs looked up from where he was staring at the carpet and said, "Yes, hello . . . 'Judy,' " as if that were the gist of it. Cook took a chair. Nobody knew what to say. At eleven, William left.

I insisted on accompanying him downstairs to fetch a taxi, as it was raining. Outside, I ran around the block, secured a Checker, and brought it back to the front of the apartment building. "Bravo, Victor!" he called as he ran past me in the rain and jumped into the cab. At least, I thought, he doesn't hold this fiasco entirely against me.

When we met for dinner the following week, the first thing I asked William was what his impression of Bill Wyman had been. Drawing himself up in his armchair and sipping from the usual two fingers of Scotch, no ice, and a dash of water, Burroughs replied "I thought he was a very rude young man coming two and a half hours late like that and not even apologizing for it. You see, that's the trouble with these rock stars: they think they're so important that everyone will wait for them; they have no sense of courtesy."

BOULDERADO HOTEL, BOULDER 1976

I was visiting William over the weekend to conduct an interview for Al Goldstein's *Screw*. Around 4:00 on Saturday afternoon we repaired to James Grauerholz's tiny attic room, because it was full of sunlight and looked out on the mountains, with two cups of tea.

BOCKRIS: When did you first meet Brian Jones?

BURROUGHS: I first met Brian Jones in the Parade Bar in Tangier. He had just returned from the Village of Joujouka, where he had recorded the Pipes of Pan music, which after his death was edited and processed in the studio at a cost of about 10,000 pounds. I went back to his room in the Minza and I listened to a selection of a tape made by a sound engineer with two Uhers. Very, very good job of sound engineering. That came out as the record and cassette of "Brian Jones Plays with the Pipes of Pan" [*Burroughs owns and often plays this cassette*].

After Jones died, the record company had no plans to do anything about this record, which was unfinished at the time of his death, although it was in pretty good shape. However, the Joujoukan musicians had a union and sent Hamri to London, and with the help of Brion

Gysin and an awful lot of finagling and phone calls with the lawyers who were handling Brian's estate, this thing finally came out and there was eventually some money for the Joujoukan musicians. You see, there was nothing of Brian Jones himself on the record and it was considered to be misleading because he didn't play. He played with them in one sense: there is a suggestion of that, you see, in playing with the Pipes of Pan, he was playing with the God of Panic. . . .

WESTCHESTER COUNTY, NEW YORK 1977

I visited Keith Richard at his country house, Frog Hollow, and asked him if he'd read Burroughs' statement: "I think I am in better health now as a result of using junk at intervals than I would have been if I had never been an addict."

It turned out Keith had actually taken the apomorphine cure with Dr. Dent's notorious assistant, Smitty: "Dr. Dent is dead, see," he told me, "but his assistant, whom he trained, this lovely old dear 'oo's like a mother hen called Smitty, still runs the clinic. I 'ad 'er down to my place for five days and she just sort of comes in and says: ' 'Ere's your shot, dear, there's a good boy.' Or: 'You've been a naughty boy. You've taken something, yes you 'ave, I can tell.' "

Of all the Rolling Stones, Keith Richard would seem to be the most likely candidate to make a real connection with Burroughs and perhaps it really is a pity that they have never met, except briefly at parties, where Bill is never very relaxed.

NEW YORK CITY 1980

I brought Bill over to The Factory so Andy could take some Polaroids of him for a portrait. Bianca Jagger was there. She spoke with Burroughs animatedly about canes, interviews and London for about fifteen minutes. After he left she came running over to me and said: "Burroughs is such an interesting man! I'd love to talk to him some more. He looks so much better now. I remember when Mick and I visited him at his flat in London to discuss filming *Naked Lunch* with Anthony Balch in 1973, he had on these pants for a man forty years younger that were much too tight, and high heeled boots. He seemed

220

Burroughs sips Coke, Bianca watches, at The Factory, New York, 1979. Photo by Bobby Grossman

very uncomfortable and was difficult to talk to. He seems much more open and relaxed now."

BURROUGHS: David Dalton, who has written a book on James Dean and edited a book on the Rolling Stones, contacted me. He wanted me to write something on the Stones with the suggested title *Their Satanic Majesties*, about two thousand words. This was to be part of an anniversary book put out by Stonehill Press—the twentieth anniversary of the Stones by the time the book is out. I cleared my throat suggestively. "Uh, there is the question of my fee." He found this a little crass but mentioned a figure—$500. I protest that I am not a music critic, can't think of anything to say that hasn't been said already. "Oh," he says "this is to be more personal." I told him I knew the Stones very slightly. But "Keith is very anxious for me to write something." Well, the Stones have shown interest in my work and I felt a certain obligation, but when I got it down on paper—my God—it ' looked so dull: *Rock and Roll music is a sociological phenomenon of unprecedented scope and effect . . . The Stones as heroes of the cultural revolution . . . front line fighters pushed around by police and customs*

221

agents. I mean, who wants to hear about the cultural revolution at this point? It's like the Vietnam War or the Irish thing. It takes me about ten days to write an article like this. It would take another zero in there to make it an attractive thing financially. Whatever the money involved on a job like this, I have to do it right or I don't do it at all. And I wasn't about to hand out platitudes about the cultural revolution and the worldwide influence of rock and roll. So Victor suggests we arrange a dinner with Andy Warhol and Marcia Resnick. However, it transpired that Mick and not Keith would be present at this meeting.

DINNER WITH ANDY WARHOL, MARCIA RESNICK, AND MICK JAGGER: NEW YORK 1980

BOCKRIS: I called up Liz Derringer and said "Could you ask Mick and Jerry Hall to come over to dinner with William at the Bunker? We're going to tape it, but it's not like an interview, it's just an informal chat." Liz thought Mick would probably like the idea and called him. He agreed. He'd be only too glad to drop by Burroughs' place on the Bowery. Liz suggested that Marcia Resnick take the photographs since they had worked together before on interviewing and photographing Mick. I also invited Andy Warhol.

Andy arrived first and began running around Bill's loft admiring the spacious rooms, Brion Gysin's paintings, the Orgone Box and the white floors, walls and ceilings, much to William's delight and amusement. I got them drinks. They sat down at the big conference table and began discussing Professor Shockley's controversial theory of artificial insemination of women with higher than average I.Q.'s in order to create a super race.

"Bill, you should sell yours!" I said. "Imagine who would want *The Sperm of William Burroughs.*"

"You could do it right now," Andy told him. "All they have to do is put it in the freezer."

"I'll do it right away!" Bill exclaimed, then mused, "I bet Mick Jagger could name his own price!" The phone rang. It was Marcia Resnick requesting entry to the Bunker with her camera equipment. She started to set up strobe lights and it soon began to look as if we were making an underground movie. We yelled at Marcia, asking her to take the lights down, stash them in Bill's room, and only bring them out when dinner was over. Everybody would by then be relaxed enough to have their picture taken.

After a couple of delaying "we'll-be-half-an-hour-late-we're-on-our-way" phone calls, Mick Jagger, Jerry Hall and Liz Derringer arrived in a chauffeur-driven Lincoln sedan. As they entered the loft, William got up from the table and crossed the room extending a hand. Andy already knew everybody. I tried to introduce Liz and Jerry to Bill, while taking their coats and making sure everybody sat at the right place at the table. Bill was sitting at the head of the table. I put Mick on his right, myself on his left, and Andy next to me. The men were at one end of the table, the women at the other.

BURROUGHS: It soon transpired that far from approving Dalton's project, Mick knew nothing about it. He assumed a suspicious attitude as if I was trying to hustle him into something when actually I was feeling more and more definitively that I wanted *out*. I ran through the notes I had made and found that Mick was as bored with the project as I was becoming. Mick apparently had been told that I had a proposition for him. I had been told by Dalton that Keith and Mick wanted me to write something for the book. So I felt that the Stones had a proposition to make to me. The result was a dead end of misunderstanding, a comedy of errors that wasn't even funny. When Mick asked, "Do you have a phone in this joint?" I thought the conversation had hit rock bottom but I was wrong.

At one point Victor said that Andy had been shot and that I had shot someone, so Jagger asked who I had shot. There was a static pause. I said, "I haven't shot anyone right lately, Mick. Been on my good behavior."

Handshakes and farewells were perfunctory. That's one article I won't have to write, I thought.

BOCKRIS: After Mick, Jerry and Liz had finally left, Andy, Bill, Marcia and I stood around dazed. Trying to be encouraging, I offered, "I find with these interviews that if I feel it was good afterwards it was always terrible, and if I on the contrary feel really terrible it was usually good. So this probably will be very good!"

"You were really terrible," Andy replied flatly.

"It was terrible. Nothing . . ." I began.

Burroughs with Joe Strummer after dinner at the Bunker, New York, 1980. Photo by Victor Bockris

"Happened," Andy finished.

"There was no connection at all!" I started. "**THERE WAS NO CONVERSATION!** There was no . . . Nothing happened again." I couldn't help thinking about Bill saying the same thing to Susan Sontag about their meeting with Beckett.

"Well, I really didn't expect anything to *happen*," Bill said fortuitously.

"I'd like to say something about Mick Jagger," Marcia Resnick piped up. But I couldn't stand to think about the concept of anybody meeting anybody and what it was all about, so I just turned around and screamed, "Marcia, you weren't supposed to be taking photographs during the conversation! It changed the concentration! How can people talk if somebody is running around taking photographs the whole time?"

THE FOLLOWING DAY

BURROUGHS: Thinking it over, I decided that an opportunity had been missed here to say something basically new about rock and roll, and about the Stones, in relation to the origin and function of language. Now a phrase like "cultural revolution" gets tossed around until it loses its meaning. "Have you seen a cultural revolution around here?" Victor asks. "No I haven't seen one," Mick says. The cultural revolution is such a bore anyhow and stuff. Mick may not see a cultural revolution but he is walking around in one. Fifty years ago jazz was confined to nightclubs, country clubs, ballrooms and occasionally, when you got to be a classic, a concert hall. You were lucky to take in $200 a week. The jazz musician had no currency outside of jazz afficionados. There were no Bix Beiderbecke T-shirts, no screaming, no groupies. The sociological and political effects of music were virtually non-existent. Now rock and roll is a mass phenomenon performed before huge audiences and associated with a worldwide cultural revolution. The comparison of rock and roll audiences with Nazi rallies is not at all farfetched. Anything that can get that number of people together is political. So Mick may be right on when he says he wants to go into politics.

Granted that rock and roll is a powerful force, just what is the nature of that force and where is it going? The simplest questions are the most difficult. I remember having dinner with Jasper Johns, 1967, in the Connaught Hotel, London, and I asked him, "What is painting really about? What are painters really doing?"

He said, "Well, what is writing all about?"

I still don't have the answer on that one. Certainly not all the answers. So here is rock and roll. And rock and roll was one of the key factors in the cultural revolution which was and is concerned with confrontation.

The young English scientist spooned some of that runny brown sugar into his coffee.

"Is there a *they* in England?" I asked, "Or is it confused like America? Every mafia capo thinks he's a *they*."

He looked dreamily at a hideous stained glass mural. "Yes," he said. "We are they."

225

"Oh," I said. "Just like that is it?"

He countered with a question. "How does it feel to know you are one of the last human beings?"

"I'm expecting another assignment," I told him primly. So we get to talking like agents will and I told him I thought singing came before talking.

"Yes," he purred "I'm sure it did."

"So what these pop groups are doing is *recreating the origins of human speech.*"

"Oh quite."

"The origin of language, in some cases, shall we say. Is a singer singing in the brains of his audience in such a way as to activate speech reflexes?"

"It had to come from somewhere. Someone had to program the machine."

"Yes of course. I am thinking now of the actual process. I see it as an illness, a virus. The ape segment under study lost most of their body hair. There were alterations in the throat which made human speech possible. The Singing Sickness had a high mortality rate. And the enfeebled apes fell prey to predators. Or they died of hunger and thirst. Those who survived the SS had gained the potential for human speech. Alterations accomplished, the Biologic Engineer packs his tools. His face expresses the utter boredom of someone who has listened to the same bad joke for a million years.

"In a jungle clearing a survivor jumps up and begins to *sing*. Blood spurts out his mouth and nose. He is *singing blood*. But the show must go on. Now the others leap about in a frenzy screaming out the words *blood* and *pus* all over as they clean out their new vocal cords for a million-year talk marathon."

"About the size of it."

"So having piped people back to the origin of all this shit what happens now?"

"This had better be good."

"It is. The Silent Sickness. The potential for silent communication is here. The Silencers will activate it."

Singing out bloody vocal cords and now he is doing the impossible, he is *singing in silence*. And now that vast audience is singing with him, silent notes ringing through flesh and nerves and bones.

226

Marcia Resnick sitting in Burroughs' lap: A First and a Last. *Photo by Victor Bockris*

Susan, Victor, and Bill after dinner, New York City, 1979. Photo by Gerard Malanga

227

The Rolling Bones have two theme songs. They improvise, tossing the words and music back and forth:

> When it gets too hot for comfort
> And the music softly means
> T'aint no sin to take off your skin
> And dance around in your bones.
> Stay all night and stay a little longer
> Take off your coat and throw it in a corner
> Don't know why you don't stay a little longer . . .

An estimated audience of ten million, racks of hammocks and bunks and tents to the sky. The Bones prance out in khakis with a suggestion of a uniform.

> When it gets too hot for comfort
> They are stripping off their clothes
> And the music softly moans . . .

They go into a hula dance. "T'aint no sin." They throw clothes to the audience. "To take off your skin." They peal off shimmering layers of flesh that float in the air and disintegrate in puffs of violet smoke and whiffs of musty ozone. "And dance." A tornado of mad jig music.

"Take off your skin and throw it in a corner . . ."

"And dance around in your bo/

"Don't see why you don't sta/

There is a silver flash and silence falls like a thunderclap. Yes, an opportunity was missed.

AFTERMATH

During the next couple of weeks, Bill was visited by Joe Strummer, lead singer and guitar player for the Clash, and David Bowie. Although he was an hour and a half late, Strummer brought a bottle of whisky, a bottle of tequila, two six-packs of Heineken, and eight enormous joints. He was bubbling over with eagerness to meet Burroughs, with whom he had a very relaxed and pleasant conversation about

English policemen. William hauled out his arsenal of blackjacks, Japanese throwing stars and knives, while Joe took a series of Polaroids of him thwacking cardboard boxes and alternately emitting an extremely wide, malevolent smile. Strummer left completely satisfied.

When David Bowie came by for a drink another evening, he was the model of gentlemanly courtesy and his entire demeanor conveyed respect. He asked Burroughs about his activities. They spoke about New York being the most exotic place in the world.

BURROUGHS: I gave David Bowie an issue of *Knife* magazine containing the Bowie knife Story. Colonel Bowie, Southern gentleman and soldier of fortune, is credited with the invention of the Bowie knife design. Experts point out there were knives of this design centuries before Bowie. In any case the Colonel did ably baptize his knife. On a lonely road three men waited with knives. They were not there just to

"I haven't shot anyone right lately, Mick." Photo by Marcia Resnick

look at him. A few seconds later all three were dead. With a powerful overhand slash the Colonel splits the skull of one assailant like a coconut. Bowie died in the Battle of the Alamo.

When we left to take a cab uptown (Bill and I were going to dinner at Debbie and Chris Harry-Stein's), Bowie graciously took Burroughs by the arm and carefully escorted him across the wide streets.

OVER THE HILLS
AND FAR AWAY

Bill finds the Bunker the most satisfactory living space he has ever inhabited, but he dreams of a country place: a fishpond, hunting and shooting, long walks. To this end he has purchased five acres in Florida near Tallahassee. His neighbors will be people like doctors, lawyers, professors. François Bucher has organized this project. All plots to be five acres and over. Positively no trailers.

BURROUGHS: My house in Florida presents itself as a shimmering mirage. It is on a wooded slope overlooking a long narrow fishpond which delineates the boundary of my land with a suggestion of the palace moat. The house is yellow cinder block. The front forms a wall with a heavy iron door and two barred windows. Doors open on the living room, dining room and kitchen area. To the right is the master bedroom behind a heavy adobe partition and a solid door. The bathroom is beyond the kitchen to simplify plumbing connections. Water supply comes from a cistern three feet off the ground just outside the bathroom. The cistern is filled from rain water draining off the roof. It goes through strainers of course but the one thing we have to watch out for, boys, is vultures, or any fucking bird for that matter, shitting on the roof. From the two back corners of the house runs a wall eight feet high with barbed wire on top back about fifty feet to form a courtyard with an iron door at the far end. The house faces inward onto this patio which contains lime and orange and peach trees, mimosa, gardenia and roses, and a fishpond with exotic goldfish, perhaps two of the large ones eighteen inches long. But I will eschew exotic pets who are, in the colorful lingo of Scientology, a "PTS: Potential Trouble Source."

Oh dear, Shredni Vashtar, one's pet ferret, has slipped out of his cage, he's awfully good at that, and torn the throat out of an infant in its pram. I tried to explain that Shredni was only playing. He didn't mean any harm. But mother became abusive. And Shredni made good his escape and has not been seen again. Then there was that terrible afternoon when Little Uttie disappeared.

Little Uttie, for Ruthie, was a horrible two-year-old that crawled around under tables biting people's legs and ankles.

"Uttie? Have you seen UTTIE?" We open the toolshed and there is Quetzocoatl, my pet python, curled around his distended mid-sections. And you can see right away by the shape and size—that bulge he is curled around with its obscene suggestion of pregnancy clearly contains Little Uttie.

The reptile lifts its head and emits a somnolent belch as foul as the latrines of hell. Calmly and rationally I explained to the bereaved parent that an infant was, after all, logical prey for a python. "Little Mother."

This epithet did not produce the soothing effect I had hoped for. Clearly beyond logic or psychological expertise, with a shocking lack of consideration for the other guests, she began screaming, "YOU FILTHY MURDERING COCKSUCKER!"

I signaled my driver to stand by to resist Furies. An awkward young deputy shot the plumed serpent in the courtyard while my driver did "Taps" on his bugle and I ordered the flag lowered to half mast. A gnawing uncertainty as to whether these funeral rites were directed towards Quetzocoatl or Little Uttie discombobulated the guests.

There is an awkward pause. Who is going to cut Little Uttie out of Quetzocoatl? Even as I formulated the question, nature yielded the hideous answer: With a rending farting sound accompanied by odors too foul for description, Quetzocoatl, in his death spasms, was voiding half digested pieces of Little Uttie per anus.

Or the time the Countess's miniature Dalmatian . . . did I hear a little yelp? She calls it Hum.

"Hum!"

"HUM!"

The old toolshed again. A canine bulge was Hum. The Countess attacks poor Quetzocoatl with her umbrella and Quetzi grabs a big hunk of thigh with his uncurving needle teeth. We have to pry him out of her a tooth at a time while her Yugoslavian gigolo rushes around screaming "You arrant cads! You utter rotters! You foul reptiles!" And apes is no better. They turn vicious at puberty. When chimpy starts wanking off with girlie pictures in the loo, walk don't run to the nearest phone and call a competent zoo.

Sand foxes? Stars splash the sky "like wilted gardenias,"—that's a quote from Bill Faulkner, an early book about New Orleans. I have arranged a tasteful little oasis, a sand dune, a pool, a palm tree. I shush my guests as my sand fox slinks in like a shy ghost. They are in fact so shy that they die if you touch one—a wise old Arab told me this at a hotel in Biskra. They had two fennecs tethered in the patio and I approached one which rushed to the end of its tether in a blind stupid panic, and the old Arab said, "No touchy pas, Mister, ou il meurt."

Clearly this could touch off some trouble. Of course I have signs up: *Don't touch the fennecs.*

But I know sooner or later some joker is going to *Touch my Fennecs.*

"Happened."

"Now Clem, you went and touched my sand fox last night and the critter's deader'n a shit bug from the contact with you."

"I meant no harm."

"Just couldn't help yourself, is that it? Couldn't keep your *ugly,* stinking, murdering sex-perverted paws off my *beautiful,* immaculate, sensitive, delicate fennec, could you now? There must be a special place in hell for people like you sneaking around touching a decent man's *fennec!*"

No other pets than a few choice cats. I favor delicate black Siamese and Ethiopian cats are so delightfully evil-looking. But absolutely no feral cats. Horrible experiences in New Mexico. This ocelot got up onto my lap, and every time I tried to shove it away it growled and dug its claws in. I eased my .380 Beretta out of an inside belt holster and told the host urgently, *"Get it off me or I kill it!"*

I provide a safe environment for my guests. I have considered keeping a few skunks in the patio since, in my opinion as a connoisseur of cuteness, the skunk is one of the cutest animals alive. Nor would I subject a cute skunk to the indignity of having his scent glands removed. If you are a Johnson my skunks won't spray you. So everybody has to pass the skunk test. If my skunks spray you, you stink right there and you get the skunk rush. I have something I can clandestinely spray on the unwelcome guests. "Oh Lydia Anne, how nice to see you," spray spray, a substance that irritates my skunks. "I'm sorry, Lydia Anne, but I simply can't have a *stinker* in my house. It's not fair to my other guests."

So we declared a moratorium on pet welfare. It is just too deadly. I content myself with two Siamese cats that cry and scream the whole time.

Here in this remote garden I create an ambiance of great luxury. Outside a discreet medley of animal sounds drifts from mikes around the garden wall. "Isn't that a wild turkey I hear?"

"It certainly is, Senator. I see you know your birds." And I have an indoor shooting range for my guests and .22 pistols with BB cap loads. Hardly any noise. They can feed the goldfish. I have two of the very large variety, eighteen inches in length, worthless luxury beasts, created in Japan by an old Master of Goldfish Culture.

Here I entertain certain key people. Will you believe me when I say my house in Tallahassee cost less than $50,000? And we have actual as well as recorded wild turkeys and even a bear, yet this retreat is only twenty-five minutes from downtown Tallahassee.

When I went down to my pond this morning I found that my overnight trout line had snared a great catfish, all of twenty pounds, snapping viciously. I killed him with a .22 Magnum in the head and I thought, I will cook this noble fish for dinner tonight. Rather a special dinner: catfish, grits, turnip greens, and fried apple and persimmon pie for dessert.

The Judge is the first to arrive half sloshed as usual. The dinner is a big success. It's important to get them into dinner before the fourth drink. So we are getting down to business after dinner and the Judge looks at me, the smeared purple veins on his nose and cheekbones glowing portentously, and his gray eyes slate cold. "Now I think that line of thought could prove productive, *very* productive indeed."

I have also looked at property in New Mexico and Lawrence, Kansas, but for now my houses are like the glittering cities of the Odor Eaters in Tibetan mythology that dissolve in rain.

IDENTIFICATION CHART

DON BACHARDY is an artist who has done portraits and drawings of Burroughs and James Grauerholz, among many other subjects. He shares a house in Los Angeles with Christopher Isherwood.

PETER BEARD is an anthropologist and photographer who has produced several books on Africa, specifically *The End of the Game*. He has known Burroughs for some time in London and New York.

VICTOR BOCKRIS is the author of *Fighter, Poet, Prophet: The Poetry of Muhammad Ali* [Freeway Press 1974], and *Nothing Happens: Photographs of Muhammad Ali and Andy Warhol* [Nadada Editions 1978].

BOCKRIS-WYLIE represents two people, Victor Bockris and Andrew Wylie. I worked with Wylie in an interview team which we called Bockris-Wylie and was referred to as a single individual from 1973 to 1975. When I first met Burroughs in 1974 I was still part of Bockris-Wylie, and it was as Bockris-Wylie that we interviewed him. Andrew Wylie is currently a literary agent in New York.

UDO BREGER is a writer living in Basel, Switzerland. He is the editor of a magazine called *Soft Need*.

ANDREAS BROWN is the proprietor of The Gotham Book Mart in New York City.

RAYMOND FOYE was an interviewer from *Search and Destroy*, going under the pseudonym of Ray Rumor when he interviewed Burroughs in San Francisco. He has also worked with Ferlinghetti on City Lights projects and is currently living in New York, where he continues his activities as an archivist, chronicler and editor.

PAUL GETTY, JR. [the notorious grandson of the late oil billionaire] has known Burroughs in London, New York and L.A. for some years. William always rather fondly calls him "Young Paul."

ALLEN GINSBERG, the poet, lives a fifteen-minute walk from Burroughs' place on Manhattan's Lower East Side. Whenever Allen is in town, he always comes over for dinner; they have remained mutually supportive throughout their long friendship.

JOHN GIORNO is a writer and performer who runs his own record label Giorno Poetry Systems. He has produced a couple of Burroughs records. He lives in Burroughs' building on a different floor and is a regular guest at his table. He is a practicing Buddhist.

MAURICE GIRODIAS is the French publisher who ran The Olympia Press in the late fifties and early sixties. *Lolita*, *Candy*, and *Naked Lunch* are among the many works published by him at that time.

JEFF GOLDBERG is a writer based in New York. He is the editor of *Traveller's Digest*.

JAMES GRAUERHOLZ is William Burroughs' full-time assistant and secretary. Grauerholz is from Coffeyville, Kansas. As a teenager, he corresponded with both Ginsberg and Burroughs after discovering their work. His arrival in New York coincided with Burroughs' arrival from London. In early 1974, the night Grauerholz arrived, Allen Ginsberg suggested he contact Burroughs, who shortly thereafter offered him a place to stay while he was in town. They soon started working together and Grauerholz became William's full-time secretary and later a real amanuensis, organizing appearances, dealing with finances, contracts and mail, aiding in the production of pieces and arranging William's social schedule. In early 1979, after producing the Nova Convention with John Giorno and Sylvere Lotringer, James moved back to Lawrence, Kansas, from where he now runs William Burroughs Communications. He continues to travel with Bill on American reading tours, handling their arrangements and scheduling, and deals with the mail and paperwork.

DEBORAH HARRY is a singer, songwriter, and actress.

RICHARD HELL is a songwriter, singer, poet, and movie star whose classic "Blank Generation" was Punk Rock's American National Anthem.

CHRISTOPHER ISHERWOOD is a novelist whose portraits of Berlin made him famous in the thirties. He moved to the United States on the eve of World War II and is currently a resident of Los Angeles. He was an advocate of the Gay Rights Movement throughout the seventies and helped introduce a finer understanding of Eastern religion through books on Ramakrishna, and his own guru.

FRED JORDAN was an editor at Grove Press for two decades. He was also managing editor of the *Evergreen Review*. He is the head of Methuen, Inc.

ANDRE LEON-TALLY is a social commentator based in Manhattan.

SYLVERE LOTRINGER is French and a professor of French Literature at Columbia and the editor of *Semiotexte*. He was the originator of the concept of Nova Convention.

GERARD MALANGA is a poet and photographer. He has published numerous books of poetry here and in Europe and shown his photographs in galleries across the country. He is also a social historian and commentator whose ability to operate in the deepest basements of literature and the highest towers of fashion has provided him with a wide angle to view his subjects through.

LEGS MCNEIL is a leading comedian on New York's New Wave scene. He started *Punk Magazine* with John Holmstrom and then created and managed America's new number one hitmakers, Shrapnel. He is also a writer.

STEWART MEYER is a fiction writer and regular guest at Burroughs' table.

MILES [his first name is Barry but everyone just calls him Miles, his surname] is a literary historian, archivist, rare book dealer, magazine editor and author of numerous cultural reports, who lives in London. A bibliography of Burroughs, co-written by Miles and Joe Maynard, was published by The University of Virginia Press, 1978, and his *Catalogue of the William Burroughs Archive* was published by Covent Garden Editions in London, 1974.

GLENN O'BRIEN is a frequent contributor to *High Times*, the avant-garde rock columnist for Andy Warhol's *Interview* Magazine, and host of his own weekly cable TV show, *Glenn O'Brien's TV Party*.

PETER ORLOVSKY is a poet and Allen Ginsberg's roommate of twenty years.

LOU REED is the William Burroughs of Rock and Roll, who has often investigated similar landscapes in his lyrics to those Burroughs covers in his novels. Among his greatest works are "Berlin," "Coney Island Baby," "Street Hassle," and "Growing Up in Public."

MARCIA RESNICK is a photographer.

NICOLAS ROEG is an English filmmaker whose productions range from *Performance* and *Walkabout* in the sixties, through *Don't Look Now* and *The Man Who Fell to Earth* in the seventies and *Bad Timing* in the eighties.

240

PATTI SMITH burst into prominence as a singer and writer around the time that Burroughs returned to New York. She subsequently became friendly with him and he has attended a number of her concerts and appreciated her work. She has often spoken publicly of the importance of his work in making her work possible.

SUSAN SONTAG is the author of two novels, *The Benefactor* and *Death Kit*. Her other books include two collections of essays: *Against Interpretation* and *Styles of Radical Will*; *On Photography*; *I, etcetera* and *Illness as Metaphor*. She has written and directed three films: *Duet for Cannibals* [1969], *Brother Carl* [1971], and *Promised Lands* [1974].

TERRY SOUTHERN is the American novelist who put laughter back into sex in the sixties. An outstanding man of letters and brilliant screenwriter and storyteller, he is a long-time confrere of Burroughs' and great companion in adventure. Burroughs always laughs when he mentions Southern. Southern and Burroughs together could almost be ready for vaudeville.

CHRIS STEIN is the lead guitarist and musical whiz-kid collaborator on the concept of Blondie, the rock band starring his girlfriend Deborah Harry. In between writing international Number One Hit Singles and playing around the world, he is the guest host on *Glenn O'Brien's TV Party*, produces *The Lounge Lizards* and *Walter Stedding*, and takes photographs, many of which will appear in his forthcoming book, *Above Fourteenth Street*.

ANNE WALDMAN is a poet and literary organizer who has worked with Burroughs at The Naropa Institute in Boulder, Colorado, and in many performances in the United States and Europe.

ANDY WARHOL is an artist, filmmaker, photographer, journalist, interviewer, and trendsetter.

CARL WEISSNER is a German writer and translator. He is responsible for producing most of the Beat literature in German and is Burroughs' translator. He is considered an active catalyst on the German literary scene.

TENNESSEE WILLIAMS, the playwright, apparently often quotes long passages of Burroughs at the drop of a hat. They have known each other since meeting in Tangier. The conversations included here were taped by Burroughs for a piece he was doing about Williams after a recent Broadway production.

Among the many people who helped compose *With William Burroughs,* I would like to thank all our actors and crew, drawing special attention to Mr. James Grauerholz, Burroughs' erstwhile factotum, who encouraged and aided the project throughout; Mr. Terry Southern, who was particularly helpful; and the *éminence grise* himself, grand, groovy and beloved William S. Burroughs.

In 1978, the National Endowment for the Arts gave me a writer's grant on the basis of an outline for this book. The late Tom Forcade, founder and owner of *High Times,* provided funds that enabled me to follow Burroughs to Colorado, Los Angeles, Berlin and London. *Interview* directed me toward the basic concept of the book as a dinner party and printed some of these conversations in earlier forms. Thanks to Bob Colacello and Robert Hayes. And in the final presentation of the text, I am especially indebted to my editor Jeannette Seaver.

Index